Wisdom With Understanding is Better Than Rubies

Lurine Karon Greenberg
Fine Arts Collection

How to succeed
in an ENSEMBLE

THÉÂTRE DE LA COUR ST. PIERRE

12me ANNÉE

FINE ARTS QUARTET

DIRECTION: M. CASETTI-GIOVANNA - GENÈVE

Program for the Fine Arts Quartet concert at the Théâtre de la Cour St. Pierre, Geneva, 3 December 1959. Left to right: Leonard Sorkin, Abram Loft, George Sopkin, Irving Ilmer.

How to succeed
in an ENSEMBLE

Reflections on a life in chamber music

Abram Loft

AMADEUS PRESS
Portland · Cambridge

Published in 2003 by
Amadeus Press (an imprint of Timber Press, Inc.)   Amadeus Press
The Haseltine Building   2 Station Road
133 S.W. Second Avenue, Suite 450   Swavesey
Portland, Oregon 97204 U.S.A.   Cambridge CB4 5QJ, U.K.

Printed through Colorcraft Ltd., Hong Kong

Library of Congress Cataloging-in-Publication Data

Loft, Abram, 1922–
        How to succeed in an ensemble : reflections on a life in chamber music /
        Abram Loft.
            p.   cm.
        Includes bibliographical references and indexes.
        Discography: p.
        ISBN 1-57467-078-6
        1. Ensemble playing. I. Title.

    MT728 .L64 2003
    785'.0092—dc21

                                    2002026024

To Jill and the family, young and old

✧ CONTENTS

✧ PREFACE

The reader will note that this book has a split personality. That is because I am aiming at two audiences. The first is the music-loving public, and specifically that large and faithful group of concertgoers, broadcast hearers, and record buyers devoted to the chamber music repertoire. You listen intently to music by the greats of old and modern times. Many of you are active players in your own right, often belying your amateur standing by the technical proficiency and musical insight of your performance. Whether you are a passive or active devotee, you must have questions about what makes a professional ensemble tick. How do the players arrive at an apparently effortless and (let us hope) convincing interpretation of demanding compositions? And just how do players get together in the first place, then stay the course—not only succeeding but *surviving* as a musical family—for the duration of the ensemble's career? Stay with me as I describe twenty-five years of my search for the answers.

The second target of this book is the young professional who yearns for—or who has indeed embarked upon—an ensemble career. There are a surprisingly great number of such performers, and I am glad this is so. For in chamber music, intelligently performed and presented, lies a major hope for the health of serious music in our future. Small ensembles, affordably maintained, can become a constant element in the cultural life of the cities and towns in which we live. Such restoration of truly competent performance in the local setting will balance the centralization of high-level music-making around our major metropolitan areas that has taken place in the course of the last century. (I might add, not too parenthetically, that the flourishing of music in the various centers would more than absorb the substantial flow of excellent performers from this country's conservatories and schools of music each year.)

In my title, I refer to "success." Defining this word in terms of a chamber ensemble's work is not a simple matter. Insightful study and performance of a superb musical repertoire is in itself an immediate reward. Playing for responsive audiences both at home and in the world at large, earning critical acclaim, issuing recordings on a prominent label to a welcoming market, teaching able students at a solid school of music—all this and more are practical rewards of the ensemble pursuit. Opportunity and emphasis will combine to make success mean different things to each performing group.

The two-fold target of this book has led me to divide my ammunition in the following way. First, I describe my own rather unusual preparation for a life in chamber music, how I came to join what was long one of America's foremost concert ensembles—the Fine Arts Quartet—and the many kinds of tasks and experiences my colleagues and I had during my quarter century (1954–1979) of membership in the group. I think I have avoided the rose-colored-eyeglass nostalgia and press-book hype of the usual musical memoir, whether of soloist or ensemble persuasion. Ensemble life is as tough as it is rewarding, and I try to picture it with a proper combination of realism and tact. Some events I recall make this the "fun" part of the book, though I myself did not always feel the bubble of hilarity at the time of the experience.

In my later chapters, I offer more concentrated advice to young musicians entering the chamber music arena. You might think that, after my twenty-five years in a quartet, I would know it all. I do not. Ensemble life is as infinitely variable as the nature and temperaments of the players who make up the group. The members themselves will hammer out rules and methods of engagement to suit the several personalities of the teammates. My suggestions stem from my own ensemble experience. I would have liked having these pointers on hand when I embarked on the many years of my chamber music career.

The first section of this book shows that I myself did not follow many of the precepts that I now offer to my successors. Hindsight is usually a sharper kind of vision. Moreover, though I was already thirty-two when I moved into an ensemble existence, I still had enough youthful impulse that I probably would have ignored my own best advice. In any case, my hard-won counsel can help ensembles avoid the frictions and outbursts that have led to the breakup of more than one ensemble of proven achievement and potential.

I hope the nonprofessional, too, will enjoy reading this longtime insider's suggestions. Here the chamber music lover can gather further insight into the workings of a concert ensemble, and the amateur performer will learn things helpful to the ensemble that meets regularly; helpful even to the casual lineup of players convening for a friendly evening of musical pleasure.

To end this introduction, a confession: I toyed with the idea of using, as subtitle, "Life in a Musical Submarine." Fearing thus to annoy more than one connoisseur of chamber music, I settled for voicing this label here and explaining it away immediately. It is clearly an irreverent way to describe the enviable pursuit of studying and performing the superb repertoire in this domain of the literature.

That pursuit, however, is carried out by a small team of musicians in close and prolonged contact with each other. It is the rare ensemble that has its members living far from one another, only getting together as necessary to brush up on their already well-rehearsed season's repertoire in preparation for a compact tour of concerts. Far more common is the ensemble that lives in or near one city, perhaps the site of a school in which the group has a residency. The members see each other week in and week out, with many hours spent in the rehearsal studio. The physical quarters are not as cramped as in a submarine, but the mental and psychological impact of long togetherness can seem almost as confining.

Each player is at the same time a director (read, "conductor") of the team, with a very personal stake in his or her own concept of the music at hand. In a duo, with just two streams of thought needing alignment, differences inevitably arise and demand resolution. Add another one, two, or more voices, and the possibilities for bumps and collisions between viewpoints and attitudes rise geometrically.

Prolong the situation over a period of months and years, and you can readily imagine that the social and musical footwork of the ensemble members must be as deft and delicate as maneuvers taken to avoid encounters with the bulkheads and torpedo tubes of an underwater craft. Fortunately, explosions of temperament are here not life-threatening, but they can do real damage to the work and existence of the group. Try not to fight for control of the rudder, and come up for air as often as possible.

With this said, I move on to my recollections of years past and my homilies on survival in an ensemble. I cannot do so, however, before expressing my thanks to those who have given me their help as I marshaled my thoughts, opinions, and words for this book. First, my gratitude to my longtime colleague and friend during my quartet years and after, George Sopkin, superb cellist both in ensemble and solo. He encouraged me over the years as I grappled with the tenor and purpose of my text. Next, my appreciation to Lois Finkel, herself a fine chamber music coach and veteran member of the Charleston String Quartet, and Mary Natvig Engelke, stalwart and knowledgeable musicologist and violinist. I have known both of them for many years and value their reactions to drafts of this writing. Again, as in past authorial effort, I have profited from the expertise and good counsel of Eve S. Goodman, editorial director of Amadeus Press, in the process of refining and organizing my manuscript. So also, I am freshly grateful for the encouragement and perspective of Reinhard G. Pauly, my friend since university days and formerly general editor of Amadeus Press. My thanks as well to Ralph P. Locke, professor of musicology at the Eastman School of Music, for the support he has expressed for the project. I extend warm appreciation, too, for the advice of my good friend during my Rochester years, Sherwin Weinstein. At the last, however, the responsibility for the opinions articulated in this book is my own.

My thanks to *The New York Times* for their permission to reprint the text of my article that appeared in their travel section in November 1977 and to Edgar Villchur for permission to reprint the photo showing him, his Acoustic Research high-fidelity speakers, and the Fine Arts Quartet in action. I acknowledge also the generosity of Sibley Library, the music library of the Eastman School of Music, in providing several excerpts from their collection of early editions for use as illustrative examples in my text.

Last, but certainly not least, my most affectionate gratitude to my wife, Jill, who has herself enjoyed and survived the several phases of my career for more than half a century. I could not have done any of it without her.

1 ✧ MY WINDING ROAD TO
AN ENSEMBLE CAREER

I n the late 1950s the Fine Arts Quartet was giving an assembly discussion-concert at the Downer Seminary, a private school for girls in Milwaukee. During our conversation with the audience, one young lady asked, "You mean you make a living off of that?" She seemed a bit startled at her own question, or at least by its grammar. We too were taken aback but made some kind of plausible answer.

I am a bit surprised myself as I look back on my career from the vantage point of my ninth decade. Chamber music was indeed my livelihood, but I came to the pursuit fairly late, roundabout, and only through a significant change in the musical track I was following. However, to begin at the beginning…

Training

It was my mother Dora's doing, all of it. As a young woman early in the last century, she had come alone to America to get away from life in her native Russia. She met my father (also an immigrant) in New York. When their children were born, she was determined they should have the benefit of musical training. She had no musical experience herself, but during her girlhood years in Odessa had seen music serve as an accessible professional avenue for some of her Jewish compatriots. Thus, here in the New World, my older brother was started on the violin; my middle brother, on the piano. For me (possibly because my mother was not too excited about any other instrument in the string family), the choice was again violin.

At the age of five, I began lessons with my violin brother, whose patience must have been sorely tried. Before long, I followed both siblings to the Greenwich House Music School. There I learned the rudiments of music theory and continued work on the violin.

When I was eight my father died, just at the brink of the Great Depression. My mother struggled to support herself and three sons. Through low-paid employment as pieceworker in the ladies' garment trade, she kept the family together; and she insisted that we keep on with

An old music school publicity photo: Abe Loft, then about seven years old, getting a violin tutorial from his long-suffering oldest brother, Jacob.

our music. We moved from one low-rent apartment to another in the course of my elementary school years, with the result that I must have attended about twelve public schools by the time I graduated.

In my last few elementary grades, we were living in Brooklyn, and I was studying violin at the Brooklyn Music School. I now know that the hardest things to learn in instrumental study are to listen to yourself objectively; practice efficiently; and give intelligent shape to the music you are playing. In my Brooklyn years I had mastered little of this. The technical requirements of the repertoire assigned me were beyond my capacity, and I developed a convulsive and perspiring playing style. In addition, the violin and bow I was using could have yielded subtleties of dynamics and tone color only to a player considerably more skilled and sensitive than I was at the time.

At thirteen I had opportunity to play for the conductor Leon Barzin. His judgment, "You'll have to start over again," was hard to hear, but I knew he was right. A fresh start was delayed, however. I was about to begin high school at Townsend Harris, the preparatory school of City College of New York. Harris had a three year curriculum, with excellent teachers and strong demands on the quality of its students' work. I had my time cut out for me and gave little thought to the violin. Also, Harris's three-year calendar meant there was room only for mechanical drawing on its program by way of an art course, and certainly no musical training. There were extracurricular opportunities, and for a time this included a school orchestra (conducted by a member of the French faculty) in which I played. The experience, however, had no impact on my instrumental prowess.

I graduated from Harris in the spring of 1938, one of eleven seniors admitted to Columbia College. While waiting for entry to college in September of that year, I resumed violin study, this time with Louis Ideler at the Neighborhood Music School. The school, then on East 104th Street, later changed its name to the Manhattan School of Music and eventually moved to Claremont Avenue when the Juilliard School left its building there for its new home at Lincoln Center. At Neighborhood I also started music theory again and played well back in the second section of the school orchestra. (By well back, I mean in the last stand. In fact, I was the only one on that stand; you might say it was a solo spot.)

At Columbia, as at Harris, the academic demands were stiff, only more so. There was, however, a university orchestra, and its conductor,

Herbert Dittler, was professor of violin in Columbia's music department. Dittler had been a pupil of the French master Jacques Thibaud and was a very well schooled instrumentalist. He took me on as student and made me concertmaster of the orchestra during my freshman year. One point in my favor was that, since I was a freshman, our conductor might count on having a known item in the lead chair for a full four years, and that is how things turned out.

Because of my renewed violin study, I began to think of a career in music. Columbia University's department of music had two avenues of concentration: musicology and composition–theory. I took courses in theory with William Mitchell, who had been a student of the eminent theorist Heinrich Schenker in Vienna. Mitchell's classes in harmony and form-and-analysis proved invaluable to me in my later performing career. Through them I learned to listen for, and to reveal in my playing, the shape and direction of a musical line. Also I was taught to seek out and understand the structure that arose from the interaction of the moving melodic strands. Without realizing it, I was being given the equipment I would later need for perceptive chamber music interpretation.

But I was drawn increasingly to the department's offerings in music history, my interest stimulated also by the chance to use the violin in the programs of the Collegium Musicum. Except for a passing thought about secondary school music teaching, I found myself heading toward a major in musicology. Paul Henry Lang was then in the prime of his long reign as professor of musicology at Columbia. I was in his history course the year his *Music in Western Civilization* appeared. The scope of the book, paralleled by Lang's ready command of an extremely wide repertoire of styles and compositions in his discourse, impressed me greatly.

My academic choice was now becoming clear, but violin was still an important part of my life. In the summer of 1941, I was a chamber music student in the first season of Yale University's Norfolk School of Music: as violist. This was my introduction to an instrument soon to become very important to me. It was also my first concentrated dose of chamber music playing. I recall especially performing the César Franck Piano Quintet in an ensemble with Urico Rossi, who would later be first violin in the Berkshire Quartet at the University of Indiana.

I was in my senior year at Columbia when the legendary conductor Leopold Stokowski embarked on one of his wide-ranging projects: a choreographed version of Bach's *St. Matthew Passion,* to be performed at the old Metropolitan Opera House. The orchestra was composed of musicians from the NBC Symphony and students selected by Stokowski from school orchestras in New York. I was among the chosen, playing next to Carlton Cooley, the NBC's principal violist. As far as I know, this novel treatment of the *St. Matthew* was never repeated. Some months later Stokowski invited me to join a symphony orchestra he was forming in New York. By then, however, I had already begun my graduate work at Columbia and did not want to be distracted from that pursuit.

In the summer of 1942, just after my graduation from Columbia College, I was at the Cummington School in rural Massachusetts. There I studied violin and chamber music with Boris Schwarz, the violinist and teacher who gained added distinction as a highly respected musicologist. The Cummington program held many temptations for someone who should have been concentrating on violin practice. As the summer wore on, I dabbled in acting, pottery, rudimentary woodturning (on an old metal lathe that I made run in the pottery shed), and so on. That summer, too, was when I signed up for the World War II draft. In the fall I began the two-year program toward an M.A. at Columbia, though I expected military call-up to intervene before completion. In the event, my army physical that fall classified me 4-F. I was able, therefore, to continue with my graduate work, turning out a thesis of some earnestness but of little consequence.

In sign of some kind of patriotic service, I enlisted in the New York State Guard, ascending to the rank of corporal—because I could type our unit's records. We would certainly have lost any actual encounter, though, if I had had to lead my troop into action. While we were on night maneuvers near the local gas works, my glasses fogged up under my rubber gas mask. When Sergeant Hammerschlag asked me where my men were, I turned to point to them—and found myself utterly troopless. So much for authority. My career in the Guard was mercifully short.

The summer of 1944 I worked for some weeks as washer-dryer in the photo darkrooms of *Life* magazine and thus saw some of the first prints of the soldiers on the beaches of the Normandy landing. Seeing those photos of soldiers lying dead along the shoreline was a chilling and humbling experience. In that context, it seems the height of irrelevancy to say that, in September, I was back at Columbia to start toward a doctorate in musicology. I was in the process of working my way from one end of the class-room to the other—and beyond.

An essential part of the transition was that of honing my ability to write and speak in an organized and intelligible way. Fortunately, the high school I had attended expected writing from its students of an amount and level that would dumbfound the student in today's average secondary school. In my undergraduate years at Columbia, the standards for both quick-reaction exam writing and the more leisurely considered essay were suitably high. Turning out a master's thesis and then the extended research and writing of a doctoral dissertation added to my abilities, though I would like to think that I have moved on, stylistically, in the fifty years since.

My writing deadlines were sometimes unexpectedly enlivened. I had met and married my wife, Jill, in 1948, as I shall recount in the coming pages. Late in 1949 she and I were in the throes of getting my dissertation ready for review and defense in time for the awarding of degrees at the May 1950 graduation ceremonies. I would follow my work day at Columbia (I was by then an instructor on the faculty there) by typing a rough draft of an installment of the study. Jill would get home from her job as editor at a science press and, after dinner, sit down to type a fair copy of what I had written. As the deadline drew ever nearer, the drill changed slightly. She was by then typing final copy, while I revised later chapters just ahead of her.

After a couple hours at the keyboard, Jill would have to let off steam by playing her cello, an instrument she had taken up a few years earlier. She was at this one midnight when our apartment doorbell rang. Jill desisted immediately and urgently motioned me to see who it was. I protested, whispering hoarsely that *she* was the noisemaker and so should do the answering. Nothing for it: I looked through the peephole and saw an impressively large policeman. When I opened the door, he regarded me sternly and asked, "Who's playin' trombone?"

Those were the days before the word processor and the photocopy machine. Consequently, multileaf layers of onionskin typing paper and carbon sheets were used to make the seven copies of the dissertation destined for the faculty defense committee. Any typing errors had to be tediously erased on the original and each sheet of onionskin before the stack was removed from the typewriter. Jill's patience held out, though, and she got the job done in good time before the deadline.

Through the good offices of Paul Lang, who was then editor of *The Musical Quarterly*, I wrote a couple of articles, as well as translations of musical literature and bulletins for that journal. It was also through Lang's recommendation that I got my biggest translating job. This was to convert, from German to English, the text of Béla Bartók's book *The Melodies of Rumanian Colinde* (Christmas Songs). During my later years at Columbia I gained more writing insights through a term as reviews editor for the *Journal of the American Musicological Society*.

As for speaking, I began to learn something about that too during my graduate years at Columbia. For one thing, the graduate students were required to deliver oral introductions to each composition in the Collegium Musicum programs. This was under the critical eye of Paul Lang, Erich Hertzmann, and other faculty members. I prefer not to remember too clearly some of these early talks (for example, the time when Lang called out to me during one of my efforts, "Slower! Not *alla breve!*")

Sooner than I might reasonably have expected, I was sharpening my speaking abilities before classroom audiences. In the summer of 1946, William Crosten, of the music faculty at Columbia, was hired away by Stanford University to be the chair of the music department there. Crosten's place in the Columbia roster had to be filled. I was appointed instructor and began teaching that September. This began my stint of eight years of classroom lecturing at Columbia, and for three of those years, at the Manhattan School as well.

In every case, I was addressing a captive audience of students who needed to complete the course for academic credit. Even so, the conscientious teacher wants to feel that the class is interested in the proceedings. As ever, the teaching experience is also a learning one; you can tell when the lecture is going over well—and when it is not. In that respect, at least, the classroom and concert platform are not too far apart.

Performance experiences

Having mentioned the concert platform, I must digress for a bit to show that I did not act entirely without reason in making an eventual change in career. Over time, I had opportunity to test my abilities as a performing musician.

When I started work toward a doctorate in musicology at Columbia in September of 1944, my mother and I were living alone in a small apartment near the university. To support the household, I needed income. With so many musicians in military service in those years, I was able to find gigs as a freelance in radio, a medium that in those days still used live music. I was hired as the violist in the band for the Pall Mall cigarette program, the one that featured vocalist Johnny Johnston, with Jim Ameche (brother of Don Ameche of movie fame) doing the commercials. Had it been the same producer's Chesterfield cigarette show, starring Perry Como, my stint would have been longer. Our band was a decent one, though, with famed Teddy Wilson at the piano. I read my part in the arrangements, played in tune and on time, and got by. Luckily, no one ever asked me to do any jazz improvisation. Johnston gave way after a time to a singing ex–postal worker from Philadelphia. The show died.

For the spring season, I was in the viola section of Ray Bloch's band on the Philip Morris show. (Cigarette advertising then was less restricted in America than it is today.) Actually, the Bloch band was more like a pop orchestra, for it had small string sections rather than the one-on-a-part setting of the band in the Pall Mall program, and fuller wind instrumentation as well.

That summer, I was again in a small studio unit, now in a Latin American music series. I was the lone violist, sitting next to a very impressive cigar. Clamped onto the end of the cigar was the celebrated Joseph Fuchs, the sole violinist in the group. I think I had more conversation with the cigar than with Mr. Fuchs for the length of the series.

By the summer of 1946, I had completed two years of coursework and passed the comprehensive exams for my doctorate. To finish the research and the writing of my dissertation would take time and money, and I had no steady job. I was, therefore, ever on the alert for the phone call from the CBS contractor's office that would summon me for a radio date. Luckily, I was assigned a pop music program (as in the previous summer, it again had a predominantly Latin American menu), led by staff conductor Alfredo Antonini. It was again a one-on-a-part ensemble, and I was the lone violist.

The instrument I played in those years was a large Bavarian viola of modern vintage, yellow-orange in color, and with a patch of reddish stain in the area around the bridge to heighten the flamboyant effect. As luck would have it, the first arrangement for the first program of the series had a short viola solo in it. I asked the conductor whether I should go to a separate microphone to play the line. Antonini gave me his instructions (I will not try to render his rich accent in print): "I tell you what to do. You stand up, move your stand close to the microphone, and play with warm, sweet, beautiful tone. You know, I don't like the color of your varnish! I hope your tone is better!" After the solo, dryly: "Your tone's better." Those lines became catchphrases in my New York circle of acquaintances.

The final arrangement of the program was always followed, without pause, by the upbeat that began the closing theme of the show. We were doing one of the later broadcasts of the series and had arrived at the last page of the last arrangement. While playing, I realized that I had not made even the slightest blooper in the entire show. Thus it remained until the last cadence, where the entire band, in rhythmic unison, had a silent eighth-note just before the closing oom-*pah*. I, however, played squarely and lustily on the silence, coast-to-coast. With his right hand, Antonini swung us into the closing theme. With his left, he gestured a dramatic slitting of the throat and pointed to the door. After the theme, I was in haste to make an unobtrusive exit. As I packed my viola, I sensed someone behind me. Turning, I found Antonini glowering at me in mock temper. "At least it was in tune!"

I must not conceal the fact that I was called for a recording date in an orchestra conducted by the respected arranger Nelson Riddle, with a young Frank Sinatra as the featured singer. Also, I subbed in an orchestra (probably the CBS Symphony, though I cannot now be certain) with Walter Hendl as the piano soloist. In later years Hendl was to become assistant conductor of the Chicago Symphony under Fritz Reiner and, later still, the immediate successor to Howard Hanson as director of the Eastman School of Music. On a different note, I played in the backup bands for two comic stars of radio days, Fred Allen and Edgar Bergen (with Charlie McCarthy, Mortimer Snerd, and friends), when they came east for a week and did their broadcasts from New York.

One last tale from the summer of 1946: when William Crosten left Columbia for Stanford, his doctoral dissertation (eventually published as *French Grand Opera: An Art and a Business*) had just been typed in the requisite seven copies. The typist in question did not have accent marks on her machine, so all seven typescripts, hundreds of pages containing many quotations in French, had to have a zillion accents written in by hand. Only then could the finished copies be distributed to the academic committee that would have to hear Crosten's defense and approve the awarding of the degree. Bill had gone to California, and hired me to take care of the accents.

The now dimly remembered Quink pen, with its fast-drying ink, was then new on the market. I bought one and settled down on a Saturday to write the accents. It was about 4:00 A.M. Sunday when I finished. I slept in, had breakfast, and then lay down on the sofa to have some more shut-eye. My mother left to walk in the summer sunshine and told me not to lie there all day, but follow her example and get some fresh air.

Hardly had she shut the door when the phone rang. It was the CBS contractor, asking me to go down to Liederkranz Hall (then a favorite New York sound studio) to sit in for a broadcast. I did the rehearsal and the show, came back to the apartment, and lay down again on the sofa. You guessed it. My mother got back, found me napping, and berated me for having spent the whole afternoon indoors.

As earlier reported, I started teaching at Columbia in September of 1946. What with the new job and having to get my own dissertation done, I would be busy and fully scheduled. It was no longer possible to respond to the sudden and unpredictable phone calls from the radio office. I told the contractor's secretary that I would regrettably no longer be available, and asked to be crossed off the list. It was the kind of request I am sure she did not often receive.

It was not long, however, before I found I needed relief from the classroom lecturing, library work, and writing sessions that now filled my time. The respite came in the form of occasional music-making. I helped manage and perform in the Alice M. Ditson Concerts of Contemporary American Music that Columbia was putting on in its Mc-Millin Theater. In the course of that activity, I got to work with a faculty colleague, the pianist Alvin Bauman. For a time we formed a viola-piano duo, giving our first concert together at the old Times Hall auditorium in the fall of 1948.

That concert was significant for me in more ways than one. To rehearse the program, I had gone up to Vermont in late summer to a house that Al had rented. After some weeks of work, we took a break and for a day visited an amateur chamber music workshop at Middlebury College. Among the participants there was a young lady with cello. This was in September and, acting with due deliberation, we did not marry until Christmas week, in the quietest of ceremonies at New York's City Hall. As I write, Jill and I have been together for more than half a century, so it seems our meeting was a good thing. Either that, or she is exceedingly patient.

In the early spring of 1950, Alexander ("Sasha") Schneider—then still in his years of sabbatical from the Budapest Quartet—was recruiting the orchestra for the first Prades Festival, which Pablo Casals would direct that summer. I was asked to try out on viola. The auditions were held at the Manhattan apartment of the musical patroness Rosalie Leventritt. Schneider listened to me and I was then called into a room where I faced Mrs. Leventritt, concert manager Thea Dispeker, Carleton Sprague Smith (then head of the New York Public Library's Music Division), and Schneider. Sasha told me they were inviting me to join the festival orchestra, and asked how much I could contribute. Taken aback, I volunteered a figure of $100. Back home, I told myself that, with our family finances, $100 might as well have been a million. I phoned to say that my instructor's salary did not allow for any monetary contribution to the Prades event, and that the fare and expenses, plus loss of summer teaching income, would already be a significant offering on my part. Some days later, I had a form letter from the festival's lawyer, no less, thanking me for my interest and inviting me to listen in at a festival rehearsal—if I should happen to be in the vicinity of Prades.

In the closing years of Sasha's life, I had opportunity to sit with him regularly for his auditions at the Eastman School for his Christmas season young people's orchestra. I never summoned up the nerve to remind him of what happened in early 1951. Recruiting was then well underway for the second Prades Festival. I had a call from Sasha's secretary, telling me that he wanted me to play that summer, but that I would have to decide by the next day. When I phoned, I got Sasha himself and essentially repeated my script from the prior year, at which point Sasha broke in with, "If you want to talk about money, maybe we'd better not talk at all!" He hung up on me, and we did indeed not have occasion to speak again until some thirty-odd years later.

I had two brushes with life in a string quartet before arriving at that goal in the form of the Fine Arts Quartet. It was probably sometime in the spring of 1945, when I was involved in my doctoral coursework, that a Columbia acquaintance asked me to meet with three friends of his who were forming a quartet and were looking for a violist to complete the group. I duly met with the three at an apartment near Columbia for an informal chamber music session. There was some reticence on both sides: they would tell me only that there was a full-time berth (unnamed) awaiting the quartet when formed; and I said that I would have to reserve time for my graduate studies.

In the light of later knowledge, I realize that this reservation alone must have cast an immediate shadow over my suitability. More important, I am sure, was my inexperience with the quartet repertoire. Whatever else we played together that evening, the kiss of death came with the finale of Beethoven's Quartet in C, Op. 59, No. 3. That movement begins with a rapid-fire, eighth-note melody in the viola, quite alone. Over the course of many later seasons, I played that finale countless times, but always as second in line after the viola. And I know from experience that there is always that little rush of adrenaline that impels each player (none more so than the lead-off violist) into the whirling rush of that theme. That night in 1945, however, when I was confronted with that line, I asked whether we could take the theme a bit under tempo. There was a polite, rather bemused response. You will understand, then, that I did not become a founding member of what turned out, in 1946, to be the Juilliard Quartet.

I was of course surprised when I learned what that audition with three newly met musicians had been about, those months back. On the other hand, when the news broke, I had unexpectedly become a member of the Columbia music faculty and felt I was on the lifelong academic path for which I had been preparing. Moreover, had Robert Mann and his colleagues by some stretch of the imagination chosen me, I am not at all sure I could have stood the strain of learning repertoire, finding a suitable viola, and jumping into what must already have been the intense schedule and obligations of their early career. What a difference just a few years would make. My entry into the Fine Arts Quartet in 1954, which I shall recount a bit later, was made under conditions rather similar in intensity to what I would have felt in 1945–46. However, I was eight years older, very self-convinced about my change in career, and—owing to playing and performance experience acquired in the interim—more ready to deal with the very real pressures of my first years (or I should say, *all* the years) as an ensemble member. What all this indicates to me is that you have to know opportunity when you see it, feel you are equipped to deal with it, and then swim like crazy when you have plunged into it.

Mann, so long the leader of the Juilliard, wrote a very favorable review of my book *Ensemble!* in the June 1993 issue of *The Strad.* I took the opportunity to write him a note of thanks, in the course of which I reminded him of that tryout evening, half a century earlier. I don't know whether he recalled it, but I have never forgotten. I also said that on many occasions, in concert with the Fine Arts Quartet, I had stepped energetically on the throttle in that fateful Beethoven finale. George Sopkin can attest to this, for as cellist he is third in line for the theme, and I would habitually hand it over to him with the motor purring very nicely indeed.

I had already been teaching for a time at Columbia when Broadus Erle, elegant musician and founding member and first violin of the New Music Quartet, asked me to join the group as replacement for their departing violist. This must still have been rather early in my teaching years. At the time, the idea of giving up my faculty appointment and changing careers was not something I was ready to consider, even though my friend and concert partner Al Bauman urged me to accept Broadus's invitation. In retrospect I know that working with either Mann or Erle, quite different though they were in musical style and temper, would have been a wonderful experience. However, it was not to be.

In 1950, two years after our first go-around, Al Bauman and I gave a second viola-piano sonata recital at Times Hall. In keeping with this spacing, 1952 proved to be a third concert year. It was then that I was in the process of changing back to the violin after ten years as violist. A feature in our 1950 recital had been the premiere of Milton Babbitt's *Composition for Viola and Piano.* Between them, Al and Milton had soon thereafter urged that I revert to the violin. Otherwise, they held, Al and I might all too soon have to pad out the relatively limited viola repertoire with transcriptions. Whether or not all of us were correct in this assumption, the changeover was not an easy decision for me, especially since the violin I owned was very far from concert caliber. For that matter, my cherry-stain viola was certainly not an outstanding instrument either, even though I had played radio dates and recitals on it in the preceding years. Rembert Wurlitzer, dealer in fine string instruments, very kindly lent me a wonderful-sounding viola for a performance of Telemann's Viola Concerto with the CBS Symphony, a feature in a Columbia University–affiliated broadcast series during those years.

Mr. Wurlitzer again very generously let me use a Guarnerius del Gesù violin from his collection for the recital Al Bauman and I gave in 1952 at New York's Town Hall. Among the works on the program was Schoenberg's last instrumental composition, the *Phantasy for Violin with Piano Accompaniment* (1949), in an early New York concert performance.

Although I did not foresee the importance that the reversion to violin would have for me, I did realize that tooling up for one "official" concert every two years was not the most satisfying way to organize my musical life.

2 ✧ COLUMBIA

My Years at the Other End of the Classroom

Teaching at Columbia was not for the faint of heart. As a freshman I had taken the required year of reading and discussion of important writings from Plato on down to recent time. In my sophomore year I took the art history semester of the sequence and, because I was already taking more specific music courses, skipped the music semester for nonmajors. When appointed to the faculty in 1946, I had to teach the music survey I had missed as a student.

I suspect that many in the course were there primarily because they had to be. Some had musical awareness, and none had any particular desire for a low grade, but there was no professional goal or career concern to inhibit their class participation. And since the Columbia student was—by habit and selection—typically of a questioning and outspoken turn of mind, the classroom experience could be pretty lively.

I found this out rather quickly. In a section that I led that first year, I had managed to graft a consideration of the ostinato type of composition into the week's syllabus. My ulterior motive was to show the class I would be no mere disk jockey, relying only on recorded examples of the music under discussion. No, I would play them the entire Bach Chaconne from the D minor Partita for Violin Alone. So there I was, well into the hour, having talked about the ostinato and ready to play a full-fledged example for them on my made-in-Cincinnati Strad. After fifteen minutes of earnest fiddling, I mopped my brow and asked the class what they thought of it. Silence. Not a word. Then a hand went up in back of the room. "Yes?' I asked." "I think that stinks!" came the reply. No student offered to discuss the merits of the case. Luckily the bell rang, and I kept quiet about the matter at our next meeting. Fortunately I did not then think that I would end up in a performing career, so did not have to regard the student's verdict as a crucial review.

As a matter of fact, that same critic suffered some comeuppance late that semester. I played a recording of Edgard Varèse's *Ionization*, a composition for thirteen percussion instruments. From where I stood, it looked as though the student had been injected with adrenaline. He made no comment whatever. In retrospect, I realize I should have drawn him out on his reaction to the striking sounds and rhythmic events of that music, for it might possibly have been a positive one.

I eventually taught thirty-two separate sections of the music survey, so I had more than one chance to gauge the alertness of my student audiences. In one class session, I described the way composer John Cage evoked special sonorities in his "prepared-piano" pieces by putting various materials between the strings of the instrument. By way of live demonstration, I inserted rubber erasers, pencil shafts, and so on, into the classroom piano and showed the effect this had on the sound of a familiar tune. Early in our next session, I turned to the piano to play a theme from a work under discussion. A succession of thunks and thuds emerged from the instrument. Sure enough, my students had repaid me in kind, and I am happy to report that we all laughed together.

By now, at least some of my readers will be wondering what value such occurrences could have for anyone who would later be engaged in concert performance. After a lifetime of auditorium as well as classroom experience, I know that conducting an effective class is as demanding as giving a good concert. Moreover, keep in mind that classroom teaching of some kind could well be part of many a player's livelihood. Whether addressing a student group or playing to a concert audience of hundreds, you are interacting with your hearers, and they with you. In the concert hall, you are meeting your public through the framework and conditions set by the composition at hand. You measure your success partly through the enthusiasm of the applause that follows the performance. In the classroom, though there can sometimes be applause after an inspiring lecture, you more often have to rely on smaller indications of the students' involvement and attention to your presentation.

For me, a mixed sign of such reaction came in a session wherein I was leading a discussion of Wagner's opera *Die Meistersinger*. For two days I had been playing excerpts from the opera, letting fall some complaints about the didactic way of the composer in making mastersinger Hans Sachs lecture his protégé, Walther (and through him, the audience), about the rules for constructing a proper prize-song. At the third day's class, we were at the point when Walther was to present the final version of the song at the mastersingers' contest. But since we had heard the preliminary drafts, I said I intended to skip the contest rendering. "No," said a student in the front row, "I want to hear it, and don't talk!" I played it and did not talk. I do not remember his name, but that student must surely have gone on to significant achievement.

In light of all the above, I was gratified to read a letter that appeared in the November 1999 issue of *Columbia Today* magazine. It was from a lawyer, now retired from a distinguished career of his own. He had been a student in one of my survey sections in 1947. Having seen my name mentioned in a *CT* report about the Columbia class of 1942, he felt moved to write his appreciation of my teaching, so long back. I value his tribute as much as any concert review I have ever had.

Paul Lang, in addition to directing the graduate program in musicology at Columbia, was busy as music editor of the publishers W. W. Norton and of *The Musical Quarterly*. In my third year on the faculty, he had me take over from him the undergraduate music history course, open to music majors from both Columbia and Barnard College. I found this to be a much tougher course to deal with than when I had taken it as student. Now I had to convey information and perspectives about a broad span of repertoires, styles, and types of composition, and hold the interest and imagination of my listeners in the process.

These were the early postwar years, and the classes included a number of ex-GIs, very intent on making up for lost time, so the course was serious business. Sometimes I felt that a given class session had clicked, though I never found it a simple matter to make verbal statements about music that approached the meaningfulness of what the music said for itself. And I could never be sure that my presentation got over to every student. A daughter of Irving Berlin was in the class one year, and after yet another session on sixteenth-century music, she asked me, "When are we going to get to the *good* stuff?"

Happily, I escaped the kind of incident that confronted Paul Lang when he was teaching the course. He told the story of ending a suitably circumspect mention of the important role played by castrato singers in a sizeable segment of our vocal repertoire. When he called for questions, a student (whether Barnard or Columbia is not known) asked, "Professor Lang, you mean they cut their *vocal* chords?" How Paul worked his way out of that one, he did not say.

My rank at Columbia was that of instructor from the start of my appointment in 1946. To advance up the academic ladder, potentially to the status of a tenured professorship, it was necessary to finish my dissertation and be granted my Ph.D. With Jill's encouragement and by concentrated effort, I completed the writing in the spring of 1950. The dissertation defense went well, except for the embarrassment of having an historian on the committee point out to me that Louis XV of France was the great-grandson, not son, of Louis XIV.

By the start of the next academic year, I had been promoted to the rank of assistant professor. Jill and I no longer had to deal with a compressed regime of research, writing, and typing, but we had new things to learn: our first-born, David, arrived in March of 1951.

My homework chores continued, for I was assisting in graduate work by coaching paleography (the reading and transcription of older forms of musical notation) and also giving a couple of lecture courses of my own. One was on chamber music, and that was a challenge. Some of the ideas I propounded about specific compositions were to change radically in later years when I had continuous, hands-on performance experience with those works.

I remember specifically the session wherein I maintained that Beethoven acted incomprehensibly in attaching the blazingly cheerful Presto coda to the intensely serious Quartet in F minor, Op. 95. Only recently have I discovered that no less a figure than composer Vincent d'Indy felt the same way about that ending. However, I recognize that d'Indy and I were both wrong. In fact, my students—including the young Ezra Laderman, later to be a recognized composer in his own right—immediately assured me that I was incorrect in my assertion. I missed a golden teaching opportunity by not challenging them to prove the correctness of their verdict. They could have shown, as I now firmly maintain, that the coda was Beethoven's personal and logical way of resolving the emotional ambivalence that permeates so much of the course of the F minor quartet.

In those years, too, I was acting as visiting lecturer in music history at the Manhattan School of Music. I was also teaching some violin students, of widely varying ability, under the Applied Music offerings at Columbia, and serving (as noted earlier) as reviews editor of the *Journal of the American Musicological Society*. Time did not hang heavy.

I had arrived at the point where I had been at Columbia, at both ends of the classroom, for sixteen years and was on my third university president. (Nicholas Murray Butler was still in office when I arrived; then came Dwight Eisenhower; and after him, Grayson Kirk). The school had been good to me, had taught me much and given me the opportunity to learn by teaching. Moreover, Columbia was an institution where many in the musicological fraternity would have been happy to find a place.

Flying in the face of all this, I was becoming less and less enthralled with what I was doing. I was transmitting information in an orderly way, and—to judge from their classroom involvement and their written work—the students were keeping up with me. More important, they were being exposed to an important repertoire of compositions. Still, I could not help feeling that, if I were to be a middleman between composer and listener, I would rather function as direct interpreter (that is, performer) than as verbal expounder. Moreover, through attendance at one or another string quartet concert, my interest in that particular kind of music-making was steadily crystallizing.

Jill had been hearing a fair amount of bellyaching from me during those months. My piano colleague Al Bauman had left the Columbia faculty in 1951 and, after our 1952 concert at Town Hall, had pursued interests of his own, so I did not have his ear to talk into. And to my knowledge, none of my colleagues at Columbia knew what was going through my mind. Thus, what happened in the spring of 1954 must have been a rude surprise to the music department: I resigned.

Having moved directly from student to teacher status in the one institution, I was so green that I did not realize I was violating the academic rule that said a faculty member should announce a move before a May deadline. Even worse, in my estimation, was my having acted without any consultation with my Columbia mentors, Lang and Hertzmann. But how could I tell them that, of all things, I was leaving to join a string quartet? Madness! Had I paused for reflection, I might even have persuaded myself that the risks were too great. But the pot had boiled too long. Even Jill, whatever inner doubts she had, did not try to stop me.

3 ✧ HOW I JOINED THE FINE ARTS QUARTET

I n the spring of 1954, the Fine Arts Quartet, a Chicago ensemble, was looking for a new second violin. The group had been formed in 1946 (the same year as the Amadeus and Juilliard, by remarkable coincidence). From the beginning, the quartet members had been on staff at the ABC network's Chicago station and, in addition to their orchestral service there, presented a broadcast of quartets and other chamber music each week. The programs were heard coast-to-coast in America and Canada and were well received.

In 1954, however, Arturo Toscanini retired from his post as conductor of the NBC Symphony. The orchestra had been formed by NBC specifically to lure Toscanini out of Italy, back to America, and to the network. Owing to the splendid reputation the symphony had established, one might think that NBC would have the orchestra continue under other conductors. However, David Sarnoff (head of RCA and NBC) had built a broadcast and recording legend around Toscanini as an individual, and apparently lost interest in sustaining an expensive ensemble after his departure. The dismissal of the NBC Symphony encouraged, if indeed it did not inspire, a general shift away from live musicians (at least for "serious" music) in the radio industry in America.

At ABC in Chicago, some enlightened soul in the front office decided that there was no place for anything as quaint as chamber music in the station's offerings. Despite the popularity of the Fine Arts Quartet series and its relatively low cost, the ensemble was dismissed in the spring of 1954. The quartet had concertized outside its home base and had been acclaimed in such venues as the Berkshire Festival at Tanglewood, the New Friends of Music series in New York, and the Coleman Chamber Concerts in Pasadena. Owing to its schedule at ABC, however, much of its stage performance had taken place in Chicago and its environs.

The ensemble was now thrust into an uncertain freelance situation and was faced with the task of building a career as a touring ensemble. The rigors of that kind of life could have been a factor in the decision of Joseph Stepansky, the original second violin of the quartet, to resign. Besides, he might already have thought of moving to California, where he was to join the select circle of musicians who made up the orchestras that played for the movie sound tracks and recordings then emanating from Hollywood.

That left three out of four: Leonard Sorkin and George Sopkin, violin and cello—founding members of the quartet—and Irving Ilmer, viola. Irv had left his post as violinist in the Chicago Symphony in 1952 and moved to the viola in order to join the quartet. (He replaced Sheppard Lehnhoff, the original violist of the ensemble, who—in a kind of game of musical chairs—joined the Chicago Symphony.) The Fine Arts Quartet threesome consulted with the New Music Quartet when that group came to Chicago for a concert. Broadus Erle, its first violin, and Claus Adam, cellist (who would move a year later to the Juilliard Quartet—more musical chairs), suggested that they try me.

I had just finished the spring semester at Columbia when Sorkin, Ilmer, and Sopkin came to New York to meet with some of the violinists they had in mind. Jill and I had rented a house in Williamstown, Massachusetts, for the summer. Jill and our two boys, David and Peter (born in 1952), would escape city heat there, and I was to commute on weekends from my summer session teaching. Before leaving town, Jill and I met the Fine Arts Quartet members and I played some quartet movements with them. What with my teaching duties and the lack of any recital to prepare for, I had not been doing much playing, so I doubted I was sounding like any stand-in for Heifetz. It was a pleasant meeting, but I did not think much would come of it.

I took the family up to Williamstown. A few days later, George Sopkin phoned to invite me to join the quartet. If I accepted, I would have to be in Chicago in two weeks in order to prepare for the quartet's summer schedule. Neither then, nor at any point during the ensuing twenty-five years (you must believe this), did I ask my colleagues why they had chosen me from among those they had tried. At that moment, I suppose I did not want to know; I only felt the excitement of changing from the classroom to a life that would focus on the concert and everything surrounding it.

My answer was an immediate "Yes," with the proviso that I first had to make certain Columbia could replace me at short notice for the summer courses I had been assigned. I drove down to New York to see Bill Mitchell, who was directing the music department's summer session that year.

I am sure that Bill was taken aback when he realized that I meant to resign my faculty post entirely, rather than take a leave of absence. Not only was I making a career shift that would surprise many in the academic world, but I was doing it very late in the calendar of the collegiate year. I am grateful to Bill's memory for not trying to dissuade me, though I imagine he must certainly have thought I was stepping off a cliff. As it was, I was leaving to Bill the matter not only of replacing me in the summer roster, but also of informing my mentors, Paul Lang, his excellent associate Erich Hertzmann, and composer Douglas Moore, chair of the music department, of the need to find my successor in time for the fall semester.

All three, along with Bill Mitchell, had known and taught me during my years at Columbia. And all of them proved to be most gracious and understanding about my move. As Paul put it to a couple of my contemporaries, he thought I just had too much "performer's blood" in me; I suspect he was right. He later had occasion to review, most kindly, concerts of ours in his capacity as music critic of the *New York Herald Tribune*. At one point, he even came to our New York hotel to hear us play through Elliott Carter's Quartet No. 1, to familiarize himself with the work before attending the concert where we were to perform it. Erich Hertzmann attended our concert at Columbia's McMillin Theater in 1955 and was very helpful to me in his advice thereafter. And Doug Moore responded very cordially to a letter of appreciation for my Columbia years that I wrote him in the summer of 1954. All four—Paul, Erich, Doug, and Bill—are now departed; I remember them most gratefully.

As for myself, things were moving very swiftly in the days following my resignation. I phoned my brothers to tell them what I had decided. If they were nervous on my behalf, they did not let on. Both allowed that, since I was a mere stripling of thirty-two, I had to get this particular experiment out of my system.

My wife, Jill, had a good feeling about my new quartet colleagues, though that could only be a guesstimate on the strength of a short get-together. She had always supported my performing activity, even after I moved back to the violin from her favorite, the viola. Most of all, my grousing about classroom versus concert had forewarned her about the move I was now making. Even so, I say again that it was truly courageous of her not to hold me back at the moment of decision.

I myself did not know all that much about what I was getting into. The quartet was already scheduled to play, later that summer, in Chicago's Ravinia Festival. Also, they were on the roster of the Colbert-Laberge concert agency, the New York management known for its strong chamber music offering. So the quartet was clearly an ensemble of some standing. Yet I could not recall having heard any of their broadcasts and really knew nothing about the group. They had in fact participated in a mixed program in the New Friends of Music series at New York's Town Hall just that February, but with the cloistered life I was leading, it had not registered on me. I went down to one of New York's big record shops, found a couple of the quartet's releases, and read the album bio, both to inform and reassure myself.

I *needed* some reassuring. On the strength of our one get-together, I could not know how we would wear on each other over the long haul. With a lifetime of experience now behind me, I know what a risk we were all taking. I said earlier that life in an ensemble might be compared to the enforced togetherness of a submarine crew. But I must also resort to another metaphor: as in a mountain-climbing team, the members of the group are roped together, absolutely dependent on each other. It takes a special turn of mind to sustain that kind of interdependence.

From New York, I drove back up to Williamstown to spend a few days with Jill and the kids. Luckily, we had co-rented the house there with a friend and her little boy, a New York sandbox pal of our three-year-old son, David. Our younger son, Peter, was still regarding the world from the safety of his playpen. I was glad Jill would not be alone, for she was already well along in her pregnancy with our third child. Especially under the circumstances, it was wonderful of her to deal with this new turn in our lives and to let me go off to Chicago by myself to get started with the quartet.

My overnight train trip to Chicago was my first time west of Buffalo. I did not sleep much, for I was heading into all kinds of uncharted spaces. That very early, sunny Saturday morning when I left Union Station, downtown Chicago was not only big, but—to a New Yorker's eye—seemed strangely deserted. After a stop to pick up a violin (I explain this strange statement in chapter 4), I took the train out to Glencoe, the North Shore suburb where the Sorkins and their two children lived. For that weekend I slept on the Sorkin sofa. Then I transferred to a rented room a few streets away.

Rehearsals began that first Monday and went on daily, either in the Sorkin basement rec room or George Sopkin's living room in neighboring Winnetka, and sometimes in Irv Ilmer's apartment in Evanston. Time was short, for our first concert together was scheduled just a couple of weeks off, at Northwestern University's Lutkin Hall in Evanston.

There was a lot to do. Between 28 June and 15 August, we had to play three concerts on the campus of Northwestern University and four at the Ravinia Festival. There were twelve compositions, shown in the accompanying list, none of them easy and most of them new to my fingers. (Our complete repertoire list appears at the end of the book.) Also, on three consecutive days in mid-July, we coached and demonstrated in a chamber music workshop at Northwestern University. Further, in the early fall we recorded the Brahms A minor quartet and Mendelssohn's octet (see Discography).

When I say that I had never played most of the works on the facing "first plunge" list, you may well wonder how my colleagues got me through the summer in live condition. I was obviously a quick study, but there are limits. A salient fact was that, in presenting those eight years of weekly broadcasts—even allowing for the occasional repeat of a composition—the Fine Arts had built up a formidable repertoire. Now all they had to do was get me to join in without rocking the boat. Thus our rehearsals during that first summer consisted of my learning, as rapidly as possible, how the others wanted to play the music that had already been scheduled. There was little time for discussion; they gave, and I took.

At the end of my second month with the quartet, Jill came out to Chicago to hear our concerts at the Ravinia Festival. At that time Jill and I put down earnest money for a small house in Ravinia, one complete with a

A first plunge into the repertoire pool

Bartók	Quartet No. 6
Beethoven	Quartet in E minor, Op. 59, No. 2
	Quartet in A minor, Op. 132
Boccherini	Quintet in C (with Paul Tortelier as guest cellist)
Brahms	Quartet in A minor, Op. 51, No. 2
Donato	Quartet No. 3
Haydn	Quartet in D, Op. 64, No. 5
	Quartet in G, Op. 77, No. 1
Mendelssohn	Quartet in E-flat, Op. 12
Mozart	Quartet in G, K. 387
Ravel	Quartet in F
Schubert	Cello Quintet in C, Op. 163 (with Paul Tortelier)

window wall looking out onto a deep, wooded ravine. It would certainly be a change for our family from our very tiny apartment in New York. Jill would be able to play cello at all hours without disturbing any neighbors. In fact, however, she found herself so busy with our growing children that the cello fell quite silent.

The day after the last Ravinia concert, I flew back to Williamstown with Jill to spend some time there with the kids. Jill and I now planned to make the move after she delivered child number three under the care of her obstetrician in New York. I returned alone to Chicago to play in the small-orchestra recordings the quartet was making for the Webcor tape recorder company.

During a break in our second day's session, I was called to the phone. It was Jill's housemate, telling me that Jill was in hospital near Williamstown, having given birth prematurely to a baby girl. I got back east as quickly as air schedules would permit. Jill was able to leave the hospital and return to the Williamstown house in a couple of days, while the baby remained in a hospital incubator. Unfortunately, despite every care the hospital staff could give, the baby died a few days later.

It was now essential that the family keep together and get into permanent quarters as quickly as possible. I drove down to New York, sold off the few things I could, junked some of the rest, and packed the remainder for pickup by the movers. Then it was back to Williamstown to collect Jill, the boys, and our summer belongings, and drive westward. We got into our Ravinia house in just about a dead heat with the arrival of the moving van. At this point, I—and Jill as well, I am sure—was ready for a South Sea isle. But the fall concert season was upon us. I was still unpacking crates and barrels when our quartet rehearsals resumed.

Jill's strength and level-headedness were rigorously tested in the months and years ahead. The move westward, combined with the tragic loss of a newborn; the need to find new friends and acquaintances and to adjust to a new lifestyle were enough in themselves. To make these changes with two—soon enough, three—very young children in tow intensified every aspect of the experience.

Deeper into the pool!

Bartók	Quartet No. 2
	Quartet No. 3
	Quartet No. 6
Beethoven	Quartet in G, Op. 18, No. 2
	Quartet in D, Op. 18, No. 3
	Quartet in C minor, Op. 18, No. 4
	Quartet in C, Op. 59, No. 3
	Quartet in F minor, Op. 95
	Quartet in A minor, Op. 132
	Quartet in F, Op. 135
Bloch	Quartet No. 3
	Piano Quintet No. 1, with Clara Siegel
Boccherini	Quartet in A, Op. 33, No. 6
Brahms	Quartet in C minor, Op. 51, No. 1
	Quartet in A minor, Op. 51, No. 2
Debussy	Quartet No. 1 in G minor, Op. 10
Dittersdorf	Quartet in E-flat
Donato	Quartet No. 3
Dvořák	Quartet in F, Op. 96 ("American")
Haydn	Quartet in F, Op. 3, No. 5

For me, the pattern of high-speed digestion of repertoire continued. The reason: WFMT, Chicago's "good music" station, had joined with the large electronics dealer Allied Radio to present the quartet in thirteen weekly concert broadcasts, held in Kimball Hall in the De Paul University building in Chicago's Loop. From 4 January through 29 March, we played the works in the list on these two pages, including some carryovers from our summer programs or I would really have evaporated in steam. Again we performed works I had never played, certainly not in concert, let alone for a microphone.

In what must have reflected a hidden vein of masochism, I had favored our taking on the assignment, thinking that it would get me to chew through another slice of the repertoire. That it did, but I had moments of

[Haydn]	Quartet in D, Op. 20, No. 4
	Quartet in G, Op. 54, No. 1
	Quartet in G minor, Op. 74, No. 3
	Quartet in G, Op. 77, No. 1
Hindemith	Quartet No. 3, Op. 22
Mendelssohn	Quartet in E-flat, Op. 12
Mozart	Quartet in G, K. 387
	Quartet in B-flat, K. 458
Piston	Quartet No. 1
Prokofiev	Quartet No. 2 in F, Op. 92
Ravel	Quartet in F
Schubert	Quartet in E-flat, D. 87
	Quartettsatz in C minor, D. 703
	Quartet in A minor, D. 804
	Quartet in D minor, D. 810
Schumann	Quartet in A minor, Op. 41, No. 1
Shostakovich	Quartet No. 1, Op. 49
Tchaikovsky	Quartet in D, Op. 11
Turina	*The Prayer of the Toreador*
Wolf	*Italian Serenade*

misgiving during the process. I recall feeling, as we waited to go onstage for the playing of the Debussy quartet (with its finale that lurches at top speed through a collage of episodes), how restful the classroom atmosphere seemed in retrospect.

With the passage of time and concerts, works from the existing Fine Arts repertoire became very familiar to me. Also, we came to play music, both from the standard and the contemporary repertoires, that was new to all of us, thus leveling the playing field somewhat. Fortunately, I was able to play with strength from the outset. Otherwise, I would have been an intolerable drag on the survival of the ensemble and would undoubtedly have been encouraged to leave. In the course of time, I could bring my own perceptions more incisively to bear on the compositions we played. Also, I came to think more analytically about our ways—individual and collective, technical and musical—of approaching our music-making.

The circumstances in which I came to a life in chamber music generally, and in the context of the Fine Arts Quartet specifically, dictate that I must look back with much gratitude to my colleagues' support in my first months and years with the group. Their seasoned experience was invaluable to all of us. I am thankful, too, that I had the perseverance to stand up to the fast-paced indoctrination process. Mine was a course that worked for me, but I would be slow to recommend its rigors to my readers.

In fact, as I look back it seems to me that the pressures of those early years became a way of life for all four of us in the quartet. Ours was certainly not the only ensemble to live under pressure of schedule and obligations. However, both through the need to survive and through force of habit, we made rather an art of loading ourselves down. This we did to such a degree that it took its toll on our way of working together. I will detail some of these self-imposed responsibilities in the pages that follow.

These pressures and our several ways of reacting to them inevitably took their toll. Suffice it to say here that, although the work we did together was fulfilling, there was too rarely a sense of the balanced give-and-take in rehearsal that I consider essential to the smooth working of the chamber ensemble. It may be that such equilibrium is attainable only in a conclave of saints; and, to my knowledge, saints are not necessarily competent instrumentalists.

4 ✧ INSTRUMENTS
Seeking the Ideal

When I took the train west to Chicago to begin my life with the Fine Arts Quartet, I was carrying an empty violin case. There was in fact a bow inside, though a very undistinguished one. I was joining an ensemble where the others played a Stradivarius violin, a Gasparo da Salò viola, and a Goffriller cello, all instruments of the highest rank. For the preceding year or so, I had been using an Italian violin, rented from the Wurlitzer firm in New York, by far inferior to the Guarnerius that Rembert Wurlitzer had so kindly lent me for my Town Hall recital of 1952. Now I needed an instrument that could hold its own against the others in the quartet, no mean assignment. The ensemble had arranged for me to borrow, on trial, a violin from the Chicago firm of William Lewis & Son.

Accordingly, my first stop that Saturday morning when I left Union Station in Chicago was at the Lewis shop to receive what I can now recall only as a very decent old Italian violin. I remember much more vividly that, a few weeks later, there arrived from Europe the instrument I was privileged to play for the next thirty years and more. It was made in Mantua by Tommaso Balestrieri in 1772, and was in a fine state of preservation. Its smooth, robust sound had a timbre slightly similar in its lower registers to that of a viola, making it wonderfully suited to the mezzo-soprano/alto role that the second violin holds in the tonal spectrum of the string quartet.

The eminent luthiers Carl Becker Sr. and Jr., who then led the restoration staff at the Lewis firm, had seen the Balestrieri at the Amsterdam shop of Max Möller during a recent trip to Europe. The violin was flown over for me to try, and that was it. Before the summer was out, I had dug into the family's small backlog of savings, obtained a short-term loan from my brother, and the Balestrieri was mine. (Fortunately, prices for fine instruments were lower—much lower—in those days.) My choice was also approved by my colleagues, for there obviously had to be compatibility of sound among all the instruments in the ensemble.

I played the Balestrieri happily in all our concerts and recordings from 1954 until 1972. This would have continued without interruption but for another violin that came into my life in the latter year. We were on tour in Europe and had arrived in Basel, Switzerland, to record a tape for the archives of the radio station there. During a free day, George Sopkin and I visited the shop of a violin dealer in the city. In his collection was an early-eighteenth-century violin made by the Venetian master Matteo Goffriller. This maker is, of course, world renowned for his cellos, less so for his violins. The particular violin in question, though, had a distinctive sound, much more of a soprano cast of tone than the Balestrieri that I had been playing for the past eighteen years. I felt so comfortable with the warm sound of the Balestrieri that I was in some doubt about switching at this point. The others in the quartet came to hear the instrument, found it to be first-class, and felt it would fit well in the ensemble. I ended up getting the Goffriller and, since the new violin was not then sky-high in price, was happy to be able to hold on to the Balestrieri as well.

This meant that I ended the tour carrying two violin cases. George had the even bigger job of wrestling with two cello cases, for—from the collection of the same Basel dealer—he was taking home on trial an old Italian cello to serve as alternate to his own wonderful Goffriller. The bevy of cases put us both to a severe test some days after leaving Basel, when, at the Munich railroad terminal, we had to make a mad dash down the platforms in a close connection between trains. For George the exercise was unprofitable, for he eventually decided against his Basel instrument and had a student shepherd it from America back to the dealer in Switzerland.

On our way home from Europe, I stopped off in New York to have some minor adjustments made to the Goffriller. Among other things, a new fingerboard was installed. Three weeks later we flew to San Juan to present the Bartók cycle at the University of Puerto Rico. The afternoon of our arrival, we assembled for rehearsal. I opened my violin case to find that the fingerboard had slipped its moorings on the neck of the violin and, in its fall downward along the length of the instrument, had knocked the bridge of the violin out from under the strings. Very fortunately, there had been no damage to the body of the instrument, for the force of the impact must have carried the bridge out of the way before it could snap down forcefully onto the top of the violin. That kind of blow can put very serious cracks into a crucial area of the instrument. Happily too, the bridge itself had not broken, for it takes a practiced hand to cut the top curve on a bridge and shape its feet to the contours of the instrument.

Nevertheless, there I was, with a violin that needed emergency treatment. A quick inquiry failed to summon up the name of a qualified violin restorer in the vicinity. I ended up at a hardware store, where I bought a bottle of glue and a couple of small C-clamps. I was able to get the violin into playable shape, and we gave our Bartók cycle without further incident. The mishap, though, meant that I had to make another quick detour through New York on my way home from San Juan, to have my amateur repair work set to rights.

In the 1950s and '60s I had been using a couple of quite serviceable bows I had purchased in America. *The* bow of my life, however, came to me by curious happenstance. It was 1971, the year before I acquired the Goffriller violin. We were in The Hague for a concert at Diligentia Hall. We had played there on earlier visits and, as on those occasions, stayed at a small hotel within walking distance of the auditorium. I was on my way to the auditorium for an afternoon rehearsal when I passed the window of a violin shop on the same block as our hotel. I had been vaguely aware of this store, but this time I noticed in the window a violin shoulder-rest I had never seen before. Since I had been a confirmed user of such a player's aid since the early 1940s, I went into the shop, inspected the shoulder-rest more closely, and bought it.

Ever hopeful, I asked the dealer whether he might have an interesting violin bow. He thereupon produced one that he identified as the work of Louis Simon Pajeot, the highly regarded French bow-maker of the first half of the nineteenth century. The dealer allowed me to take the bow along to our rehearsal. The others looked at it, and our *primarius*, Leonard Sorkin, said that if I did not buy it, he would. The upshot, naturally, was that I returned to the dealer after the rehearsal and bought the bow. The Pajeot was a wonderful match for my Balestrieri, as well as for the Goffriller, and I used it with great satisfaction for almost the next thirty years. I am happy to think that the bow is now enriching the life of a younger violinist.

My string-playing readers will already know something that seems strange to the general public: namely, that a given violin, viola, cello, or bass, in the hands of a given player, will sound differently with different bows. The change in sonority can be so subtle that it will not be apparent to the untrained ear, but it is there. One scientist has maintained plausibly that the stick of the bow vibrates in response to the vibrations of the string and of the body of the instrument. The interaction between these vibrating elements and the physical impact of the particular player's physique, his hold of the violin, and his manner of stroking the string with the bow all add up to the production of a unique sound.

Quite aside from its effect on the sonority of the instrument, a fine bow will respond very sensitively to the player as the music calls for the various kinds of strokes in the arsenal of bowing: legato, staccato, spiccato, martelé, and so on. In making a traditional bow, the artisan fashions the stick from wood. No two pieces of wood, even if both are from the favored species used in bow-making, pernambuco, will behave exactly alike. (The same, of course, is true in making the violin-family instruments themselves. The unique nature of any given piece of wood, coupled with the artistic judgments of the luthier, combine to give each instrument its own, inimitable sound character.) So the player will be very happy to find the bow that feels comfortable and responsive, and that draws the best possible sound from his instrument.

The others in the quartet had been as fortunate as I to find and purchase bows that suited both their own playing and the requirements of their particular instruments—even when they changed instruments. In the search for the ideal, during my years with the quartet, our first violin gave up his Stradivarius for a Guarnerius. The violist of my last eleven years with the ensemble moved from a fine old Italian viola to an equally fine J. B. Guadagnini, again a master luthier of eighteenth-century Italy. My own fling with the Goffriller violin ended in the middle 1970s. By then my Balestrieri had undergone adjustment, including replacement of its bass bar, by the master restorer Vahakn Nigogosian in New York. The violin sounded better than ever, and I was happy to go back to my first love.

The only quartet member who stayed with instruments by one luthier in all my years with the ensemble was George Sopkin, our cellist. He played beautifully on his Goffriller cello when I joined the group and continued to sound that way, always. He did, however, a few years after I came to the quartet, trade his Goffriller for another cello by the same maker that had even more beautiful varnish and was in a finer state of repair. This second Goffriller was the "ex-Hamma," so named because it had at one time been in the collection of that renowned dealership in Stuttgart. I think there is a moral here for all of us in the performance fraternity: we must make sure our instruments are in the best possible adjustment, learn to play them so they give their best innate response, and resist the urge to rush around in an endless quest for the "perfect" instrument.

We also make a mistake if we try to improve an already fine instrument with arbitrary alterations to one or another characteristic physical detail of its structure. Not only do such modifications seriously diminish the market value of the instrument, but they also reveal a quirky disregard for the integrity of an irreplaceable work of art on the part of the owner. Such aberrations have taken place over the centuries and continue on into our own time. It is what Nigogosian called instrumental butchery.

Everyone in the profession is aware that fine old violin-family instruments were discerningly reengineered to meet the acoustic demands of performance in the increasingly large auditoriums that arose in the nineteenth century. The softer, intimate palette of sound of the original design of the violin family was fine in the small halls of earlier centuries, whether in the court, the aristocrat's mansion, or the town chambers. For the sound needed in the new auditoriums, changes were made in the violin and its cousins. A longer and more tilted neck was grafted to the original scroll and body of the instrument. The neck carried a longer fingerboard to accommodate playing the higher ranges of the instrument's register. A higher bridge supported longer and thicker strings; and those strings had to be kept at higher tension for a given pitch, thus again allowing for a higher sound volume. The tuning of the instrument was itself gradually raised for increased brilliance of effect, and the bass bar inside the instrument was replaced with a stronger one for proper physical support and acoustic response. These modifications, carried out by expert and careful artisans, became the standard in the production of more recent instruments. In making the changes I have described, the truly qualified luthier did not presume, for example, to tamper with the shape of the instrument's body, its f-holes, or any of the other details (including the varnish) that identify the instrument as the work of a master maker.

Today's impressively high prices for fine old instruments and bows have had the salutary effect of turning the attention of young artists to the work of our very able modern makers. Whether it be instruments or bows, very fine and responsive specimens can be found, dating from the twentieth century and now, the twenty-first. A brand-new instrument may need rather extensive overhaul as it begins to age and settle into itself. But it will reveal its character and quality even during its very early years. More than one prominent artist performs just as happily on a contemporary copy of his fine old violin, viola, or cello as on the original masterpiece.

As for bows, interesting experiments have led to the use of manmade composite materials in place of pernambuco wood. This Brazilian species has been the central resource of the bow-maker since the days of the master who perfected the modern bow, François Tourte, in the early nineteenth century. Players may want to consider bows made of new-age products, though it should be recognized that many fine bows are still being made today of the older, traditional wood. It is all a matter of how the individual bow feels in the hand and of the sound that it evokes from the instrument. The most usual sequence of events has been to find the instrument of choice, then look for the bow that best produces the desired sound when used on that instrument.

The prospect of all members of a string ensemble searching, all at the same time, for suitable instruments raises visions of chaos. It is to be hoped that some in the group already own superior equipment and only the others will need to find instruments of suitably matching sound character. It can happen that a complete family of instruments, all from one modern maker, becomes available or can even be commissioned by the group. There is no guarantee, however, that such a freshly minted set of siblings will provide the required balance and blending of tones. The experience of our own and other ensembles, moreover, shows that a mix-and-match assembly of fine instruments can yield a convincing community of sound.

As for ensembles with piano, there is the inescapable fact that the size and weight of the piano makes it likely that the ensemble, when on tour, will be performing with a different keyboard specimen at each successive concert. Very few pianists are willing or able to pay to have their own piano trucked from city to city on a concert itinerary. Having to use a different instrument at each concert of course tests the technical mastery and the musical alertness of the player. Even so, much will also depend on the ability of the other instrumentalists to match their playing to the acoustic environment established by the particular piano and the sonic response of the auditorium in which the concert is being given.

In the case of today's wind instruments as well as the piano, we are not dealing with instruments that go back as far as the violin family. For both keyboard and winds, current instrument specifications trace largely from the nineteenth century. Here again, fine instruments are being produced by modern makers. As always, however, each player will look for the particular instrument whose action and sound best suit his or her taste.

5 ✧ THE FREELANCE YEARS

When I joined the Fine Arts Quartet in 1954, they had just become a freelance group, relying solely on their own efforts to survive. From this time until 1963, when we were appointed tenured faculty members at the University of Wisconsin–Milwaukee, we found income, sometimes rather creatively, from a variety of activities. It was a merry dance that kept us hopping.

Television

Our quartet benefited from opportunities we had on both sides of the television aisle—commercial as well as educational. These days, such opportunity comes rarely to musicians in the small-ensemble sphere, even on educational television.

Commercial television

Our first appearance on NBC's early-morning program, the trendsetting *Today* show, was in November 1955. It came about because earlier that season we had made two short movies (*Listening to Good Music* and *Playing Good Music*) for Encyclopedia Britannica Films. The EBF publicity office engineered the invitation to appear on the television program in order to tout the film. That debut had a ripple effect. Listening to excerpts from the quartet repertoire while drinking one's morning coffee apparently struck a responsive chord with the show's listeners. The producers reported that the write-in votes of support for our appearance were exceeded in number only by those for the famed black singer and actress Ethel Waters.

For that first appearance and those in the next few years, the host was the show's original master of ceremonies, Dave Garroway. The program was given, as are all such morning talk shows now, in a street-level store-front in the NBC building in Radio City, with the passing public able to view the proceedings through the large plate-glass windows, although onlookers then did not go through the silly hand-waving and screaming that now marks the morning shows. The program, in fact, gave up the storefront for some years, moving for a time into old studio 8H, where Arturo Toscanini had conducted the NBC Symphony during the heyday of that orchestra. With the audience seats removed, the hall had been converted into a large, gaunt room where various sets could easily be constructed and rearranged.

The program still emanated from the storefront the early morning of 16 January 1957, when Garroway, during a break for a commercial, got the news from the control room that Toscanini had just died. Garroway asked us whether we had anything appropriate to play as a musical memorial to the maestro. Luckily, we had with us the music for Haydn's Quartet in D, Op. 20, No. 4. We played the slow movement, that lovely and very affecting set of variations in D minor, and I think that might have been the first musical testimonial to the great conductor.

We had another macabre experience with a television memorial in November 1963. It was two days after the assassination of President John F. Kennedy. We had been called to a commercial television station in Chicago to play some quartet music in a program mourning the nation's loss of its leader. We had rehearsed in the studio, taken our place on the podium, and were waiting the short time before we were scheduled to play. Suddenly, on the studio monitor, the control room patched through the news video from Dallas, Texas, where Jack Ruby had just shot Kennedy's killer, Lee Harvey Oswald. Very soon thereafter, we were on the air, playing while wondering inwardly what was happening to the world around us. Adding to the tragic irony of the moment was the memory that we had given a concert in the auditorium of the Library of Congress on the night of President Kennedy's inaugural in January 1961.

Heading toward the *Today* show studio, 1959. Left to right: Irving Ilmer, George Sopkin, Leonard Sorkin. The quartet flew on to Paris later that day.

Turning back to the *Today* show: it must have been in December 1961, not long after our return home from our first visit to Australia and New Zealand. The program was then moderated by John Chancellor. His production office asked us whether we could talk about our visit to the "down under" countries. We had brought along an aborigine bark paint- ing to show, and I also had an Australian bull-roarer with me. This is a flat, canoe-shaped wooden object, mine being about two inches across at its widest point and a foot long. It is tied to a string through a hole at one end and, when whirled through the air, produces a roaring sound. At Chancellor's request, I demonstrated the effect during rehearsal. However, the braided vegetable-fiber cord broke, and the roarer went sailing off into a corner of the studio. Nobody was hurt, and a stagehand replaced the broken string with a length of nylon fish-line.

At the appropriate point in the telecast, I whirled the bull-roarer, producing a convincing noise that suddenly and mysteriously stopped. I still had the nylon cord in my hand, but it pointed straight up. There was an overhead grid of pipes in the studio, to which lighting units could be clamped as needed. The bull-roarer, ascending too high as a result of my efforts, had wrapped the cord around one of the pipes. There I was, my arms held protectively over my head, with a grinning John Chancellor as in-studio spectator and a bemused coast-to-coast audience looking on. We went on to several concerts in the south after we left New York, and I was asked more than once what I was doing in that guarded stance on the *Today* show.

Leopold Stokowski happened to be a guest on one of our *Today* show appearances in those years. After his interview spot and before he left the studio, he stopped near our quartet to listen for a moment as we played a selection. The show's producer called up a superimposed shot, showing both Stokowski and the quartet. I could see the image on the studio monitors, and thought it effective in a quietly dramatic way. Stokowski might possibly have remembered me from our acquaintance back in the 1940s, but there was no chance to converse during the program. In any case, he left as we were finishing playing.

George Sopkin, incidentally, tells me that he also had had direct acquaintance with Stokowski, at the time when the maestro was holding auditions for his All-American Youth Orchestra (1940) for that symphony's tour of South America. Stokowski asked George to play the cello part of Tchaikovsky's Fourth Symphony, and in fact conducted him as he played through virtually the entire work. When George finished, Stokowski seemed favorably impressed and told George that he would be hearing further word. And that was the end of that. (Leonard Sorkin and Irving Ilmer, by the way, were selected for the group and made the tour aforementioned.)

I must confess that the things our quartet had to do to keep itself afloat in the years before our university residence were not always edifying. A musician cannot always live on Beethoven and Mozart alone. During my first couple of years with the quartet, we were hired to play in the band for a local Chicago program on ABC television. It was sponsored by an auto dealership in Chicago, and its emcee was actually the owner himself. The program that stands out in memory came during the Christmas holiday season. When we arrived at the studio for the pretelecast rehearsal, our host told the four of us, "Wait until you see what a great idea I've thought of for you!"

A set had been constructed on the TV stage that represented a living room, complete with a hearth in which a merry blaze was burning. Arrayed in front of the fireplace were four stands and chairs, where, at the appropriate time, the quartet would be seated, playing a Christmas carol. Came the telecast, and there we were, about to play our assigned carol, whereupon our host introduced us with these deathless words (less likely encountered, one hopes, in today's TV world): "Where but in America could you find four Hebrew boys playing a Christmas carol?"

Educational television

It is hard to believe that, some forty-six years back, there was room on educational television for entire programs about the quartets of Beethoven, Bartók, Mozart, Debussy, Haydn, Hindemith, Brahms, and the like. We were fortunate to be the ensemble featured on those programs.

A producer at the New York office of National Educational Television, and himself a Columbia alumnus, had known me during my university years. This connection, along with the established reputation of the Fine Arts Quartet, led to our signing in 1957 to present a series of television programs on the Beethoven string quartets for NET. These were produced at the Chicago station of the network, WTTW, in its studios then located in the Museum of Science and Industry. In line with the technology of the time, the programs were done on kinescope—that is, photographed on movie film, then telecast from that source.

Each of the six hour-length programs in the series was devoted to one Beethoven quartet (we chose two quartets from each period of the composer's career—early, middle, and late). The first part of the hour was devoted to a discussion about a given Beethoven quartet, carried on between a moderator and the members of the quartet, ostensibly extempore but actually from a script written by me. There were no teleprompters, but we had our scripts unobtrusively placed on our music stands.

The idea was to focus our attention on each other, our studio colleague, or at times on the TV camera, and thus, by extension, on the home viewer. Our aim, within the existing constraints of time and technology, was to produce as free and easy a mood as possible. (When I muffed the playing of a theme at the piano and had to try it a second time, the program's producer even decided to leave the mix-up in the finished program.) In the remainder of the hour, our quartet played the entire work, uninterrupted by comment.

The success of the Beethoven series led, in 1958, to the production of a second set of six hour-long programs, in similar format, with each program given over to one of Béla Bartók's six quartets. This, in turn, gave rise to a third series, *Four Score* (I disclaim responsibility for the title). Now there were eight programs, presenting quartets from Haydn to Hindemith, each again with preliminary discussion by the four of us in the ensemble. The scripts were again mine, and again the chore not only of dreaming up the material but of typing the resulting texts took time and midnight oil.

As an offshoot of this NET series, we issued recordings of the Bartók cycle. And, to accompany the discs, I wrote a pamphlet of notes about the quartets. Those were the days before the seemingly automatic issue of a booklength paperback tome for every series of programs on public television, whether the subject be carpentry, cooking, sewing, or whatever. I am happy to report that the album notes for the records we issued in connection with the *Four Score* series were by the excellent critic and annotator Michael Steinberg.

We made several additional programs for WTTW in the early 1960s. One was in collaboration with the New York Woodwind Quintet. In common with some of our live concerts together, the television program had the ensembles doing a string quartet and a woodwind quintet selection individually, then joining in the playing of a portion of J. S. Bach's *Art of Fugue.* Another program, on the subject of teamwork, was divided, half and half, between an excerpt from a game by the Chicago Bulls basketball team and a quartet played by our foursome. I'm sure their stuff-shots were better than ours!

Back in January 1958 we were in the middle of videotaping the Bartók programs. The night before a morning session at the WTTW studios, we gave a concert at Carleton College in Northfield, Minnesota. We had traveled to Minneapolis by train, rented a car for the drive to and from the

WTTW studio, Chicago, 1963: the New York Woodwind Quintet, ready for taping their part in a television program shared with the Fine Arts Quartet. Left to right: flutist Samuel Baron; oboist Ronald Roseman; French horn Ralph Froelich; bassoonist Arthur Weisberg; clarinetist David Glazer.

college, and were due to take a sleeper that night from Minneapolis to Chicago, arriving there early enough to get to WTTW on time.

All was going according to plan, except that we were getting uncomfortably close to the train's scheduled departure as we drove into Minneapolis. George Sopkin was at the wheel. He dropped Irv Ilmer and me off at the railroad terminal. George and Leonard would return the car to the rental office, near the terminal. Meanwhile, Irv and I were to get a porter and baggage truck, board the train with all the valises, briefcases, and instrument cases, and implore the conductor to delay departure a few minutes if need be, so our two colleagues could get on board.

Irv and I peered nervously down the platform, but the missing two were nowhere to be seen. Perhaps the conductor did indeed hold the train very briefly, but not long enough. When George and Leonard came pelting onto the platform, they saw the train disappearing down the tracks.

Rising to the emergency, the two marooned players obtained tickets to Chicago on the first plane out the next morning. That meant they had to get a hotel room in Minneapolis for the night. Because their unexpected expenses were mounting up, they asked for one double room. Now, because we knew we were going to have a close connection on our way from Carleton to the Minneapolis train station, we had decided to drive while still in our full-dress uniform so as to make a quick exit from the campus. Consequently, George and Len, without luggage and clad in soup and fish, presented a strange sight at the hotel check-in desk. They drew a baleful stare from the night clerk.

There was a baleful stare again the next morning. This time, it was from George and Len, who had arrived in Chicago early enough to get to the railroad terminal in time to watch Irv and me coming down the platform with the fully loaded baggage truck. There was some pungent questioning about our failure to hold the train. We assured them that it would have required throwing ourselves onto the track in front of the locomotive.

Hi-fi shows

In the late 1950s our quartet took part in an annual hi-fi show at a downtown Chicago hotel. Those attending the show would wander from one exhibit to another, listening to the latest equipment and to the still novel sensation of stereo sound. A Chicago hi-fi dealer dreamed up the idea of having our quartet supply live music by way of demonstrating his lines of playback equipment. The stunt involved alternating between our live playing and our recorded sound in pretaped excerpts, heard via a stereo speaker setup that framed us on the exhibit stage. For example, we began the second movement of the Ravel quartet, then fell silent, played, fell silent, and so on, with the speakers taking over as needed. Our listeners were properly amazed at the effect. But the real dazzler came at the end of the demonstration. There, we played the finale of the Mendelssohn string octet. The four of us were abetted by our four alter egos, heard in stereo via the playback. It was a super wind-up, though it palled a bit on the four live players in the course of repeat shows during each day of the exhibit.

Among the observers of this demo was Edgar Villchur, the head of the Acoustic Research firm and inventor of its speakers and turntables. He adopted the demo idea and presented us in the early 1960s not only in Chicago but also at a hi-fi show in New York, Cambridge, Massachusetts, and elsewhere. For greater reality of effect, he had us record all our musical examples afresh, this time in the open air on the grounds of his country home. That way, there was no room reverberation on the tape. As a result, both our live playing and the sound coming out of the speakers responded identically to the acoustics of the exhibit room in which we happened to be giving the demonstration.

I imagine that these demos helped sell hi-fi equipment. I am not aware that many of those who sat, spellbound, in the exhibit room became part of our concert audiences. Maybe some did, or had even been dedicated listeners beforehand.

Funeral music

I do not know how he heard about us and our recording activities, but we were approached by a Minneapolis vendor of funeral parlor supplies. He had come by the business naturally, as an outgrowth of his family's long service as funeral directors. His firm sold everything needful for the trade, from pews to parking-strip painting machines and other much more arcane items. What he asked us to produce was a library of tape recordings of music that would be appropriate for funeral parlor use, whether as background for visitation hours or for actual funeral and memorial observances.

Our own part in the funerary library consisted of such selections as the Cavatina movement from Beethoven's Quartet in B-flat, Op. 130. String quartet music was only one item on the menu, however. We engaged a prominent church organist of the Chicago area to provide selections on that instrument. As usual, we made the recordings at night, when

Early 1960s, Woodstock, New York: the Fine Arts Quartet recording a demo tape outdoors to avoid room reverberation. Left to right: Abe Loft, George Sopkin, Irving Ilmer, Leonard Sorkin. Third from right is Edgar Villchur, inventor of Acoustic Research speakers. Helping him are Eduardo Chavez, painter and sculptor, and Roy Allison and Sunshine Timrud, Villchur's plant manager and secretary, respectively. PHOTO COURTESY OF EDGAR VILLCHUR

the church was not needed for services and traffic noise was at a minimum. We also arranged with a Chicago choral conductor, a friend of the quartet's, to lead his small chorus in the singing of hymns and other inspirational music.

When the library was complete, we turned the master tapes over to the quite businesslike funeral executive. I have no idea what the later history of the library was, or whether its sale kept pace with the other offerings of the Minneapolis firm. It is a good thing, though, that I was not asked to provide album notes for the recordings, for I would have been at a loss for words. I much prefer live, or at least lively, audiences.

Jingles

In the 1950s and '60s there was a large recording studio on the near north side of Chicago where radio jingles were taped. Those were the days when sizeable orchestras, with actual string sections, were used for such work. Even when the music in question was decidedly of the jazz or pop persuasion, the ensemble often included a respectable number of strings. Every so often our quartet would be called for such dates. We were expected to play accurately, give the conductor what he asked for by way of shading the flow of the arrangements, be alert for any cuts or additions that were needed, and above all avoid time-consuming mistakes. At the prevailing pay scale, routined players were needed, for time was an expensive commodity. The income from these studio dates was welcome for our quartet.

Even after we had moved from Chicago to Milwaukee in 1963 for our new residence on the university campus there, we were still occasionally called for the odd recording in Chicago. Making the 180-mile round-trip drive for the single engagement, though, began to feel burdensome, especially in winter weather, so we eventually begged off.

Radio

My introduction to radio station WFMT in Chicago had come during my first year in the quartet. A leader in the circle of "good music" stations across the country, WFMT was then in its early years. After our thirteen-week broadcast concert series for the station in 1955, we continued to give occasional broadcasts for them, no longer on remote signal from a downtown auditorium, but in the studios of the station itself. The rooms were small and the acoustics not reverberant, but we were happy to be playing chamber music repertoire for a station that still thought it a good idea to pay homage to live music. It was during those years, too, that we made occasional appearances on Studs Terkel's interview program, long a renowned feature of WFMT's offerings.

(It is a pleasure to report that early in the twenty-first century WFMT retains its status as a commercial station devoted to a high level of program offerings, both musical and otherwise. In addition to broadcasts of recorded music, it regularly presents live performances by various ensembles appearing in Chicago's musical scene.)

The 1950s still featured the weekly program of the *Chicago Tribune* on radio station WGN, with the owner of the *Tribune,* the redoubtable Colonel Robert McCormick (then in his last years) as the regular speaker. This was radio, not TV, mind you, but there was a studio audience, and the station's symphony orchestra held forth in full dress. We in the quartet were called a few times to serve as added men in the string sections of the orchestra.

Fortunately or not, depending on your viewpoint, we were never witness to the kind of jape that we understand took place during one of these broadcasts. The concertmaster rose from his chair to play a short solo spot and experienced momentary difficulty. A helpful orchestra-mate had tied the tails of his full dress jacket around the back of the chair.

Schools

Among the most meaningful things we did for income, not only in our early, freelance years, but on for a time into the period of our university residence, was to visit the Music Center of the North Shore (in Winnetka, Illinois) several Sundays during each season. The school was directed by Herbert Zipper, who—during a long and fruitful life—was widely known for his leadership in the community orchestra movement and his innovative ideas about the musical training of young people. Our sessions at the school were for the purpose of hearing and coaching its student ensembles. Among these were the three brothers and their sister who were to grow into one of today's outstanding chamber music groups, the Ying Quartet. The hours we passed at the music center were enjoyable and well spent.

We occasionally made school appearances under the auspices of Young Audiences. Especially satisfying here were the occasions when we played for the younger listeners, as early as kindergarten age. They had not yet built up the habits and prejudices of some of their elders, and were ready to enjoy a Bartók movement as much as they did more conventional fare.

Whether meaningful or less so, the things our quartet did in our free-lance years to keep our heads above financial waters were at least concerned with music. Though often without the challenge that lies in the interpretation of a fine piece of chamber music, our varied activities still called for the same skills that we brought to bear in our professional ensemble work. We never had to resort to waiting on table in restaurants or selling merchandise, as some actors and musicians have done to get by between engagements. Besides, as I report in these pages, we were also busy with concerts, recordings, and touring. Throughout these years, however, there was the uncertainty that came with the lack of a solid and predictable income base.

Who did what in our quartet

Here and there in the course of my narrative, I refer to activity by one or another member of the Fine Arts Quartet in areas outside our central function of playing our assigned parts in the quartet performances. These other chores, though, were scarcely less important to our existence as an ensemble. For the sake of clarity, I want to draw together some of those threads and describe how we took care of them.

To begin with, I must emphasize that never, as far as I can recall, was there anything like a quartet board meeting to bestow on each of us an official cap and badge designating our area of responsibility. There were things that had to be done in the process of getting through successive seasons, and each of us rather automatically gravitated toward the area(s) that suited our abilities and inclinations. If I supply greater detail about my own activities, that is only because I was most aware of those that concerned me. There were more than enough jobs to keep all of us busy.

When I joined the quartet, I brought with me the early-model electric typewriter with which I had gathered my research notes and on which Jill had typed my dissertation. Since I had been typing from the age of twelve (starting on an old Underwood machine), I was reasonably good at it and also had had a fair amount of practice at putting words together. Thus, I naturally fell into the role of the quartet's scribe. This led to my handling the correspondence with our managements, both in America and eventually in Europe. In the latter connection, moreover, my fairly fluent reading of French and German came in handy.

Both in America and abroad, the various managements with whom we dealt over the years were small enough that I would be in touch with the person in charge. This was also true of the New York agency that figured in the last ten years or so of my membership in the quartet. It was with the owner of that management that I argued the question of commissions on European tours (see chapter 13). I do not know that the rest of the quartet cared as much about the matter as I did. For one thing, they were not handling the correspondence with European management (that was my job); and for another, the amount of money involved was not tremendous. Yet with the rather minimal net income we were gleaning from our European touring, as well as on the sheer merits of the case, I felt strongly about the issue.

Concerning the handling of fees: again, it just seemed to happen that the care and feeding of the quartet checking account fell to my lot when I joined. In America the fees—with management commissions and expenses deducted—would come to me by check from the management's office. European concert fees are ordinarily paid in cash immediately after the performance. In reflection of my checkbook and record-keeping function generally, the quartet tacitly designated me to receive the fee. I would immediately divide it among the four of us, either withholding amounts owed to the managements involved or squaring that accounting at intermittent points in the tour. The cash distribution was made for two reasons: we each needed the money for living expenses while on tour, and I did not want to be carrying the whole amount around with me. European concert officers would sometimes caution us against leaving any cash in the dressing rooms. And, for that matter, our first violinist's wallet once was stolen from the minuscule greenroom at Carnegie Recital Hall while we were onstage. (This was in the days before that auditorium was remodeled as Weill Hall, and I remember that there were a couple of doors from that small offstage room, giving on to the labyrinthine ways of the Carnegie building. Things have no doubt changed since then.)

Leonard Sorkin was much involved with technical recording matters and—in the years when we were still seeing to the distribution and sales of our records—running that end of things as well. George Sopkin was also concerned with distribution and sales questions and was always active, and very effectively so, in the vital area of maintaining relations with friends and supporters of the quartet. George also was active in planning our season's programs, keeping in touch with guest artists and our Chicago-area auditorium administrators, coordinating the several schedules, and making sure that they meshed with the calendar of the Milwaukee campus. At the university, also, he was our point man in discussions with our dean and other administrative officers. During his years with the quartet, Irv Ilmer shared record-editing chores with Leonard and was also active in other details of the production chain of our record releases. I was handling cash flow for the quartet (not for the recording end of things; for that, we had a small office staff during the company years), program notes, script writing—as for the television programs we turned out—and much of the speaking at our talk-and-music events.

In our years at the university in Milwaukee, of course, we all taught our instruments and organized and taught the chamber music end of things at school. Leonard, because he liked to conduct, would lead occasional concerts of a small chamber symphony made up of students and faculty. For a time, we other three in the quartet served as principals in that orchestra but eventually withdrew to a spectator's role.

In addition to the quartet's concerts (including both our regular concert series and periodic noontime concerts for students and faculty at large) during the academic year and the summer session, we individually—whether in solo, duet, or other context—gave occasional recitals. As I describe in chapter 11, Armand Basile (a faculty colleague) and I gave a series of programs presenting the mature Mozart sonatas, as well as the Beethoven cycle of ten sonatas. And so on.

I led our discussion in our quartet-repertoire courses during our later years on campus, and took care of exam grading. There were also various classroom lecture assignments for us over the years and committee meetings galore, both in the music department and the university at large. I recall with special feeling a university graduate faculty committee meeting that ran for all of five hours. There is a German word for perseverance (consult your dictionary), *Sitzfleisch*. Rarely was mine more sorely tested than on that occasion.

The travel arrangements for our concert tours were always in the hands of travel agencies, though of course we had to keep them apprised of our concert schedules and the cities on our itineraries. Here too,

George kept in touch with the agents. And, again as a consequence of my role as scribe, it was my responsibility to draw up our point-to-point calendar and distribute copies to my colleagues and to all others needing information about our travel and whereabouts.

Our tasks in connection with our Milwaukee-Chicago-Wilmette concert series, our concerts away, recording activities, and so on are described at appropriate points in the course of this book. Dealing with our individual family responsibilities during all these years was of course a parallel theme in our lives, though I must leave any treatment of that to our respective journals and recollections. Suffice it to say here that our days, weeks, and months never ceased to give each of us things to think about, worry about, appreciate, and enjoy.

6 ✧ RECORDING

Pioneering in the 1950s and Beyond

Over the past centuries, much human intelligence and energy has gone into inventing machines that play music. To be sure, the violin, piano, organ, and all the rest of the instrumental arsenal are machines. But they sound only with the direct and continuous intervention of the human performer. The challenge has been to construct machines that play music on their own. Here, the human participates only by powering the mechanism: turning a crank, pumping away at pedals, and so on. Even that amount of immediate, live participation is gone if the operating energy is supplied by a motor, whether run by waterpower, weights, clock spring, or electricity.

Composers as eminent as Haydn, Mozart, and Beethoven either composed directly for such machines or sanctioned the use of transcriptions of their music in this way. It was a kind of publicity as well as the source of some extra income. There was no question of the machine-made performance taking the place of the live player. The sound was never the same as that of an instrument played with the subtlety only the human brain can supply.

Perhaps the most pervasive of the music machines of the later nineteenth century and on into the twentieth was the player piano. Here (as in a less widespread violin-playing machine) the sound was that of the actual instrument. Moreover, in its most advanced stage of development the player piano could capture an impressive amount of the nuance of live performance.

However, it was the ability to reproduce the sound, shading, and flexibility not only of the musical instrument but—for the first time—of the human voice, that enabled the phonograph recording to displace all the mechanical devices that had gone before. And when high-fidelity electronic recording replaced the acoustic type, the dominance of recording in our musical world was firmly established. The blessing has been a mixed one. Recordings have made accessible a very wide repertoire, performed by the world's great soloists, ensembles, orchestras, and opera companies. At the same time, however, the recording accustoms the listener to the unchanging, ever-repeatable performance, the antithesis of the live concert experience. Further, modern editing technology gives the recorded performance a literal perfection that does not prevail in live playing. This flawlessness comes at the cost of that very variability we should most prize in our hearing of music, drama, or oratory.

Finally, the recording is seductive. It is now easy to pop the CD into the player, dial in the acoustics of a favorite concert auditorium—large or small, local or abroad—and settle down to listen in the informal comfort of the home living room. It is even easier to turn on the radio receiver and let someone else turn on the playback. Why bother going to a concert?

Having expressed these sentiments, how can I now turn to describing our quartet's active involvement in the production of recordings? In my early years in the ensemble, the reservations I describe above did not even occur to me. For all of us, the primary concern was one of continued existence.

The early 1950s witnessed the gradual emergence of commercial tape recording. For the Fine Arts, the making and sale of stereophonic recordings on reel-to-reel tape promised a source of income to keep our independent ensemble going. The quartet had established, and were joint owners of, Concertapes, Inc. Because the day of the LP was not past, the title of the label was extended to include Concert-Disc.

The quartet members were the production staff of the company. Our Ampex tape recorders were portable: that is, they were mounted in large trunks with a handle on either end so that we could lug them into and out of our cars, along with microphones, cables, playback speakers, and related paraphernalia. We carried all this equipment into school gymnasiums, church buildings, and other venues that had promising acoustics. This was always in late night hours, when the space was not needed for regular activities and when traffic noises were at a minimum.

As I have mentioned, in my first months with the quartet we were even involved in recording light classics for small orchestra for Webcor, a Chicago manufacturer of consumer-level tape recorders. Leonard was our conductor. Like many instrumentalists, he enjoyed conducting and got the job done in good, musical fashion.

But Leonard had a more central function in our production hierarchy. He had familiarized himself with recording technology, including the new techniques of stereophonic sound reproduction. Not only did he supervise our recording setups, but he also spent hours editing the tapes. At first, this meant long sessions in a temporary workshop in the basement of his home. In addition to the grunt work of carrying and setting up equipment, we all had various chores. I wrote album notes, some very good, a few that I would be pleased to forget. George and Irv (who also did some editing) helped keep track of contact with pressing plants and distributors, and so on. At first, Leonard served as recording engineer, and we all functioned as a team of record producers.

In the usual recording process, the producer sits in the control booth alongside the recording engineer, keeps track of the "takes," and decides which ones should be used in making up the master tape from which will come the eventual release copies of the record. A good producer has informed musical judgment, keen and discerning hearing, good memory, and the ability to organize his tally sheet of takes so that the eventual editing process will move efficiently. When, instead of one producer, you deal with stitching together the opinions and verdicts of four, five, or more players acting as a many-headed arbiter, life can become pretty tricky. You end up playing more takes than might actually be necessary, and the late-night hours have a way of extending into the wee hours of the approaching dawn.

Our operations eventually had a fixed locale, first in the small auditorium of the Masonic Temple in Wilmette, Illinois, and later in the recital hall of the Fine Arts Building at the University of Wisconsin–Milwaukee when we had become resident faculty there. In both these locations, we gave ourselves the luxury of a recording engineer, but retained the production responsibility for our own. This continued, with few exceptions, even after we had sold the company library to a buyer in Los Angeles. It held true whether we made recordings for the new owner or for other labels. Almost every release in the Discography was produced the same way: we recorded, and Leonard edited the master tape and supplied the finished tape for transfer to disc, packaging, promotion, and distribution.

The full extent of the roster can perhaps be better understood if I say that it represents a total of almost sixty LP discs. And the Discography does not include other works that we produced, whether of serious repertoire not involving the participation of the quartet members, or of some small orchestral and pop releases that we produced to fill out the company catalog.

I recall vividly the time and effort we put into our do-it-yourself recordings. When I listen to the results, all these years later, I am gratified at how well the recorded performances sound. The fact is, though, that we were producing them on the fringes of an already busy schedule. The fringe itself made the schedule all the tighter and accounted for many a sleepless hour. Also, the pressure to record ate into time that might otherwise have been available for more predictable and more extended vacation periods, when the four of us could have had longer escape from the constant togetherness of ensemble life.

The intensity of our pace did not lend tranquility to our rehearsals. Indeed, it is a tribute both to the experienced routine of the group and to our willpower that we were able to juggle a number of activities, recording included, for so many years. We made it work, but I do not urge a similar lifestyle upon any ensemble that can avoid it.

In my first autumn with the quartet, and with the kind of temporary setup described early in this chapter, I made my first recordings with the ensemble. The list included the two Brahms quartets, Op. 51, and a number of Mendelssohn works, among them the octet (with guest artists from the Chicago Symphony and the music faculty of Northwestern University). Other titles followed. Not until August 1957, however, after our summer series and chamber music workshop in Milwaukee, did we begin to record the Beethoven cycle, in reverse, starting with the late quartets, from Op. 127 through Op. 135. In summer 1964 we recorded the middle period quartets of Beethoven, Op. 59 through Op. 95. Finally, in August 1966 we completed the cycle by taping the six early quartets, Op. 18. Irving Ilmer was our violist in the late quartets; Gerald Stanick (who succeeded Ilmer as violist in 1963) for the middle and early sets. As usual, we ended work on the Op. 18s very late one night, just before separating for a short end-summer break.

Jerry Stanick went off with a remark indicating his disdain for the process. It left me with an uncertain feeling. In retrospect, I believe that it was the first apparent sign of Jerry's resolve to leave the ensemble, even though his actual departure did not occur until two years later. I do not think it was just our recording load that bothered Jerry, but it certainly must have contributed to his discontent. Our recording of Mendelssohn's Quartet in D, Op. 44, No. 1, made with Stanick about a year earlier, had elicited a superlative review in *The New York Times* in October 1965: "The splendid Quartet in D is given the performance of a lifetime." Success in the narrower sense—a well-received recording—clearly was not sufficient to ensure our survival as a group.

I was surprised to learn, a few years ago, that Leonard was not the only quartet leader doing the editing of his ensemble's recordings. This was apparently true also for Zoltán Székely, for many years the first violin of the Hungarian String Quartet until it disbanded in 1972. He edited even though he could no doubt have delegated the task to the staff of the commercial labels that produced and released the recordings of his ensemble. Still, I believe that among the leaders of the relatively few prominent quartets in that era, Sorkin and Székely were unusual for functioning in this way.

As for ourselves, I always felt we had missed the boat. We should have tried vigorously to establish a connection with a large record firm. The issues on our own label had been receiving very good reviews, but perhaps our association with a minor label made us less attractive to a major house. In any event, Len—and we with him—continued to keep record production in-house. Recording in the auditorium of the music building at UW-M had built-in problems. The hall had satisfactory acoustics, but it did not exclude noise from the nearby parking lot and quadrangle of the school. Consequently, we had to schedule recording sessions for the late night hours, when external sounds were at a minimum.

After a day of teaching and a quick trip home for supper, we would gather at the hall to set up microphones and playback speakers and run the cables to the control booth (the lobby checkroom, where we had installed our recording machines). We had a local engineer to help with this and to run the machines, but had no actual producer in the control room. When the sound seemed properly balanced, we would begin to record the music at hand, appraising the playback ourselves as the evening progressed. More often than not, we would have to end the session by helping move microphones, cables, and playback speakers into the control room, both for the safety of the equipment and because the hall would be in use the following day. And this was just the beginning.

When recording, musicians have to deal with the feeling that every sound they make may be held against them in perpetuity. Is my part heard enough? Did I play the solo as immaculately, as beautifully as I would like? Did the duet passage come off well? Is the trading of line between the voices in the ensemble smoothly, temperamentally, dramatically done? Does the development, the variation, the minuet, or whatever, fit properly into the musical context? Without the ear of an outside producer, differences in viewpoint between ensemble members are not always easy to resolve.

In our case, Leonard resolved some issues as he edited the recorded takes into the final, assembled tape. He did an amazingly good job of it, but at the expense of long work and concentration. How he was able to manage this and still do the amount and quality of playing he did is cause for wonder. At best, however, it was not a happy situation for the four of us.

Just when Stanick left us and the very fine violist Bernard Zaslav succeeded him in the quartet (1968), we took on one of our biggest recording projects: the completion of the first full recording of the Haydn quartet cycle. Such a project was not a new idea. Among others, Alexander Schneider—during the years when he had withdrawn from the Budapest Quartet—had begun a similar venture with a string quartet headed by him in the 1950s. No one had yet succeeded in reaching the goal, however. Now George Mendelssohn, head of Vox Records, took up the challenge. He found four musicians in Holland who were willing to undertake the job. Calling themselves the Dekany Quartet, they began, recorded three fifths of the cycle, and then broke up!

That left thirty of the quartets, early through late, still to go. (This number, I should point out, still included the six quartets of Op. 3, though in 1964 the musicologists Alan Tyson and H. C. Robbins Landon had claimed that this opus was not by Haydn, but by his younger contemporary, the Benedictine monk Roman Hoffstetter.) Mendelssohn asked us to take over and finish the assignment. By early fall of 1968, our Vox recordings of the Op. 50 quartets and the unfinished last quartet, Op. 103, were already in the record shops. We went on, in succeeding months, to add the remainder of Op. 2 and all of Op. 3, 64, 74, and 76, a fairly sizeable job. At this point I cannot recall which quartet it was that came last in our production line, but I know that we had recorded all but its finale when, owing to the long hours we had put in, we had to break for the night. I was superstitious enough to worry that the Haydn-cycle jinx might prevent our actually recording that one remaining movement. We did, in fact, return to the task the next day, taped the finale, and at last completed George Mendelssohn's dream project. Our Vox Haydn recordings were duly appreciated. No less a critic than Paul Henry Lang wrote in *High Fidelity*, June 1972: "The ensemble work is irreproachable; each member of the quartet is a finely honed instrumentalist with impeccable technique and intonation and each knows when to defer to the other."

We went on to other recording sessions in the years following, and always in the context of a full schedule of activities. For me, the breaking point came during our recording of the cycle of Mozart's viola quintets, with violist Francis Tursi as guest artist. (Francis had already collaborated with us in concert performances of all the Mozart quintets, as well as in the quintets and sextets of Brahms and other works.) When we were all seated in front of the recording microphones for the Mozart sessions, I was appalled to note that musical suggestions were being made from within our foursome and, without time for real reflection or discussion, immediately accepted and committed to tape.

Now, years after the release of the quintets on disc, I listen again to the recordings and must admit that I find them very convincingly performed. I still rebel at the thought, however, that we allowed ourselves to be so last-minute in our approach to recording these consummate compositions from the pen of Mozart, that most subtle and nuanced of musicians. After those sessions, I refused to be party to any further recording of the classic repertoire. In any event, we did make some additions to our list of twentieth-century quartet releases in the few years that remained before George Sopkin and I left the ensemble.

Some of today's enlightened recording companies are issuing remastered, CD versions of LP chamber music records produced years ago. It must have been in the summer of 1994 that I had a phone call from a woman on the staff of the Omega Record Group in New York. A critic who knew our quartet from the old days had acquainted her with the fact that I was not only among the living, but holding forth in Rochester. (This certainly made me feel my age.) She was delighted to reach me, for her firm needed information for the album notes of the Omega release of our Beethoven quartet cycle on CDs, planned for that year. I phoned George to let him know about the Omega project. It turned out that the one-man record conglomerate in California to whom we had sold our library all those years earlier, and for whom we completed the Beethoven cycle, had sold all his record holdings to an outfit in Canada. It was from the Canadian firm that Omega had purchased the license to reissue our Beethoven recordings on CD.

Deadline or no, however, there proved to be a problem. Our Californian friend had been flogging the cycle, under various labels, through discount bookstore chains for years. In the process, the master tapes had gone through several generations of copying and recopying, had apparently been improperly stored, and were in poor shape. As I understand it, Omega had engaged Sony engineers to remaster the tapes in 20-bit digital technology, and those experts reported that the tapes at hand were simply not good enough. This, however, was not the end of the road.

After Leonard Sorkin's death in 1986, his widow decided to move back to her native Chicago. In the process of closing her Milwaukee home, she had the original master tapes of our recordings moved from her house to that of John Friedman (George Sopkin's son-in-law), long a faculty member of UW-M's department of physics. It was from each of these master tapes that Leonard had made the very carefully processed, splice-free tape supplied to the firm issuing the release in question. George flew to Milwaukee and, among this collection of our decades-long output of recordings, found the masters of our Beethoven cycle. Owing to the passage of time, many of the original splices had to be replaced, but otherwise the tapes proved to be just what was needed. Only the tape of Beethoven's Op. 18, No. 4, was missing. Here again, a solution emerged: a tape we had made of that quartet with Irving Ilmer, the violist of my first years in the quartet, that happened to be in George's own library.

Not only has the Beethoven cycle appeared, but some other works from the library were brought out by Boston Skyline Records, under the expert technical supervision of its owner, Wayne Wadhams. These were again issued under license from the Canadian firm that now owns the library. Perhaps other titles from our library will yet be reissued. This takes money, however, even though—with the mysterious ways of the recording world and of contracts—we quartet members do not receive any royalties on all these reissues. Boston Skyline, in fact, has gone out of business as a result of the costly funding of rereleases of titles from various record libraries.

Today probably more than ever before, the record business, including that surrounding art music, is a difficult, highly competitive affair, with a volatile market. Despite this problematic climate, an ensemble fortunate enough to negotiate a commercial recording contract would do well to seek provision for compensation from future sublicensing sales. In any case, George and I enjoy hearing ourselves in newly resplendent plastic, and have had the pleasure of contributing to our second coming by buying multiple copies of our latter-day releases.

I am happy to confess again that I enjoy hearing all those records we turned out during my years in the Fine Arts Quartet. But I would never want to relive the experience of making them under the conditions, pressures, and constraints that surrounded their production. As for today's young ensembles, filled as they are with enthusiasm and energy, they would be well advised to think carefully before becoming involved in a long-term, in-house musical cannery operation.

7 ✧ CONCERTS, TRAVEL
Our Tours in the 1950s

T he concert is the chamber musician's reward. You have been through the rehearsal process; discussed, debated, argued, *fought* over details of intonation, dynamics, inflection, tone color, pacing, projection, mood, and whatever else—more than you could ever imagine arising in any composition. You are safely at the concert hall, actually seated onstage in front of an expectant audience. You start the program, with the excitement of a combined burst of adrenaline and expectancy about what will unfold during the performance. And you know that no one in the group, not even you, can stop the creative process by saying, "No! Let's try that passage again." The composition must make its way to its end, with all the interplay between voices, the happy accidents of the live performance, and the sense of uninterrupted growth and continuity of the music that the word *concert* implies.

This is the payback for all the hassle, the business of dealing with your colleagues, your management, travel agents, the airports, railroad terminals, critics, rented cars, bad weather, flight cancelations, all the other niggling details that surround the oasis that is the concert experience. If you cannot enjoy that sense of control and personal fulfillment that comes from your role in the ensemble's free-flowing reconstruction of a truly fine piece of music, then you have been wasting your time—not just the months and years you have spent in the ensemble, but all those years of study you expended to be able to function within an ensemble in the first place.

But do not even think about it. Think only of being lucky enough to do what you are doing, even if it *is* the tenth time this season that you are performing the "Death and the Maiden" quartet of Schubert. There is again that pleasure of hearing the work build itself from first note to last. You have made the music come alive, even if it does vanish with its last vibration.

You do not pull off this bit of magic in a vacuum, however. Part of the excitement and release a performance gives the musician stems from what happens before, after, and—I confess—sometimes even during. So, let me turn now to some comment on travel.

Getting there

Musicians have been on the move for a long time. In 1705, at the age of twenty, Johann Sebastian Bach walked—at least some of the way—from Arnstadt (where he was then employed as organist at the Neukirche) in central Germany to the city of Lübeck, on the northern coast of the country. He made this jaunt of some 430 miles, round trip, to meet and hear the famous composer and organist Dietrich Buxtehude. When Haydn was pensioned off in 1790 after thirty years of service at the Hungarian court of Prince Esterhazy, he not only moved to Vienna but crossed the English Channel twice for triumphal visits to England. Mozart traveled to many cities in Europe during his early years, going even as far as London in search of the recognition and fortune that his father, Leopold, felt was rightfully due the blazingly talented youngster.

Mendelssohn crossed the English Channel no fewer than ten times between 1829 and 1847 for his warmly received visits to England. In his day, of course, the steam railroad was already in development, so travel was gradually becoming easier than before. This was the era of ever-larger concert halls and the touring virtuosos who filled them, including such formidable stars as Paganini and Liszt, not to mention singers and conductors.

In our own time, the dominance of air travel has made it possible for musicians to jet their way across continents, oceans, and hemispheres. It is now almost demeaning for a prominent conductor to devote his entire schedule to one orchestra. If not music director of two widely separated ensembles (preferably one in America, another in Europe), he must at least commute between his main appointment and guest appearances in far-flung cities and countries. The same holds true for a relatively small number of instrumental virtuosos, opera singers, and chamber ensembles. Entire symphonies, complete with luggage, instruments, and music trunk, must make pilgrimage abroad if they are to count themselves among their nation's recognized musical great.

It is now almost mandatory for any musician, and certainly for the ambitious chamber group, to gather plaudits far from home. The ensemble that does not include in its publicity some glowing review excerpts from appearances in large metropolitan centers of America, Europe, Japan, and elsewhere will probably find its career to be slow in the building. The young group will probably play for low fees to introduce itself abroad. Its travel and living expenses, however, will be high, for airlines, hotels, and restaurants are not in the business of subsidizing aspiring musicians.

The logistics of an extended trip are formidable, what with many cities in various countries, strung out along geographic lines that are typically not the shortest distance between two points. Add to this the rigors of eating cuisine that varies wildly in flavor, spicing, type of foodstuffs, and quality of cooking. Then there are the wide shifts in weather conditions that challenge the players' health in the course of their journey. And, especially for linguistically challenged Americans, there is the problem of dealing with tongues and dialects that fall strangely on the ear. Considering all this, you may wonder at the wisdom of undertaking such a regime for the pleasure of giving concerts near and far.

Consider also that a concert tour is not the ideal way to get to know the countries through which the musician passes. To drive or fly to a city, check into the hotel, play at the local auditorium, then leave town as soon as the following morning affords a very narrow view of place and people. It was only by dint of repeated visits to the cities in our various tours, and the occasional open days when we did not have to press on to the next engagement or a new spot on the map, that our quartet had a chance to build some sense of the locale.

Fees for leading ensembles are now higher than they were in our day, but all expenses, from air fares on down, have risen enough to cancel out some of the seeming advantage. Nevertheless, such is the game in our time, so the modern ensemble still has to train itself to pack lightly, look for the cheapest available flights, and have robust constitutions. Be aware, moreover, that your audience, whatever the city in question, will neither know nor care if you had a tough time getting there. They have paid to hear the concert, and they expect to be transported or at least edified by your performance.

I have been asked why musicians would want to subject themselves to all this, and how they deal with the stresses involved. The short and honest answers are: a) it is part of the job; and b) you grin and enjoy the fun experiences en route, bearing your way through the tough spots. No psychologist can force you to enjoy the rigors of travel. You have to be interested enough in new things, new faces, new customs, new sights to make you want to keep going through the passing seasons. Sooner or later, the physical toll may come to seem too great; players have, after all, chosen to curtail their touring or leave the field altogether. As long as the demand for your performances continues, however, the high of hearing the response of an enthusiastic audience will be a powerful stimulant—especially if there is enough cash involved to help pay the mortgage.

During my twenty-five years' membership, the quartet performed in twenty-eight countries, commonwealths, or protectorates, as the case may be. Though I do not list them here, we played in some 270 cities in the process; in many of them, more than once.

In pages that follow, I will summon up some of those funny-annoying-mundane things that our quartet experienced. Any ensemble that has already been in action will be able to match my reminiscences. Yet those about to set out for podiums near and far will gain some idea of what to expect. As I said early in this book, memory—and the passing of years— softens the rougher edges of recollection. In the actual event, we somehow managed to retain our resilience, even with increasing age.

Our quartet tours in the 1950s

One of our road concerts, early in the 1956–57 season, took place in Memphis, Tennessee. A southern management bureau had arranged it, and we had been given the name of the school where the concert was to take place. We arrived by train at the Memphis terminal, got into a cab, and asked to go to LeMoyne College. The driver turned and asked, "Why do you want to go there?" We neither understood nor liked the way he

Where we played

America (48 states)	Great Britain	New Zealand
Australia	Greece	Norway
Austria	Holland	Portugal
Belgium	Hong Kong	Puerto Rico
Canada	Ireland	Spain
Denmark	Israel	Sweden
Finland	Italy	Switzerland
France	Japan	Taiwan
Germany	Korea	Thailand
	Mexico	

asked his question. When we got to the college, though, we saw why: LeMoyne was a black college. Though I have not been back to Memphis in all this time, I assume that attitudes have since changed.

We were on campus two days, enjoying the gracious hospitality of our hosts and using the time to rehearse ahead for a Beethoven-Bartók cycle we were presenting in Chicago. On the last evening of our stay at LeMoyne, we gave our concert in the college auditorium. It was presented to a barely integrated audience: that is, there were a few white listeners in the assemblage.

The following afternoon we were back at the Memphis terminal, to board an overnight train for our return to Chicago. A limousine delivered another passenger for the same train: Elvis Presley. Young, trim, and dressed in a smart gray suit, he looked every bit the sophisticated traveler. Noticing our instrument cases, he had a few friendly words with us, but he was soon surrounded by a crowd of young couples who were going to ride the train a few stops for the sheer pleasure of seeing Elvis on his way. After dinner, we in the quartet were sitting in the club car. Presley was at the bar, still surrounded by his admirers. Eventually he had enough of the crowd and walked through the car on his way toward the sleeper. As the young things chased after him, I heard one girl say to her beau, "This will be a naht to *remembah!*"

Elliott Carter's String Quartet No. 1 raises some special memories for me. In February 1957, at Chicago's Fullerton Hall, we gave a program that wound up with the city's premiere (and our first performance) of the work, a forty-minute composition of great fascination and complexity. The concert gave rise to a priceless comment by an important Chicago patron of the arts: as he left the hall, he said of the Carter, "It'll never replace 'Mother Machree!'"

But the Carter had a further, ripple effect on us. The next night, we were scheduled to give a concert at Wisconsin State College at Stevens Point, well up into the center of the state. That morning, we met in George Sopkin's living room in a North Shore suburb of Chicago to rehearse the forthcoming program. Our session got as far as the unpacking of the instruments. We were so busy discussing the Carter performance of the previous day that we just sat and talked. Suddenly someone noticed it was time to catch the train for the trip to Wisconsin. We packed the instruments, got into a large taxi with our cases and luggage, and left for the station.

We were then in the habit, during long train rides, of tipping the train porter to let us use a bedroom compartment in which we might do some rehearsing (quartet players do strange things). This time, we were still so involved with our Carter reminiscences that again we just sat and schmoozed. We detrained and were met by a station wagon from the college and driven across the snowy wastes to the campus. During the ride, Irv Ilmer said he thought he had forgotten to bring a white tie. I told him I had an extra tie to lend him, but jested that I had only one pair of evening pants with me. Backstage at the concert hall, Irv checked his suitcase and found he did not, in fact, have his white tie. I gave him one, whereupon he continued to unpack and discovered that he had also forgotten to bring his pants! No way out—he played the concert in black tailcoat and medium-blue suit pants, complete with cuffs.

Something else happened just after we arrived at the hall. An usher came backstage to tell George there was a phone call for him. George returned from the phone doubled over with laughter. He asked Leonard to open his violin case. Len cried out that he had forgotten his bow. George asked him to look again. The reply: "I forgot my violin!" When we had hurried out of George's living room, Leonard had clapped shut his violin case, leaving both instrument and bow on George's table. Luckily for us and for the imminent concert, we learned that a lumber mill owner in Stevens Point was a musical enthusiast who owned a quartet of Amati instruments. A quick phone call elicited the loan of a violin (Leonard luckily had a spare bow) for the evening, so all four of us were able to sit down to the music at hand.

For our first concert tour in Europe, in 1958, we were a party of seventeen (four quartet members, each accompanied by wife and two children, plus Carol Sopkin's niece). Jill and I brought both boys along, but our daughter, Marah, then just three years old, remained at home with a trusted babysitter. The crossing on the *Queen Elizabeth*—predecessor of the *QE2*—was comfortable enough, except for one rough day that kept most of us away from the dining table. Irv Ilmer, our violist, did not take well to wavelike sensations, so spent much of the crossing resting in his cabin. As a consequence, he did not do much eating on the voyage, but complained nonetheless about the cuisine. He felt so strongly on this point that, toward the end of the tour, when we were in Berlin, we all marched into the United States Line office and exchanged our Cunard tickets for space on the *United States* for the journey home. Because of the last-minute arrangement, it turned out that the Loft family had a windowless cabin fairly far toward the nose of the ship. From the sound of the crashing waves, we must have been close to the waterline, so it was not a terribly restful crossing for us.

Our tour had ended in England, so we boarded ship at Southampton and crossed the channel to Le Havre to pick up passengers there before setting out across the Atlantic. The channel was docile that day, and at Le Havre the water was smooth as glass. There were to be a couple of hours with the ship tied up to the dock, and we decided to pass the time by seeing a movie in the ship's theater. The film turned out to be *All at Sea*, starring Alec Guinness as a British naval officer who could not stand the ocean. There we were, seated in a theater as stable as Radio City Music Hall. As luck would have it, each word of the title of the film emerged in a rocking motion from a rather turbulent sea. By the time "Sea" made its appearance, Irv rose to his feet, said, "Well, that's it," and repaired to his bunk. I do not think he ate any more on this crossing than he had on the *Queen Elizabeth*. But at least he did not complain about the food.

This first European tour had begun in March with two concerts in Paris. In the first, a mixed program at the Comédie des Champs-Elysées, our share consisted of Beethoven's Quartet in B-flat, Op. 130 (with the replacement Allegro instead of the *Great Fugue*). The second concert, all ours, comprised three Bartók quartets: Nos. 1, 6, and 4. The cordial response of the audience at both programs gave us a heartening sendoff for the impending journey.

The day after the second performance, the four families set out, each in its own well-loaded sedan purchased for the trip. Our fleet—not a caravan, for we were driving independently—included three small Mercedes (George's and mine with roof luggage racks), and Irv's Renault. A mixture of snow, rain, and sleet came up when I was a few hours south of Paris. Luckily, we were on an open stretch of road when we started to skid, oscillating wildly for a hundred feet or so, then coming to stop with no hurt or injury to us, our auto, or passersby.

All four cars arrived in Bordeaux the next afternoon with little time to spare before the concert at the Foyer du Grand-Théâtre Municipal. In what was to be routine procedure at the various hotels we would visit, the kids in our party tested the workings of the elevator, then played games or did some schoolwork or reading before supper. Food was no problem, for David and Peter usually opted for hamburger and *frites* on the hotel's menu. Jill's bouts of laundry in the bedroom sink involved some heroic labor, especially when it came to the kids' corduroys. All I had to do was drive and play the concert.

From Bordeaux it took us two days of driving, partly through nighttime fog and across mountain road, to get to Geneva. Three days there, with a radio broadcast and a concert at the Théâtre de la Cour St. Pierre (a fine auditorium in the city), gave us a chance to rest up. Then on to Bern for an evening concert-broadcast.

We traveled via auto-train through the Simplon Tunnel to Italy, and then drove eastward for a concert at Verona's Castelvecchio. In the audience was an acquaintance from Chicago, Manoah Leide-Tedesco, a distant relation of the Italian composer Mario Castelnuovo-Tedesco. We had played a quartet of Manoah's back home in Chicago. Learning that we were going from Verona to Belluno, a resort town in the Dolomite mountains, for a performance there, Manoah swung into action. He persuaded Belluno's chamber music society to request the addition of his quartet to the program that had already been announced. Dr. Vinante, a Belluno physician and president of the society, had a deep and extremely resonant voice. At concert's end, his bull-horn cries of "*Bravi! Bravi!*" whipped the audience into paroxysms of applause. We four innocents responded with several encores, so a long evening grew longer still.

Vinante hastened backstage, shook hands warmly, and suggested we have some refreshment back at our hotel. He and an associate joined us and our wives in the hotel restaurant and urged us on with cries of, "Have wine! Have cheese!" Next morning, the treats were on our hotel bills.

Our next stop was at Turin, for a concert in the auditorium of the Verdi Conservatory. Then we dispersed for a two-week Easter break, a lull time in European concert schedules. In true ensemble fashion, we all drove through Pisa and ended up in Florence. Our family stayed at a pension just across from the Boboli Gardens, with a pleasant vista from the building's terrace. At last, though, it was time for us to set out on the drive to Paris, where the quartet was to reconvene.

After some rest and a brush-up rehearsal, we drove to Holland for concerts and broadcasts, and into Germany for concerts and broadcasts at points ranging from Berlin to Cologne to Stuttgart. These included introductory concerts at several U.S. government Amerika Haus auditoriums. (The various America House locations in postwar Germany were centers for information about American life and culture.)

Near the end of the tour, we drove to Baden-Baden to tape a program for the radio station there. At 10:30 the following morning, we were to be at the television studios in Brussels to rehearse a telecast scheduled for the evening of the same day. The trip would involve hours on the road. Accordingly, families rested up beforehand in day-rate rooms at a Baden-Baden hotel while we did our stint at the radio studio, and we decided to break the journey with a stop in Cologne for the night.

It was past 2:00 A.M. by the time we were in our rooms at the Cologne hotel, just a few hours before we had to resume our way to Brussels. We left so early that there was no possibility of breakfast. When we at last pulled up in front of the Brussels television building we saw—and joined—the Ilmer and Sopkin families at a sidewalk food-cart, wolfing down coffee, cocoa, and rolls to blunt our hunger. Up to the studio then, where the production crew awaited our rehearsal. It was a strange ses-

The Fine Arts Quartet on the steps of Berlin's Amerika Haus in 1958 during our first European tour: Irving Ilmer, George Sopkin, Leonard Sorkin, Abe Loft.

sion, for we had no first violin. Leonard arrived only shortly before the end of the designated time slot. He and his family had stopped for break-fast at a roadside restaurant en route.

The city was filled to overflowing with visitors to the 1958 Brussels Exposition. Reservations had been made for us at what turned out to be temporary housing put up specifically for the season. In the television parking lot we huddled over a Brussels map, trying to figure out the way to our destination. We finally decided to follow George in caravan as we searched for our digs. Leonard's car was last in line, and he lost us as the cortège wound through traffic. Luckily, the family managed to find ac-commodation somewhere, but it was Leonard's turn to be morose when we gathered for the evening telecast.

We closed the tour with four afternoon concerts at London's Royal Festival Hall. The programs comprised two Bartók quartets, four by Bee-thoven, and the clarinet quintets of Mozart and Brahms. Our guest in the quintets was famed English clarinetist Reginald Kell.

At the end of the last concert, our quartet was surrounded backstage by four wives and nine excited children. Looking on were David Oistrakh and his pianist, Victor Yampolsky, who had arrived to perform their own evening recital. What the Russians must have thought of the ways of American ensembles can only be imagined. In any case, the London con-certs were a great wind-up, but we had been away from home for three and one-half very full months and were ready to return home and settle down.

An interesting footnote about the 1958 European circuit: the ridiculous fact that we stood ready to offer no fewer than fifty quartets to the clients in this tour! In part, this was made possible because we were traveling by ship and auto, so that the weight of the instrumental parts each of us car-ried was not an issue. The reason behind the madness, however, was that we wanted to be ready to program works of regional interest in the vari-ous countries we would visit. We performed in France, Switzerland, Italy, Holland, Belgium, Germany, and England; and, in the final analysis, played works by Bartók, Beethoven, Bloch, Boccherini, Brahms, Britten, Carter, Chausson, Haydn, Hindemith, Holmboe, Leide-Tedesco, Mozart, Piston, Prokofiev, Ravel, Riegger, Rosenberg, Schubert, Shostakovich, .Vaughan Williams, and Walton. This range was spread over several months but was still beyond the call of valor. That we did it and still got audience and critical response that was generally very favorable was heartening. We made many European tours after this, but never again with so bloated a repertoire in our briefcases.

In April 1959, however, we set our quartet's endurance record. At the Mid-American Symposium of Contemporary American Music at the University of Kansas, Lawrence, we presented eight quartets in one day, by Walter Aschaffenburg, Wayne Barlow, Parks Grant, Robert Kelly, Leon Stein, Burnet Tuthill, Maurice Weed, and Norma Wendelburg. We had given normal-length programs incorporating contemporary music at the U. of K. in preceding seasons and would do so again in following years. This marathon event, though, was a tour de force that I for one refused to repeat in the future. Our usual season's doings were strenuous enough.

For our second European tour, in the last months of 1959, several families again came along (only Irv made this trip alone). Carol's second niece joined the party in place of her sister, and our daughter, Marah, now a few months past her fourth birthday, filled out our own family group. Wives and children had traveled ahead, via ship, while the quartet remained behind in the States to finish up musical chores and close up house. I was so strained by this wind-up that I got to Europe with the makings of a terrific cold. We arrived in Paris by plane, joined the families at the hotel, and, still feeling jetlag, rehearsed in one of the rooms. Under the circumstances, four zombies could have done better; the rehearsal soon ended.

Early the third week of the tour, we were in Copenhagen for a concert. Jill and the kids interrupted our rehearsal to reveal that while David and Peter were playing tag in the park, David had fallen against a parked bicycle and knocked off half of an upper front tooth. He took this in much better spirit than did I. We got him to a dentist that afternoon, and a very presentable temporary cap was installed on the offending chopper.

In the course of that European tour, we made one of those point-to-point connections that seems logical only to a concert management. We had taped Andrew Imbrie's Quartet No. 3 for Dutch radio in Hilversum, Holland. The next day we drove (again with each family in its own car) from Hilversum to Paris and installed the troops in a hotel. The day after *that*, the quartet itself flew to Lisbon for an evening concert.

Our plane was about a half-hour late as it made its approach to Lisbon airport. Checking through his briefcase, Leonard found that his part to the Imbrie (which was scheduled for the evening's concert) was missing. Hurried reflection reminded us that, since we had no score of the Imbrie with us, Leonard had left his quartet part with the people in Hilversum to help them in editing the tape. We quickly refashioned the program and decided to open with Beethoven's Quartet in C, Op. 59, No. 3.

We had assumed the concert would begin at 9:00 P.M., a usual hour for an evening program in Europe. Even though we were late getting in, this would give us a chance to get to our hotel, wash up, and get a quick dinner. I was first in line when the plane door opened. Confronting me was an airline grounds-man. Seeing my violin case, he asked, "Are you in the Fine Arts Quartet? Hurry! Your concert starts in five minutes!"

This was news to us, for we had not been given any warning by the Valmalète agency, our general manager in Paris. We hastened into the terminal. The Portuguese manager, Mr. Quesada, looking harried, waved to us from the terminal crowd. He had arranged with the customs officials to pass our luggage through first; our bags, though, were in the bottom layer on the baggage cart, so some precious minutes elapsed before we were at last in the cab on our way to the concert hall.

There was no time to go into the dressing rooms. Bemused security and fire guards watched us fling open our suitcases on the backstage floor, hurry into our white tie and tails, unpack the instruments and music stands, tune up, and make a quick entry to the stage. By now the audience had been waiting the better part of an hour for the program to begin. The first chord, an F-sharp-diminished-seventh (already an unusual beginning for a work in C major) of the Beethoven came as a special shock. It begins in *forte*, and is marked for an immediate decrescendo. This time, though, the chord did not just dwindle; it disappeared. There was simply no perceptible reverberation of sound. George Sopkin and I exchanged glances and had to bite our lip to keep from giggling hysterically.

The four of us soldiered on and eventually left the stage for the intermission. Quesada, standing in the wings, urged us to keep it short. For the second half of the concert, we were dismayed to note that the audience had significantly diminished. And when we came off after the final work, Quesada said, "Fine concert; but no encores!" At last came the explanation of the strange events of the evening. The concert was part of a twilight series. Our late start threw off the evening schedule of the audience, which explained why so many had left during intermission. Further, the reason for no encores was that the auditorium was a movie theater and had to be cleared for the evening's screening. The fact that the hall was a well-upholstered and draped movie theater of the old school (we would have noticed if we were not so hurried) accounted for the miserable acoustics we had endured.

In the cab on our way to our hotel, Quesada told us we were to be dinner guests of the Marquesa de Sadoval at a Lisbon restaurant. Would Mr. Quesada be joining us? "No," he replied, "I have to go home and rest!" He had spent a very nervous day awaiting our arrival in Lisbon. Having heard that we were driving from city to city on our itinerary, he had been phoning the border crossing-points to ask whether musicians in four cars had made their entry to Portugal. At last he called the Valmalète office in Paris and learned that we were coming by plane. Between his lack of information and our own, confusion reigned supreme.

The following day was open on our calendar, and the weather was wonderful. We enjoyed seeing Lisbon and resting up after the excitement. On the *next* day, however, we proceeded by train to the city of Oporto; and there the concert was indeed set to begin at 9 P.M. This was again unsettling, because we had to be at Lisbon airport the next morning for a flight back to Paris, where we were scheduled for a matinee concert in Salle Gaveau the day following. And to make the connection, we had to take a sleeper train from Oporto to Lisbon. Unfortunately, the train would have left Oporto before we finished our concert.

The sponsors put us in touch with a local travel agent, who told the railroad officials we would board the train at a local stop, a ways out of Oporto. To facilitate this, the agent arranged to have a taxi waiting for us outside the concert hall to whisk us to the appointed station. The reader can be sure our tempos at the evening's performance were not the slowest in our career, though we did chance a well-paced encore before hurrying to our dressing rooms to pack our instruments and throw on our coats. There, however, were the concert sponsors, waiting to express their thanks by toasting us in the celebrated tipple of the region: Port wine. We knocked back the testimonial shot while wearing our coats, grabbed our luggage, and made our exit to the waiting cab.

It was raining. And we found not one, but two cabs, for the driver of the first had decided that he alone could not accommodate four passengers and paraphernalia. Both drivers spoke very little English, but they conveyed the idea that we would make the train in good shape. George and I were the duo in the second cab. When we reached the designated train-stop, the drivers leaped out, peered down the track, and made us understand that we had, after all, missed the train. Back into the cabs; on to the next stop—and the next. The same scenario had been enacted a few times before we reached a station, apparently miles from nowhere, with a small group of rain-sodden passengers awaiting the train.

We paid the drivers a fare that had swollen appreciably, then joined the queue on the platform. When the train pulled in, the conductor, upon seeing our instrument cases, burst out, "Where were you? We *waited* for you!" Moral: never underestimate the power of a cab driver.

As the train pulled into the Lisbon area the next morning, it was clear that it would be arriving late at the city terminal; we were sure to miss our plane. The conductor advised us to debark at a suburban stop and proceed directly to the airport by taxi. Although this ploy did not get us there in time for the scheduled plane departure, the flight had fortunately been delayed. We boarded, got to Paris in decent time, and even had time to recover before the Salle Gaveau appearance.

The day after the Paris concert, we all—musicians and families—took train, channel steamer, and train again to London for tapings at the BBC. After another day's respite, we retraced our chain of transportation back to Paris, picked up our cars, and set out for the drive to Switzerland for several days of concerts and radio tapings, then drove back into France, this time heading for the town of Gap, southeast of Grenoble and just to the west of the Alps along the Italian border. It was from the *gavot* or *gapot*, folk dance of the Gap region, by the way, that the stylized dance we know as the gavotte descended. Our *Concert de gala*, arranged under the enthusiastic leadership of the town priest, took place at Le Centre, Gap's new movie theater. I think the weather was as much on our minds as music, for we were due to drive over the Alps, via the Mont Genèvre pass, the next day on our way to Turin. We had been reading the paper and listening to radio bulletins about impending snow and ice, and all of us, except George, had bought tire chains in Gap in preparation for our attack on the mountain.

When I started out the next morning, the roads around Gap were still clear, so I delayed putting on my new chains. Our family stopped for lunch in a town that was noticeably higher up than Gap, and the roads there were already coated with snow and, as I should have suspected, some ice as well. We got back in the car and continued through the center of town on our way toward the pass. The street took a sharp jog around the sturdy masonry-and-wrought-iron fence that surrounded official town buildings. I had every intention of following the jog, but the car wheels started slipping on the icy roadway, and I proceeded, slowly and inexorably, into a very immovable masonry fence-column. When Jill and I could bear to look, we saw that the brightwork on the front of our new Mercedes, from the top of the grill-frame right on down through our now butterflied bumper, had a very definite crease. The saving grace was that none of the sheet metal of the car had been affected.

It was now painfully clear that tire chains should be mounted. I drove along some distance to a garage and had them put on. To add to the upset, David and Peter had meanwhile had a tussle in the back of the car, and the cap on David's busted tooth had been knocked off. After all this, our navigation of the twisting road up to the top of the pass and through the border checkpoints seemed almost a restful anticlimax.

Such was not the case with George, however. He started up the road to the pass without chains. Irv drove behind him, accompanied by Carol's niece. There came a point when the road was so steep that George's car lost traction. Both George and Irv then had to back down until they got to a lay-by in the road where they could turn around. Then both cars descended to the town of Briançon, where George was able to buy chains. At that point, Carol's niece found that she did not have her passport. Thinking quickly, George devised a plan he thought would get them across the border. He was driving a large, front-wheel-drive Citroën sedan. He had his younger daughter, Paula, lie down on the flat floor in front of the rear seat. Coats were piled over her for concealment. On the seat were George's older daughter, Nicky, and her cousin, with the latter holding Paula's passport. Though the girls did not really resemble each other, George hoped that the usual, quick inspection of passengers at the border would let him get away with this ruse. As it happened, there were no fewer than four checkpoints at the top of the pass, two French and two Italian, and every passport was inspected at each barrier. Even so,

George's group got through. When they stopped at the coffee shop on the Italian side of the border and released Paula from her igloo of coats, she was in tears.

There was some explaining to do about the girl with no passport when we checked in at the hotel in Turin. A call was made to the American consulate, which phoned the authorities at Gap. It transpired that the missing document had been discovered on the floor of the movie theater/concert hall. The consulate arranged to have it brought to Turin in diplomatic pouch. "By the way," asked the consul, "how did you cross the border?" I wonder if George told him the truth. Besides, who would believe it?

George was kind enough to accompany me to a Mercedes agency in the few hours before the evening's concert. The manager said that his service department could make my car look like new. Great! But it would be two weeks before they could do the job. This kind of conversation ensued at the other towns where we played on our way south. It was not until we got to Rome, the last stop before we left Europe, that I was able to have the bumper and other front chrome replaced.

One stop en route to Rome was at Brescia, where Irv Ilmer's Gasparo da Salò viola had been made in the late sixteenth century. I knew in advance where the evening's concert would take place, for Jill and I had taken the kids to the town zoo that cold December afternoon and found that the auditorium building was very close by. The auditorium's heating system was out of action that day, and by concert-hour the hall was absolutely freezing. For comfort during our performances, we always played in tropical-weight full dress. Brescia in December, and especially in that auditorium, was not the tropics. The audience sat in hats, coats, and gloves. (Have you ever heard the sound of applause delivered by gloved hands?) Their breaths steamed in the cold air and so did ours. An iron stove in the greenroom maintained a glowing temperature. Going from there onto the stage was like taking the icy plunge that follows a sauna.

In Rome we turned in our cars for shipment back to America. We ourselves, though, were not headed in that direction. An invitation to visit Israel had been cabled to our Paris management when we were already on the road in Europe. And a concert management in Greece became involved when it was learned we might be going from Italy to Israel. Cables and phone calls ensued, and we agreed to extend the tour to include concerts in Greece as well as Israel. Our entourage flew to Athens, where the families stayed while the quartet went off for concerts in other cities.

Our first stop was in Kozani, a small town at the juncture of Greece, Yugoslavia, and Bulgaria. A native son had made his fortune as restaurateur in Baltimore and had endowed his hometown with a small music conservatory building. Our concert took place in the auditorium of the school, and the audience represented a cross-section of townsfolk, including the officer in command of the local garrison. I remember this concert, apparently the first ever by a quartet in Kozani, because what seemed to be the entire audience, officer and all, filed through the greenroom during intermission to shake our hands and thank us.

There were concerts also in Larissa and Salonika, then it was back to Athens for a couple of days to rejoin the families and proceed to Israel. Before the departure, Jill and I went to the airline office to settle some detail. While at the counter, I turned pale, felt faint, and had to sit down for a time. The weakness passed (though it proved to be harbinger of a bout of illness to be described in chapter 12), and we made the trip to Israel without incident, landing at Tel Aviv airport on Christmas Eve.

In addition to concerts at Tel Aviv, Haifa, the Weizmann Institute, and at kibbutz Givat Hayim, we also paid a visit to the Jerusalem Conservatory. The director of the conservatory invited us to become the resident ensemble there. Though the achievements of the country and its people were highly impressive, Jill and I were personally disinclined to move our family from America and were relieved that the ensemble declined the offer.

A postscript to the Israel visit: at our suggestion, the New York management had been in touch with *Time* magazine, telling them of our European touring successes and our travels with family. The outcome was that a photographer-reporter in Israel was assigned to do a write-up on us during our stay there. A *Time* issue containing the piece appeared the day we landed at New York airport on our way home. It was the kind of publicity an ensemble would kill for, and we had high hopes from it. It did in fact have an immediate repercussion, to be detailed in my next chapter.

During our first tour of Israel, December 1959–January 1960: Jill Loft, toting Abe Loft's violin case and camera tripod, as well as her own straw sack, on the steps of Jerusalem's King David hotel. Abe is busy taking the picture.

8 ✧ A LANDMARK CONCERT SERIES

In Chicago the *Time* magazine article just mentioned led quickly—the following season, to be exact—to something that would affect the group for all the remaining years of my stay in the quartet. The item inspired four prominent women in Chicago's cultural scene, already supporters of the Fine Arts Quartet for some time previously, to embark on a new project.

The four in question were Lucy Montgomery (at that time the wife of Chicago financier Kenneth Montgomery); Jean Evans, wife of the eminent professor and author Bergen Evans; Eleanor Martin, wife of the architect Albert Martin; and Ruth Roberg, wife of Leo Roberg, photographer. These four women, noting that a Chicago ensemble was being recognized for its work abroad, felt that the quartet should be properly signalized in its home city. Their idea was to establish a full-fledged series of concerts featuring our quartet, both in the string quartet repertoire and, with the collaboration of guest artists, works for mixed ensemble from the extensive repertoire of chamber music generally.

The four women were seasoned musical commuters, traveling often into the city for concerts of the Chicago Symphony Orchestra and other downtown cultural events of every variety. However, they all made their homes in the North Shore suburbs of the city. And they knew that many working men and women who resided in those suburbs would not be inclined to travel back into the city for an evening concert after having made the commute to and from the day's work. Accordingly, the downtown series was to be matched, concert for concert, by a parallel subscription series in the North Shore area.

The location for the suburban series was chosen at the outset and remained in force for all the years I participated in the concerts: the auditorium of the Howard School in Wilmette, Illinois. In Chicago proper, the setting shifted several times: at first, the auditorium of the Prudential Building; then, the Studebaker Theater; and for all the remaining years until 1979 (when I left the quartet), the Goodman Theater of the Art Institute.

For each of the parallel series, there were never fewer than seven concerts per season. In the very first years of the venture, the number was higher, encompassing also participation by a small orchestra of Chicago musicians conducted by Herbert Zipper, director of the Music Center of the North Shore. Soon, however, the series adhered more literally to its title, The Fine Arts Quartet Concert Series. That meant that our ensemble was involved, either alone or in mixed works, in fourteen concerts (seven pairs) in the Chicago area each year. This had implications for the number of works performed over the years, and I refer to them in my repertoire chapter. As to guest artists, we were joined by such eminent musicians as pianists John Browning, Lorin Hollander, and Richard Goode; flutists Jean-Pierre Rampal and Paula Robison; violist Francis Tursi; cellist Robert Sylvester; bassist Gary Karr; and ensembles including the Berkshire Quartet, the Pro Arte Quartet, the New York Woodwind Quintet, and the Modern Jazz Quartet. (A complete list of guest artists appears at the end of the book.) The series also gave rise to new works by composers Milton Babbitt, Charles Wuorinen, Ben Johnston, and Karel Husa (whose Quartet No. 3, written for us, won the Pulitzer Prize for Music in 1969).

I must emphasize the great debt our quartet owes the four women aforementioned. Not only did they lend their own considerable energies to the realization of the series, but they involved other movers and shakers of the Chicago community in support of the project. The list of patrons quickly grew to sizeable proportions, and I hope I may be forgiven for not giving the roster here. Kenneth Montgomery contributed both financially and in the form of commissions of new works, as did attorney Lee Freeman Sr., later so prominently active as a sponsor of Chicago's Lyric Opera.

Various metropolitan centers in America, I am sure, have been home to chamber concert series over the years. As a rule, however, these have centered on a school, university, performing arts center, or other host organization. That a series the size and longevity of ours in Chicago (1960 to 1979 and beyond), let alone one dedicated to a single ensemble and supported entirely by community sponsorship and subscription sales, should have been instituted and maintained so effectively must surely constitute an exceptional event.

Over the years, the audience for these concerts remained large and faithful. Some of our listeners aged along with those of us in the ensemble. However, there seemed to be a fresh infusion of younger listeners each year to help fill the auditorium, both in the city and in the suburban series. For us in the quartet, the series offered not only vital income but also some considerable obligations. There was the basic chore of finding concert dates that meshed with the calendar of the Goodman (busy with its own schedule of rehearsals and theatrical presentations) and with our touring commitments. There were also such matters as planning programs for each forthcoming season, selecting and inviting guest artists, and scheduling their participation on suitable dates. There were board of directors committee meetings to attend and coordination with the manager's office on various facets of the series operation.

During the first years of the series, the travel involved was not too strenuous. All four quartet members lived in or near the North Shore suburbs, so the drive into Chicago and back for the city series covered a distance of only thirty miles each way. Getting to and from the Howard School was even easier, since Wilmette was itself a northern community. The physical factors changed, however, after we became faculty members at the University of Wisconsin–Milwaukee (see chapter 10). By 1965 we were all living in Milwaukee and commuting to Chicago and Wilmette for the series performances. In the earlier years, rail service from Milwaukee was fairly convenient. Over the course of time, however, the train schedule was sharply reduced. Moreover, we could not always stay over in Chicago after the Monday night program to be on hand for Tuesday's Wilmette concert; we had teaching duties in Milwaukee that did not predictably allow for missing a day in the academic week.

In addition, it became part of our campus assignments to present a third parallel concert series, in the recital hall of UW-M's School of Fine Arts. The schedule, then, included concerts on three successive evenings (Sunday, Milwaukee; Monday, Chicago; Tuesday, Wilmette). And along with this, there was a 180-mile round trip by auto on Monday and often again on Tuesday. I want to tell you that this can wear a guy down. During the fall and winter months, the weather on the road between Chicago and Milwaukee can turn rather grim. Driving north at night after the Chicago or Wilmette concert demanded alertness that was not easy to come by after the day's events. I would often get through Milwaukee and into the garage of my home with none too clear an idea of how I had attained my goal. There is an old saying that one must suffer for art, and I think I have described one specific way of so doing.

I do not know which of us would have been prepared to throw in the first towel for this kind of schedule. In actual fact, though, the crucial step was taken by our first violin, Leonard Sorkin. In February 1974 he demanded that we take a sabbatical from the following season's concert series. There followed some intense discussion within the quartet, during which we pointed out, among other things, that this would still leave us with the obligation of providing the traditional concert series on the university campus. The upshot was that we reduced our participation in the 1974–75 series by one Sunday-Monday-Tuesday package, with the Beaux Arts Trio taking our place in that set. This first departure from what had become the standard premise of the series (adherence to one core ensemble) opened the way for a changing perspective on the original purpose of the series. A year or so after George Sopkin and I left the ensemble in 1979, the Fine Arts Quartet was completely dropped from the series, and the name of the project was changed accordingly. Leonard expressed his dismay at this turn of events in a rather frank newspaper interview. The trend he had initiated, however, could not be reversed.

During the twenty-odd years it lasted, the Fine Arts Quartet Concert Series was among the very few of its kind in this country. It demonstrated what can happen when a community and a resident ensemble dedicate themselves to the common end of maintaining a sounding board for chamber music. If I were to do it over again under the circumstances that prevailed, however, I believe I might indulge myself to the extent of hiring a chauffeured limousine to get me to and from the concerts. That would be expensive, to be sure, but possibly cheaper (and certainly more optimistic) than paying the premiums on a sizeable accident and disability policy.

9 ✧ REVIEWS

Read 'Em and Weep?

A s earlier recounted, the *Time* magazine piece about the Fine Arts Quartet in January of 1960 helped inspire the founding of the long-run concert series in Chicago that began the following season. Clearly, media coverage plays an important role in the career of the performer, whether the exposure is in the area of general publicity or specifically related to the artistic merit of the artist.

Edward Rothstein, a prominent music critic at *The New York Times* but here writing in the 2001 edition of the *New Grove Dictionary*, assessed the recent musical scene thus: "The power of critics to influence acceptance of new compositions or the careers of performers seemed much weaker than before, particularly in comparison with the forces of mass marketing." I am not fully persuaded that this is true, for I believe that the review continues to be a critical factor in the professional health of the artist or ensemble. In a word, performers live with reviews, music lovers read them, and critics should study them.

Let me start by referring my readers to the articles entitled "Criticism" in the *New Grove Dictionary of Music and Musicians* (1980 edition) written by English critic Winton Dean and in the *New Grove Dictionary of American Music* (1986) by Edward O. D. Downes and John Rockwell. Dean surveys the history of music criticism in Europe; Downes, the history of the field in America (Downes for 1800 to the present, Rockwell for jazz and rock). It will be helpful to read what Dean and Downes, both experienced critics, have to say about the subject and about the overall differences between music criticism in Europe and America: in the European tradition, a leaning toward partisanship and polemics regarding composers' styles and musical trends; in the American, an early emphasis on news and reportage. Moreover, and possibly in reflection of these contrasting attitudes, the European tendency to have the review appear several days after the event, as against the British and American habit of the next-day report.

Dean, as forthright as he is knowledgeable, plausibly names the critic's first responsibilities to be toward art, society, and the composer, in that order, with the performer next and the promoter (manager) at the bottom of the list. He recognizes the powerful impact of the critic on the fate of the performer, while offering the rather shadowed advice that "the critic would do well to bear in mind the benefit of the doubt."

For my part, I can assert that performers sometimes need all the help they can get in their effort to understand their relationship to the reviewer. It is all too easy for the musician to think that the reviewer is an enemy. Just consider what can happen: in America, the reviewer covering a concert often has to leave before its end in order to write and file the critique in time for the next day's issue of his newspaper. Unless the critic has heard the given artist on earlier occasions, the review must be written on the basis of the impressions gathered from this single—and sometimes incomplete—exposure to the work of the performer.

If the write-up is favorable, the performer is of course gratified. Should the review be negative, there is no recourse; the concert is over. A theatrical presentation can possibly survive an unfavorable review of an early performance by attracting enough ticket buyers to the continued run of the drama or musical. The concert, however, is a one-night affair; the critic's "pan" hangs over the performer, negating the months of preparation for the concert. If the performer has had to finance the concert appearance himself, then he has little to show for his investment. Further, after receiving a poor review, the performer will find it difficult to summon up the energy and willpower to prepare all over again, and even more of a stretch to get any outside backing for future presentations.

The performer's situation is the more precarious because many cities now have, to all intents and purposes, only one newspaper. This is true even of some metropolitan cities whose reviews carry the greatest clout in the concert world. Where there were formerly several morning and afternoon papers, the high costs of publishing, the drain on public allegiance toward print journalism exerted by television, and the trend toward the swallowing up of journals by publishing conglomerates has seriously thinned the number of newspapers. The result for the concert-giver is that, if a critic from the one important paper in town does not get to the concert, the impact of the event is just about nullified.

The reason? The concert public has been conditioned to trust the verdict of the critic almost as much as, and sometimes even more than, the evidence provided by its own eyes and ears. In the large cities, home to the more prominent papers, a lukewarm (let alone, negative) review will strongly weaken the resolve of a music lover to attend a later concert by the performer in question. Hire a babysitter, drive downtown to a concert-hall, pay for parking, buy a ticket for the performance, and in all likelihood also have the expense of a preconcert dinner? It is all too much like work; especially if the jaunt is for the purpose of hearing a comparative unknown on the musical scene. How much easier it is to put on a CD of an already celebrated virtuoso and sit at home, listening to a recording. As for the smaller city and town, there is little chance that local concert presenters will take a chance on engaging a performer from afar who cannot offer a brochure with quotes from favorable reviews by the big-town critic.

Does the critic merit the power he or she holds? In some cases, maybe so. There are reviewers, today as in the past, who have the requisite musical training and discernment. They have broad cultural interests, acquainting them with the span of the musical repertoire, of many types and styles, old and new, and also with the arts and literature generally. They have had long experience in listening to, and writing about, musical performances by soloists, orchestras, chamber ensembles, singers, and opera companies. Some critics have been through the mill of teaching serious courses about various musical subjects and have written meaningful books on important musical topics. Over the generations, composers—some of them quite prominent (for example, Schumann, Berlioz, Debussy)—have turned their hand to criticism, both for love and money. For people who are thus qualified, the power that rests in the critic's role can be justified. Power, however, also brings responsibility.

Good criticism recognizes and applauds beautiful, communicative performance, whatever the medium. Let it be that wonderful combination of a singer who reveals the very core of meaning in the text of a song and the pianist who evokes from the abstract sounds of the accompaniment nuances that complete and intensify the meaning of the poem. Or it can be the string quartet that follows the composer's lead through every tangent of thought, mood, and temperament, without ever blurring the structural clarity of the music. Yet again, it will be the symphony orchestra that plays as though it is a large chamber ensemble, responding to the lead of an able conductor not slavishly, but as though there is a meeting of informed, sensitive, flexible musical intellects. (Let there be no human metronome beating relentlessly "square" time on the podium.)

Good criticism also recognizes technical accuracy, properly gauged rubato, and polished and subtly colored tone, whether from the instrumental arsenal or the human voice. Precise intonation must of course be valued. Unfortunately, since poor intonation is so readily apparent, it will attract the attention even of the reviewer who is not discerning enough about other aspects of performance.

Above all, the conscientious critic will not let irrelevant factors color his appraisal of the performance at hand. The temperature in the auditorium may be too hot, too cold, the air too dry or too damp. If such discomforts do not bother the performer, they should certainly not distract the reviewer from his or her job: to appraise the performance. The report may contain mention of the untoward conditions surrounding the concert. It should not let such concerns mar the central purpose of the review: to convey a sense of the event, a personal response to the music-making, an evaluation of the technical and musical integrity of the performance. The review should certainly comment on perceived shortcomings in the performance, while at the same time offering whatever brief remedial advice the critic is qualified to give.

Such instructive advice may seem out of place to the publication's editor, to its readers, and perhaps (or even especially) to the performer. On the other hand, it enables everyone, including the critic himself, to get some perspective on the validity of the review overall. Unless the critic is ready to dismiss the performance outright as being a fraud inflicted on the public, the expectation of some helpful counsel helps level the playing field. On one side stands the concert-giver, who addresses the listeners only through the performance. On the other, there is the critic, whose words are available not only to those who attended the concert, but to that larger audience, the readers into whose hands the publication may make its way. The debate, if such it can be called, is between one who must not speak, and the other who is paid not to remain silent.

The situation is no better if the performer in question is already firmly established in star status. Here, unless the critic is also of well-entrenched repute, the tendency may be to pull the punch, to gloss over any reservations about the performance. That, however, is not likely. The reviewer is aware that, even if his serious carping about a revered artist should evoke protests, the publication will side with him in the name of freedom of the press. In fact, the outspoken reviewer may actually be counted a boon to the subscription rate.

Depending on the print space allotted the reviewer in a given publication, the critic may use the particular concert as a springboard for a fairly wide-ranging historical artistic essay. This can be of great interest to the reader but should not blot out the proper consideration of the performance that occasioned the review in the first place. To be "proper," the reviewer should not be cruel. There was a report by one sharp-tongued critic that held—without any further comment—that three members of the string quartet in question were "professionals." What this crack did to the next rehearsal of the ensemble, let alone its longevity, can only be guessed.

Unfortunately, newspaper administrators cannot always afford to hire a fully qualified critic, nor are they necessarily discerning enough, when engaging a less expensive, younger reviewer, to gauge whether the candidate has the necessary instincts for the job. Thus, it will happen that a neophyte reviewer adopts the magisterial tone of the established critic without having mastered the same level of artistic insight. The printed and negative commentary of the novice critic, however, can be damaging, whether it reflects a snap judgment or a carefully considered, informed opinion.

Performers must recognize all of this at the outset. In a very distant way, there is an air of the old gladiatorial combat about the modern concert scene. Thumbs up, the player has his or her reprieve or triumph. Thumbs down does not mean death but, in professional terms, something vaguely like it. Anyone seeking entry to the performing world knows that privacy ends when one goes through that door onto the stage. You are there to convince your audience and, of necessity, the critic(s) that you belong there. Their reaction to your performance will either confirm or contradict your own self-conviction about your artistic right to hold the stage. Be advised, however, that if you do not have that conviction to begin with, there is little reason to present the concert.

How should performers read reviews? Dispassionately. For one thing, they must not let an approving review make them giddy. It is hard to predict what response the next concert will bring, even from the very same critic. Moreover, if more than one reviewer covers a given concert, one journalist might applaud, the other decry that very same performance. It is the performer's job to evaluate the appraisals, looking for the reservations in the positive report and the kernels of advice lurking in the chilly write-up. As the late, lamented, and much-traveled pianist Victor Babin put it to me, "The most important word in a review is 'but.'"

I need scarcely tell the members of a chamber ensemble that if reviewers consistently single out one member of the group for praise, there is something out of kilter with the band. The ensemble should be heard as an integral musical organism. If one participant stands out above the others, there are three possible explanations. First, the standout is truly in a different league from the rest of the group. Or, second, the individual is grandstanding or scene-stealing (and shame to the critic who does not recognize and condemn such behavior). Or, third, the others are not giving their all. If there is no "all" to give, the ensemble should do some serious soul-searching, for its demise cannot be far off.

Suppose the converse is true: one member is frequently criticized for one or more faults in performance, and not just by one reviewer. That member, whether leader, inner voice, or whatever, dare not ignore such comment. The entire ensemble must be able to discuss the situation, determine whether the observations are valid, and if they are, decide what to do about the matter. Certainly the solution of taking the reviewers to court, as one victim of persistent criticism urged upon the rest of the ensemble, is self-defeating. The attendant publicity would be ruinous, and the court would in any event most likely decide that the concert artist must accept the challenges of a public career. The immutable principle for the ensemble must be to avoid litigation, whether between members of the ensemble or by the group against those outside (except in the case of outright fraud, of course). There can be no winners in any such proceeding.

When it comes to meeting the challenges of dealing with reviews, I trust that my readers will join with me in hoping there is truth in an anecdote I heard about Fritz Kreisler's handling of one particular critic. Kreisler's inimitable artistry was in fact usually treated by the press with a reverence that matched the adoration given him by his audiences. A certain American critic, however, tempered a laudatory review of the first of a pair of concerts that Kreisler was giving in a local auditorium by saying that the master was, after all, playing on a fine old violin. Before the second concert, Kreisler went to a dealer in the city and bought a run-of-the-mill fiddle. At the end of the program there was a standing ovation. At that point, Kreisler is said to have thrown the violin to the floor and stamped on it. Again, I fervently hope that this tale is true.

Whether the general European practice of having a concert review appear two or three days after the event is an improvement over the American tradition of next-day printing is not an easy question to answer. Again, much depends on the insight of the reviewer. When you translate and/or read such a review, you might find that the extra writing time has allowed the critic to indulge in rather flowery prose, not always entirely clear in its commentary on the actual performance. It will also happen that the critic, apparently knowledgeable, gives chapter and verse on what he found wrong with the playing. Then at the end of the review comes the phrase, "enthusiastic applause from the audience." Which is the performer to believe: the adverse view of the critic or the acclaim by the audience? The player was onstage, with an insider's perspective on the performance. He has to analyze the review as objectively as possible, to glean what help it offers. That is true whether it is a write-up in English or any other language. And if the review in essence merely reports that the event took place, it can simply be ignored.

Sidelights from our reviews

We left for our first European tour in 1958 with some heartening American reviews in our file, including one from *The New York Times* (8 October 1957) with this quote: "Airiness, grace and high polish were everywhere. Nothing in the evening gave more pleasure than observing a group of fine musicians delightedly and cautiously preparing one in particular of Beethoven's elaborately sly modulations."

In Paris, at the start of our European circuit, I saw that we were up against listeners of strong opinion, to say nothing of the print reviewers.

An officer of the Paris chamber music society came backstage to lead us to the postconcert reception. As we walked, he told me how much the concert had been enjoyed. The Allegro finale of the Beethoven Op. 130, however, he found to be absolutely "*trop vite.*" I tried to question this view of the matter but desisted after a couple more cries of "too fast," having met my match.

Our Geneva concert, a bit later in that same tour, earned us a rather mixed review. Since I had some command of French, it fell to me to offer a live translation for my quartet-mates. It went, in part:

> If we have to declare the slightest reservation, we would say that the tone of the first violin sometimes lacks a certain encompassing charm—something which the cellist, on the other hand, has in full measure. Very strong musical personality in the second violin, and impeccable performance by the violist (*Journal de Genève*, 19 March 1958).

Two other reviewers conferred laurels on the cello and second violin. And a fourth took all four of us to task:

> [Their] central attribute . . . seems to be a kind of mechanization of performance, with a remarkable perfection of ensemble that starts, leaps, breathes, and stops with admirable synchronization. This, however, at the cost of a heaviness of speech and a lack of poetry on the simplest level that seems rather surprising (*La Suisse*, 19 March 1958).

All these reviews were for one and the same concert! Since an ensemble stands or falls as a single organism, the analyses provided by the critics gave scant pleasure to those singled out for praise and were certainly no fun for the others.

Still, the quartet went on to give seventeen more European tours during my years in the group. I suppose this shows that performers can co-exist with critics. Moreover, we came in for reviews such as the following, manna from heaven for all four of us.

> No public place in London has a mellower atmosphere for chamber music than the Wigmore Hall; otherwise anyone could be forgiven for wondering why artists of this calibre were confining themselves to so small an audience—though needless to say it was as large an audi-

ence as ever comes to Wigmore Street for anything other than a gui-
tar (*London Times*, 3 April 1971).

and

> On any count this is one of the great quartets of the world, and its
> greatness came home to me the more forcefully after I had heard
> another in the top flight so recently—the sweet-toned Quartetto Ital-
> iano. . . . Much as I love to have my ears soothed by Italian tone, the
> precision and honesty of the Fine Arts sound is something even more
> exciting, particularly when heard in the ideal Wigmore Hall acoustic.
> These are players who hit every note ping in the middle, whose pitch-
> ing provides an exact match even when they reduce or (on occasion)
> eliminate vibrato (*Manchester Guardian*, 29 March 1971).

Our first concert in New Zealand, in 1961, was in Wanganui, on North
Island. The local critic was taken aback by my moving about a bit in my
chair as I played. I will admit that, in my younger years as performer, I was
a tad more active than some. Even so, I felt that the reviewer's description
of "the second violinist, who at times almost groveled on the platform
floor," was rather extreme.

For our concert at the Kaufhaussaal in Freiburg in 1958 we played
the Allegretto pizzicato movement from Bartók's Fourth Quartet as an
encore. A loud chord seems to end the movement, only to be followed by
a few teasing, additional measures that actually lead to the double bar.
Many in our audience fell into the trap and applauded before the movement was truly ended. They were taken to task in the review, wherein the
critic expressed surprise that this should have occurred with initiated
music lovers, especially with professionals among them. How nice to be
told that there is artistic responsibility at both ends of the auditorium.

In The Hague in 1961, we shared a concert with the New York Woodwind Quintet. Each ensemble played a work from its respective repertoire, and then for the second half of the program, we joined together for
the first ten sections of Bach's *Art of Fugue*. I asked our good friend the
Dutch manager Harry de Freese to be sure to send me copies of any
reviews of the concert. He promised not only to do so but also to supply
a translation, though I said that I would rather attempt that myself. Harry

was as good as his word, and sent us a translation that began with the headline, "The Blowers and the Bowers." I ended up doing my own version after all.

In this year the quartet received plaudits mirrored on both sides of the world. On 22 January 1961 *The Washington Post* critic called us "one of the finest string quartets to come to Washington in a long time." And 24 August 1961 in the Melbourne *Herald*: "This is easily the best American quartet to visit Australia, and it is a long time since we have heard chamber music playing of such distinction from visitors of any nationality."

An away concert in February 1963 was at Town Hall in New York, where we gave a piano quintet program (Bloch, Schumann, Dvořák) with Frank Glazer. We had an appreciative audience, but from the performers' perspective the concert remained in a kind of limbo: a newspaper strike in New York coincided with the date of our appearance, so no reviews were printed. The only reaction we had on the journalistic front was the typescript of a favorable write-up, very kindly sent to us by its author, the critic of the *Christian Science Monitor*.

In June 1967, toward the end of a tour that our quartet and the clarinetist David Glazer made under the auspices of the U.S. State Department, we gave a concert in Melbourne, Australia. This time around the reporter from the Melbourne newspaper *The Australian* devoted his entire brief review to the program notes.

Though they were unsigned, the notes were by me, and I cannot deny my readers a quote from the barbs flung in my direction. Among other things, the reviewer cites an excerpt from my notes about the closing movement of Beethoven's Quartet in E minor, Op. 59, No. 2, and offers his own commentary thereon.

> "The final Presto is Beethoven the steamroller, personified. You stop this one at your own peril. It moves mightily forward, but is not so much of a juggernaut that it can't pause now and then for kittenish dialogue. The kind of repartée that makes quartet playing the reckless pleasure it is."—Oh boy, the next time I want a bit of reckless pleasure, it will not be wine and women for me. I'll just grab three of my friends, a couple of violins, a viola and a cello, and have a bit of reckless quartet playing.

Oof! What I really resent is that the review was well written.

We left Australia for New Zealand the next day, and it was at the airport that I got the paper and saw the review. Though somewhat abashed, I was not so crushed as to keep from buying several copies of the newspaper in order to have extras of the write-up. Perhaps that marks me as the quintessential performer.

10 ✧ THE FINE ARTS QUARTET IN
A UNIVERSITY RESIDENCY

During my first months in the Fine Arts Quartet, the ensemble gave several summer concerts at Northwestern University's Lutkin Hall, with six more during the academic year that followed. These programs were an extended swan song, for 1954–55 was the third and final year of the quartet's adjunct residency at the university. In view of the end in early 1954 of the quartet's employment at ABC, we would have been happy to have the university attachment not only prolonged but converted into a full-time appointment. There was, I believe, division of opinion on this score within the faculty of the university's school of music, and our days there were definitely at an end. I had arrived in the quartet just in time to witness all this, and I think the experience educated me for our next and very long-term installation in academe.

While I was away on my emergency trip east in the summer of 1954 to gather and move my family to the Midwest, Leonard, Irving, and George visited the Milwaukee campus of what was then Wisconsin State Teachers College. They met with the administration to discuss a possible series of summer concerts. This led to the concerts we gave there in July 1955. We were joined in this short series by the excellent New York Woodwind Quintet and the equally distinguished pianist Frank Glazer. (A native of Milwaukee, Glazer studied with the celebrated Artur Schnabel in Europe and went on to a concert and teaching career in his own right.)

The quartet and quintet had appeared together in New York in a Town Hall concert of February 1954 in the New Friends of Music series. Our quartet suggested to the academic administrators at Milwaukee the inclusion of the quintet in the summer roster. With the addition of Frank Glazer, this corps of ten musicians, along with occasional guest artists, made possible the programming of a broad variety of chamber music works.

Out of this collaboration were to come some of the important mixed-ensemble releases issued by our quartet's record company. These included the Beethoven septet, Schubert octet, Hindemith octet, Spohr nonet, the Schumann, Bloch, and Dvořák piano quintets, the Beethoven quintet for piano and winds, Mozart's horn quintet, oboe quartet, and flute quartets, and especially J. S. Bach's *The Art of Fugue*, in the sensitive transcription by the quintet's flutist Samuel Baron. Sam also played in the recording of the four Mozart flute quartets, and the quintet as a whole recorded a number of woodwind works for the label.

The summer concerts were given in Marietta House, the college's large mansion on Milwaukee's handsome Lake Drive. The ground floor of the building held an audience of some two hundred. The listeners sat on folding chairs, ranked on three sides of a low platform that could accommodate a piano and the various ensemble groupings drawn from among the four strings and five winds.

The living quarters on the upper floors of the mansion easily took care of the entire complement of players and (in the case of the quartet members) their families as well. Jill, I, and our two boys, David and Peter (they were then four and three, respectively—our daughter, Marah, would be born only on the last day of that July), were quite comfortable in one very big bedroom–dressing room–bath complex on the second floor. The bedroom itself was larger than the entire three-room flat near Columbia in which Jill and I had started our married life.

This collaboration of quartet, wind quintet, and pianist went on successfully for some years. The Marietta House concerts were fully subscribed by Milwaukee music lovers. All participating musicians presented afternoon talks about the music featured on the evening programs. The string and wind players conducted chamber music workshops as part of the summer offerings. Matters could have gone on indefinitely this way. After 1965, the tenth anniversary of the summer concerts, however, Frank Glazer had to bow out, owing to the pressures of his own teaching and concert schedule.

The campus had meanwhile become part of the University of Wisconsin system, changing its title to the University of Wisconsin–Milwaukee and very soon growing into the second largest component of the system after the parent campus at Madison. Because of the lack of sufficient faculty string forces and our proximity in the not-distant city of Chicago, our participation in the summer events at Milwaukee continued. For the year 1962–63, indeed, we were appointed visiting quartet-in-residence for the academic year. Railroad service between Chicago and Milwaukee was on a much fuller schedule then than it is today, so we were able to cover our campus schedule by a combination of rather lengthy commutes and periodic hotel overnights.

As we began our accustomed summer concerts in 1963, however, it appeared our own presence in Milwaukee was about to end. The dean of the School of Fine Arts (to which the music department belonged) informed us that our role at the university, and specifically the summer concerts and chamber music workshop, would be taken over by a quartet made up of the principals of the Milwaukee Symphony Orchestra. We knew there had been pressure from the symphony's administration toward this end. We pointed out to the dean the inevitable differences between the two ensembles. On the one hand, there was the style and polish of a dedicated quartet with many years of performance experience. On the other stood an ensemble whose first obligation was to an orchestral schedule and whose playing could not match the integration and sound palette of a seasoned chamber group. Though clearly uncomfortable over the matter, the dean was just as clearly feeling the pressure from the Milwaukee Symphony and its supporters within the city. We felt our Milwaukee days to be numbered.

Partway into what promised to be our last summer series in Milwaukee, we gave a lecture-concert in the school auditorium on Bartók's Quartet No. 6. Among those present were the provost of UW-M, Charles Vevier, and a high administrative officer of the parent campus, Madison. I was surprised when, the next day, George Sopkin told me that we had been invited to join the faculty on a continuing basis, year-round.

Pleased though I was at this sudden turnaround, I thought back to our fate at Northwestern University, not an experience I wanted to repeat. I chanced upon a hallway conversation between Dr. Vevier and George. When Vevier looked at me for comment about the UW-M invitation, I said something like, "Fine, but not without tenure."

My words were instinctive and instantaneous, though I was certainly aware that what I said had implication for the quartet as a whole. The remark reflected not only my concern about potential frictions in the halls of academe, but also my discomfort over the knife-edge on which we had been perched for several weeks in our relations with the university. I felt that our established reputation as a concert ensemble, with our work long known on campus, merited the long-term assurance that tenure would offer, the more so because the addition of an ensemble of four to the music department faculty must inevitably be regarded as an intrusive threat by some of the incumbents. Fortunately, and I suspect because of the support of Provost Vevier, the university did indeed install us with immediate tenure for the three older members, and with the prospect of tenure in future for our new (and considerably younger) violist, Gerald Stanick.

It was grimly ironic that our appointment should come only after Irv Ilmer, who had been our violist since 1952, was in process of withdrawing from the group in order to follow an individual career, with renewed emphasis on his original instrument, the violin. He had, after all, been involved in the years of summer residencies that had made us familiar on the UW-M campus. Yet we had already made a commitment to Stanick to serve as Irv's replacement, so there was no possibility of reversing course even if Irv had so desired.

Now came another ripple in the waters: Leonard asked the three of us—George, Jerry, and me—whether we thought the university's offer should be accepted, tenure or no. He was afraid that a full-time residency at the campus would somehow diminish our effectiveness as a concert ensemble. George and I were both surprised at Len's doubts, for we felt the faculty appointment would at last give us a predictable base to help support our continuing investment in the expenses and hard work of a concert career. On my own account, I immediately said that I would have to give up the quartet if we did not take hold of the university's offer. The steady income from the academic post was vital to the needs of my family, with three young children in school. There was also the appeal of helping college-age students prepare themselves for a career in music.

Len yielded to our view, and matters moved ahead. I must recognize that his reservations had merit, for we were adding to our work responsibilities. He shifted some of the burden by finding the California buyer who took over our tape library and its distribution. The recording chores for further releases in the rest of the 1960s and '70s, however, remained with us. Consequently, we would be significantly spreading our energies. It was going to be a tall order.

At the departmental faculty meeting that opened the academic year 1963–64, our dean paid us a signal and no doubt advisable courtesy. He attended the meeting and endorsed our tenure status as recognition of our established reputation and our value to the work of the department and the growth of the department's importance both on campus and in the community.

Our appointment was to an annual, rather than academic year, schedule. This meant that we were on duty for the eleven months from September through July, rather than just the two-semester span of September through May. This was so we would continue to be responsible for the summer concerts and chamber music workshop. Our salary, of course, was scaled to match the extended calendar of service. For our first year as full faculty, we took unpaid leave for the second semester, because our concert and touring schedule—compiled before the teaching appointment was even thought of—filled too much of the spring term to allow for effective handling of teaching duties.

The departmental faculty made its own recommendations for raises in salary, meeting for such discussion each year during the spring term. Since we were away that semester, we had no hand in the matter that first year of our residency. When the list of increases was made known, each of the four members in the quartet had been allotted the princely increase of $300 for the following year. The dean made an adjustment to the department's decision and continued to oversee our raises in the years to come, but I had had fresh confirmation of my opinion about the ensemble's need for the safeguard of tenured status.

In the late 1960s there was pressure from within the music department to have the New York Woodwind Quintet replaced in the summer festivities by a quintet formed by the wind instrument teachers who had been appointed to the faculty. We in the quartet argued with the dean that a newly formed faculty ensemble could not, for some time to come, approach the seasoned artistry of the New York group. There was nothing for it, however, but that the visiting wind ensemble must bow out. We in the quartet felt it was a loss for Milwaukee's music-loving community.

With its appointment to the faculty in 1963, the Fine Arts Quartet had added a new and demanding element to its workload, and we were all the busier as a result. Over the years, we taught our several instruments and organized and coached the student chamber music ensembles. Before the department acquired musicology faculty, I gave one or another classroom course, and the entire quartet took part in team-taught lectures. We sat on academic committees, attended departmental and university faculty meetings, and presented noontime lecture concerts during the year for the general student body (with faculty from various university disciplines usually in attendance as well). We also recruited new string students and conducted year-end juries for string majors. This was in addition to our formal concerts on campus and the continuation of our concert series in Chicago and its North Shore, our domestic and foreign touring, and our recording activity. Along with all this, our kids were growing up and had to be listened to, tended to, sent off to college, and so on.

For the first two years of my faculty appointment, our family stayed on at its home in Ravinia on Chicago's North Shore. Jill and I wanted our kids to have some more time in their familiar schools before we moved up to Milwaukee. This meant that I made many trips by rail or auto between the two cities from the autumn of 1963 through the spring of 1965, some of them during harsh winter weather.

When we found a house in Milwaukee, I got a new slant on tenure. It came when I applied for a mortgage at a local bank. The mortgage officer asked how long a contract I had at the university. "I have tenure," I replied. His response was the question, "What happens *after* the ten years?"

In 1967 we were in Tokyo as part of our U.S. State Department tour of the Far East with the clarinetist David Glazer. It was then that we got word from UW-M that Len, George, and I had been promoted to the rank of full professor. It must also have been about this time, or shortly before, that Jerry Stanick was appointed a tenured associate professor. Very soon after our return home to Milwaukee, Jerry announced his decision to leave the quartet. Though we had had some earlier warning signs of his unrest, it was still a shock to think that we were to lose the benefit of the already more than four years invested in the process of integrating a young musician into the ensemble. He was a truly gifted player and a very quick study, but he had been unfamiliar with the extent of our chamber repertoire when he joined us. In the face of our dismay at his announcement, Jerry stayed on, but in the course of 1967–68, his resolve to leave us grew firmer.

Now there was a further complication. Owing to his tenure status, we faced one of the problems I warn about in chapter 21. Jerry could have left the quartet but stayed on in the music department. This, however, would have meant that we could only hire his quartet replacement if the university would fund an additional position in the department. Because there were scarcely enough viola students for one teacher, let alone two, appointing a second viola position was obviously out of the question. The impasse was resolved when Jerry decided to resign his faculty post as well as his position in the quartet.

Besides, Jerry might have realized that his tenure inhabited a cloudy legal area. The impact of a member's departure from the quartet on the matter of continuing tenure certainly would have raised concern had it occurred to us. Did we enjoy tenured status as individuals, or only as part of the ensemble? Fortunately, it would never prove necessary for any of the older members of the quartet to look for the answer; retirement and resignation made the question irrelevant. For his part, Jerry went on to a distinguished performing and teaching career in other venues. Our quartet was able to find a very fine new violist, Bernard Zaslav, and get on with its work as an ensemble.

In the spring of 1972, the quartet had a semester's leave from its work at UW-M. There was no mandatory sabbatical process in force in the Wisconsin University system. Paid leave could be granted only for work on a suitable academic project. Our own proposal was to work on an annotated, performing ensemble's edition of the Beethoven quartets. I am afraid that we did not make much progress on the task during our leave.

In fact, our itinerary in all these months was so full, and the spacing of Milwaukee-Chicago concerts so little interrupted, that I cannot now really define it as a leave. This was positively stupid on the part of the quartet. Instead of using the time as an opportunity for the four of us to have some relief from our busy round and from each other's constant company, we did our best to fill the months with concert and recording activity. What could have been a safety valve in our ensemble life was left tightly closed.

With the benefit of hindsight, I recognize that residency was a mixed blessing for our ensemble. This was partly our own doing and partly imposed on us. The faculty appointment came at a critical juncture in our career and, I know, helped us stay together. However, our response during all the sixteen years that ensued before my departure from the quartet was to try to juggle two very full-time schedules. To make room for our teaching duties, one sensible solution would have been to scale back on our concertizing activity and recording output. Quite aside from our own inclination, however, that would have taken the bloom off our publicity value both to us and the school.

Or we could have asked for significant reduction in our campus assignments. I doubt whether this would have been possible in those years in a university system dependent on the state legislature for funding. Events surrounding residencies in more recent time also suggest that a fortuitous combination of circumstance and sheer brass is needed to skew conditions toward a sustainable ensemble presence on campus. The world is not always a logical place.

11 ✧ THE 1960s
Playing Far and Wide

Memory is sometimes too clear. When I read over what I have written here and recognize that the playing and travel described took place along with recording, maintaining a multiprogrammed concert series, moving the family from one city to another, and—from 1963 on—the addition of teaching duties at a university, I question the individual and collective sanity of our ensemble. I realize that one does what has to be done, but I still shake my head in disbelief. If I add the fact that for the last couple of years of the 1960s I was also working on a book, I truly wonder what made me do what I did. Could it have been fun?

In the early 1960s we served, with the New York Woodwind Quintet, as principals in the UW-M Chamber Orchestra, led by the conductor Thor Johnson. I will never erase the memory of the concert of January 1961, in which Johnson had us perform the Quartet Concerto, Op. 131, of Louis Spohr. It was to become a continuing item in our repertoire, but never again would it elicit the special excitement that it brought on this occasion.

The concerto puts the quartet of soloists through some active paces, especially in the finale. In the first section of that movement, there comes a moment when first and second violins, viola, and cello, each one absolutely alone, take off in succession in four individual, ascending, three-octave flights of arpeggios, with a one-measure orchestral interlude before each soloist's entrance. In the recapitulation section, a similar maneuver takes place. Now, however, after a longish passage by the orchestra, the second violin leads off, followed by cello, first violin, and viola. In our very first orchestral rehearsal of the work, I had muffed this arpeggio and had developed a psychological hurdle about it as a result.

Comes the concert, the Spohr, its finale, and the recapitulation section thereof. The orchestra begins its seventeen-measure *tutti* passage, and I am keeping count while at the same time psyching myself for the approaching arpeggio by dint of repeatedly tapping my left index finger on the initial note of the passage, the low A of the violin. While indulging in this figurative pawing of the ground, I lose count of the measures but tell myself that it is only necessary to let the orchestra end its passage, then begin my flight. This, however, was our first performance of the piece, and I had not yet internalized the fact that my takeoff coincided immediately with the orchestra's last downbeat. Thus, when the orchestra stopped, there was a pregnant and ominous silence. Johnson remained frozen with baton in midair, and the orchestra wondered what was about to happen.

For me the silence was deafening. I saw my childhood pass in review, wondered what had made my mother push me into music, and at the same time, pondered how to get out of the moment's impasse. George, who was waiting to follow me, wondered whether he should set up a diversionary action by knocking over his music stand. Eons of time seemed to be passing, but it was only the length of one measure. I decided to blast off into my arpeggio on that very downbeat. So I did, in the most perfect and incandescent arpeggio of my career. Johnson whipped the orchestra into action, George and the others launched their arpeggios in turn, and we continued on in triumph to the end of the movement.

As we were taking our first bow, I wondered how I was going to face our conductor when we got offstage. In the wings I went up to Johnson and tried to disarm him by saying, "I bet I had you scared!" To which he fervently replied, "You sure *did!*" While the orchestra was packing up, flutist Sam Baron came over to me with a mischievous grin and said, "Abe! What an arpeggio! It had determination, chagrin, remorse!"

In any event, I had two consoling thoughts: I had survived; and the audience had no inkling of what had transpired in the performance, for I doubt whether any among them had ever had occasion to hear Spohr's Quartet Concerto before.

In early March of 1961 we were off to Europe for our third visit, taking us to Austria, France, England, Switzerland, Holland, Denmark, and Germany, with a finale at Paris's Salle Gaveau, for an all-Russian program: Lopatnikoff's Quartet No. 3, Op. 36; Tcherepnin's Quartet No. 2, Op. 40; and Shostakovich's Quartet No. 4, Op. 83.

This time around, my family was the only one accompanying us on the trip. Our kids were the youngest in the quartet circle and thus would be less affected by the time away from school than their older counterparts. For this tour we would be down to two cars: one for George, Irv, and Len, the other (a VW minibus) for Jill, the kids, and me. Just before leaving, we had a concert at Mt. Holyoke College and, on the morning of the flight to Europe, another turn on the NBC *Today* show.

Jill and the family flew to New York on their own and met me at the airport there. As we waited for the departure of the evening flight to London, we had a pleasant surprise. Our friends, the duo-piano team of Vitya Vronsky and Victor Babin, were there to take the same flight. Before boarding, Victor and I had a conversation during which he delivered a wonderful line. "Very often, after a concert, people from the audience will ask me, 'Don't you just love your work?' And I often think to myself, after twenty-five years, *must* I love it?" As matters were to turn out, it was a thought I must have filed for future reference.

The most exotic experience that spring was reserved not for the quartet, but for George and me. The director of a Bach group in Chicago engaged the two of us to perform J. S. Bach's *Musical Offering*, along with Ray Still, principal oboe of the Chicago Symphony, and with the director at the harpsichord. In the original edition of the work, specific instrumentation is given only for the trio sonata portion and the canon immediately following in the lengthy composition, with flute and violin named to perform the two upper melodic lines and harpsichord and cello to provide the basso continuo. As the director explained in a program note, "Since oboist Ray Still was engaged for this concert before the *Musical Offering* was decided upon, we are substituting the oboe for the flute." This seemed to me a remarkable explanation, perhaps advanced to cover what I assumed to be the reality—that the director's favorite flutist, principal in an eastern city's symphony orchestra, was unavailable. We performed the work at a house concert on Chicago's

North Shore, and Ray did his characteristically masterful job in this very demanding assignment.

When the opportunity arose of repeating the performance at the University of Chicago, Ray's Chicago Symphony schedule did not permit his participation, and the distant flutist was again not available. Rather than give up the engagement, the director said the three of us would perform the *Offering* by ourselves! That George and I did not hang back is incredible to me now. Maybe we wanted to see what would happen.

Just as we were about to go onstage at the University of Chicago's Mandel Hall, our leader surprised me by asking that I explain to the audience the unusual performance that was about to take place. Improvising at such short notice, I gave what I hoped were some halfway plausible comments about the freedom of choice of instrumentation in (relatively) early music, and we launched into the work of the evening. To cover the absence of the missing high-register instrument, not only in the trio sonata, but in the various canons of the work, the harpsichordist was especially adroit and George was athletic in his journeys up into the rosinous stratosphere of the cello, while I held forth in the comparatively normal duties of the violin. Luckily for my peace of mind, I did not know that Donal Henahan, one of Chicago's first-string critics, was in attendance. Luckier still, the resulting review likened the concert to a three-legged horse running in the Kentucky Derby—and winning. It was an interesting evening, but not one that George and I would choose to repeat.

In early August 1961 we left for our first visit to Australia and New Zealand. Two families accompanied us on this tour: the Sorkins and Lofts. The kids had study books with them and would be missing only the very opening of the fall semester at school. Since there was a stop in Hawaii en route, both families arranged their itineraries so they could spend a couple of days there before going on. When Irv and George came through, we boarded their flight so that we could all arrive in New Zealand together.

George and Irv left the plane while it was being cleaned and refueled in Hawaii, then reboarded. Unfortunately, their luggage not only left the plane, but stayed off. Thus, when we got to New Zealand, our cellist and violist were without both full-dress and general wardrobe. Even worse, they had each packed their music in their suitcases (the last time they did so). Consequently, they had to play the first few concerts with music bor-

First Australian tour, 1961. Left to right: Loft, Sorkin, Ilmer, Sopkin, waiting to enter the gallery of Melbourne's Museum of Art.

rowed from local quartet enthusiasts. It was a couple of days before the missing luggage was sent on from Hawaii. Meanwhile, with some emergency purchases, George and Irv were able to take part in the first concerts of the tour. For uniform appearance, we all played in informal wear, or what the reviewer called "lounge suits."

The awareness of things musical down under is evident from an experience Jill and I had at the Taronga Park Zoo in Sydney. We had taken the kids there to have a look at, among other inhabitants, the koala bears. The koala house was closed for the noon hour when we arrived. A keeper, however, gave my name to the zoo director. He immediately came out of his office and said that any member of a quartet giving the first Bartók quartet cycle in Australia (two programs, planned and announced just a few days earlier) merited special courtesy. David, Peter, and Marah were not only given entry but also had the pleasure of holding and petting a couple of the koalas.

We all enjoyed the warmth and hospitality of the people we met in Australia and New Zealand. In retrospect, we were especially glad to have made this trip, for it was the last tour abroad on which our kids accompanied us. They were getting too old to continue missing part of the school year. This way, before their "retirement," they were able to add new memories to go with their recollections of Europe.

In October 1961 we started the second season of our Chicago-Wilmette concert series. In the first two concerts, we presented Bach's six Brandenburg Concertos, in one-on-a-part setting. Guest artists from the Chicago Symphony and others of the city's musical elite joined us not only for the Brandenburgs but also for the other mixed ensemble works. The New York Woodwind Quintet came out to take part in *The Art of Fugue*. The chamber orchestra works on the programs (and Schoenberg's *Pierrot lunaire*, with Alice Howland as the *Sprechstimme*) were conducted by Herbert Zipper, then director of the Music Center of the North Shore and formerly conductor of the Brooklyn Symphony.

These programs included the twenty-nine works shown on page 122, in most of which we participated. With the repeat series on the North Shore, that meant we played twenty-four concerts at home in addition to our other Chicago activities and programs on the road. I think we must have set a record for perseverance.

As newcomers to Australia, we take direction from a very informative signpost. Left to right: Irv Ilmer, Leonard Sorkin, George Sopkin, Abe Loft.

This kind of calendar in Chicago could not continue. For one thing, the high number of concerts in a single locale enforced the performance of many different works within the confines of a single season. Moreover, even in a city the size of Chicago, it is doubtful that the schedules and the daily round of life of the concert-going public could long have sustained such a concentration. As I reported in my chapter on this home-city series, it was not long before the orchestral programs were removed from the series and the concerts settled back to what was now to be the norm: two parallel series, each comprising seven concerts. It was still a sizeable package.

One among the more outlandish of our experiences on the road came in March of 1962. We finished a concert at Union College in Schenectady and set out for New York in a rented station wagon immediately after the program. We had to be at the NBC studio early the next morning for

Chicago-Wilmette series repertoire menu, 1961

J. S. Bach	*The Art of Fugue*, the first ten counterpoints
	The six Brandenburg Concertos
Bartók	Quartet No. 3
	Quartet No. 4
	Quartet No. 6
Blackwood	Quartet No. 1
Brahms	Quartet No. 3 in B-flat, Op. 67
	Viola Quintet No. 1 in F, Op. 88
	Viola Quintet No. 2 in G, Op. 111
Debussy	Quartet No. 1 in G minor, Op. 10
Dvořák	Piano Quintet in A, Op. 81
Haydn	Quartet in D, Op. 50, No. 6
	Quartet in C, Op. 54, No. 2
	Quartet in B-flat, Op. 76, No.4
Hindemith	*Hérodiade*
Leide-Tedesco	Quartet, Op. 23
Mendelssohn	Quartet in D, Op. 44, No. 1
Mozart	Quartet in B-flat, K. 458
	Quartet in C, Op. 465
	Horn Quintet in E-flat, K. 386c
Partos	Quartet No. 2
Schoenberg	Quartet No. 3
	Pierrot lunaire
Schubert	Quartet in D minor, D. 810
Spohr	Nonet in F, Op. 31
Strauss	Prelude to *Capriccio*
	Metamorphoses
	Oboe Concerto
Tcherepnin	Quartet No. 2, Op. 40
Wagner	*Siegfried Idyll*

another *Today* show appearance. George was at the wheel, driving at speed down the highway. In the light of auto headlamps, I could make out a deer loping along the embankment on the far side of the northbound lanes. Then the deer suddenly crossed all four lanes of the road and was directly in our path. The animal almost made it, but not quite. After the impact, George pulled over to the side of the road so we could assess the damage. Another motorist stopped and helped pull the deer carcass off the roadway. None of us was hurt, and the car, with only some surface damage, was able to continue. We kept on to New York, returned the car, got to bed about 1:00 A.M., and were on our way to NBC at 5:00. We were rewarded for our zeal by being seated for our "spots" on the show against a black backdrop (signifying outer space) and next to a mockup of a planet.

We began the winter 1962 European tour in October—this time, just the four quartet members quite alone in one rental car—with a concert in the small, beautiful baroque theater at the castle in Celle, Germany, northeast of Hannover. That same month we returned to Bruchsal Palace, in the city of that name (near Karlsruhe). The hall was less spectacular than that at Celle, but the stage attendants' costumes were quite atmospheric.

In this 1962 tour we also performed in the auditorium of the large chemical manufacturing firm BASF (Badische Analin- und Soda-Fabrik) in Ludwigshafen. At our hotel that afternoon, George and I decided we would fortify ourselves by having a full dinner, with wine, before going to the hall. Accordingly, it was with some concern that immediately after the concert we heard the BASF representative tell the quartet, "And now we have supper!"

We repaired to a private dining room where George and I manfully put away our second dinner of the evening, complete with beer. (Again, one suffers for art.) During the table talk, the BASF officer told me that, in the war years, technical people had not been required to join the Nazi party. Even so, I asked, had not he and others like him heard anything about the evil deeds that were taking place in Germany and Europe under the Hitler regime? "We heard rumors," he said, "but could not believe that Germans were capable of such things." He seemed sincere in his statement, and that made the conversation the more unsettling to us in the quartet.

October 1962, Bruchsal Palace, Germany. George Sopkin, Leonard Sorkin, Irving Ilmer, with the three page-boys (girls!) who would be ushering the four of us into the hall for the broadcast concert.

The Fine Arts Quartet rehearsing onstage in a broadcast concert studio at Radio Saarbrücken, Germany, 1962. Left to right: Leonard Sorkin, Abe Loft, George Sopkin, Irving Ilmer.

A week after this, we had a somewhat related experience after a concert in Trier. We were invited out for a beer with the chamber music society officer, the local district attorney, and another citizen of the town. Somehow the conversation turned to holiday visits our hosts had made to Spain, and they commented with some disdain on what they said was the mistreatment of animals by the Spaniards. The following day, as the quartet was driving to the next city on the itinerary, one of us recalled the prior evening and—in light of the Nazi years—the strangely obtuse statements we had heard. We taxed each other for not having said anything pertinent in response.

I must point out that we did indeed meet Germans who were overtly aware and concerned about what had transpired in their country in the years leading up to and during World War II. Among them was a musicologist on the staff of the important music publisher Bärenreiter Verlag in Kassel. This scholar, who had been in his early teens in the war period, told us, "There are those who tell you it was not so bad, here in Germany at that time. They are wrong! Things were very bad!"

Later in that tour, we arrived in Brussels the very week of the Cuban missile crisis, with the world teetering on the brink of nuclear war. Evincing the strange reactions of people dreading a horrendous catastrophe, Brussels housewives had cleared market shelves of such staples as sugar. Despite the tension, our scheduled concert was to proceed. We got to the city the early afternoon of the concert day and reported to the *pension* where reservations had been made for us.

Harry de Freese, our manager for the Low Countries, always sought lodgings for us at moderate cost. Whether by Harry's instructions or owing to the landlady's available space, we found that she had set aside two double rooms for us. This we could not accept; it was enough to spend days together traveling, rehearsing, and performing. Listening to each other snore at night was beyond the call of valor. (I have read that some ensembles even refuse to have their members' hotel rooms located on the same floor.)

Leonard and Irv immediately took a cab downtown to check into a hotel. That left George and me to toss for the choice of room at the *pension.* George called it right and got the bedroom with bath. For me, there remained the room with sink and bidet. The room was large enough to accommodate not only a large iron bedstead but also, right next to it, an iron folding bed. On the wall was a gas water heater that switched on when the tap was opened. You had to run the water slowly enough so that it could pick up sufficient warmth as it ran through the tubing in the heater.

What with the one-night stands we had been doing, I had come to Brussels with a valise filled with clothes that needed laundering. The day after the Brussels concert, we were to go on to Holland for a concert at The Hague, and I wanted to catch up on my washing beforehand. I did the laundry and left the clothes to rinse in the bidet, with the warm water flowing slowly through. At the same time, I plugged my noisy electric razor into the 220-volt outlet next to the washstand. There I was, in my underwear and oxfords, looking into the mirror and shaving with this very loud contraption—so loud, in fact, that I did not hear the sound of water falling (the wash had plugged the overflow outlet in the bidet).

Then I happened to look down, and I saw to my horror that there was water seeming to reach almost up to my shoelaces. I was able to get the razor disconnected from the outlet before electrocution could take place. But the floor of my room looked like a tranquil pond. Worse still, I knew that the landlady's apartment was directly underneath our rooms. I could picture water cascading through her chandelier and felt sure that I might never get to the concert hall that evening.

Since mine was the room without bath, I had only a small towel. With this I proceeded to sponge up water as rapidly as I could, wringing the towel out into the sink between-times. In addition to the towel, I also had to squeeze water out of small scatter rugs that adorned the floor. I could not reach far under what now seemed to me a football-field-sized array of beds. With inventiveness never taught me in my violin lessons, I opened my folding music stand and used it as a mop handle to shove the towel around under the beds. The only saving factor in all this was the fact that the floor had two layers of linoleum on it, one old, one new. Apparently I was able to get enough mopped up so that there was no percolation through the floor coverings.

At this point, though, I was one tired violinist. Just then, George knocked on my door to say that Len and Irv were waiting downstairs in a cab and that it was time to leave for the concert hall. (George later told me he had been wondering what the strange noises from my room could mean.) I said only that I would be right down, threw on my full-dress, folded my music stand, grabbed fiddle and briefcase, and joined the others in the cab. I said nothing about the events of the preceding hour because I did not want the guys worrying about my ability to function at the concert.

When we got to the auditorium, I put my stuff in the dressing room and ducked out to a neighboring bar for a strong coffee before facing the evening's event. As luck would have it, this concert was part of a Beethoven cycle, parceled out among various visiting ensembles. To make the cycle complete, one ensemble had to perform four quartets; we were the chosen ones. I do not have a copy of the program in my files, but it must have included Op. 95, that short and pungent quartet in the Beethoven series, for otherwise the concert would have been endless. For me, the program seemed not only long but irrelevant, for I saw visions of a bedroom floor that still needed attention.

After the concert, I got back to my room, did some final mopping, and put my violin case, valise, and briefcase on some edges of the new linoleum layer that were beginning to curl. In the morning, I dressed, paid the landlady, and fled to the train. I hope only for two things: that everything dried sufficiently before the room had to be made up and that the landlady has forgotten my name.

The next night, in The Hague, was even worse. After the concert, I sat in my hotel room looking out the window at a still, moonlit, unpeopled street. The Cuban situation had not yet been resolved, and—with family four thousand miles away—I wondered if I would ever see Jill and the kids again. We all know that disaster was averted. It was only a few days later that I was back with the family, feeling mighty grateful.

In August the quartet coached chamber music and appeared in concert at the Aspen Music Festival. Our family, including David's dog, drove from Milwaukee to Aspen in our minibus. It was fun, but this, except for a round-trip by train to San Francisco the following summer for concerts at the Berkeley campus of the University of California, was the last concert tour with everyone in tow.

The 1964 European tour was our first with Jerry Stanick, and we kept him busy. In Holland, Belgium, Germany, Switzerland, and Italy, we made music in twenty-six concerts and radio tapings in twenty-nine days (and on one of the three free days we attended a concert by the Amadeus Quartet!)—an insane schedule, now that I look back on it from my advanced years. The quartet traveled alone again for this tour, but our wives joined us for a short vacation in Europe thereafter. The spouses of Len, George, and Jerry were with them for the last few days of the tour, but Jill and I had arranged to meet only after all concerts were complete. I arrived alone at Milan airport, rented a car, and started out toward Lovere, which was to be the scene of our last concert. It was unsettling to learn that the people at the car rental agency had never heard of the place, and I drove into Milan in hopes of getting some driving information. Several queries proved fruitless, until at last I happened on someone who was able to point me toward the proper road.

Lovere turned out to be a small town northeast of Milan, perched on the edge of Lago d'Iseo. Perched is the word, for the mountainous terrain sloped steeply toward the water. I wondered, in fact, how the town was

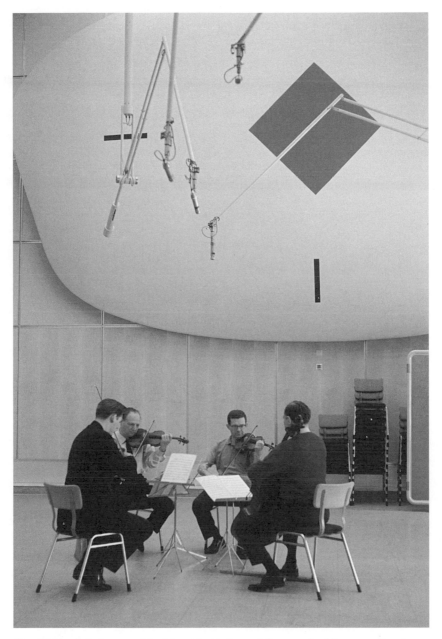

Gerald Stanick, Leonard Sorkin, Abe Loft, and George Sopkin preparing for an archival taping in a radio studio during the 1964 European tour.

Spring 1964: warming up onstage in the chamber music hall of the Concertgebouw, Amsterdam. Left to right: George Sopkin, Gerald Stanick, Abe Loft, Leonard Sorkin.

able to maintain its footing on dry land. My colleagues arrived, we gave the concert and—as is the habit in Europe—were paid immediately after the concert. To my dismay, however, the chamber society officer handed me the fee not in cash but in the form of a check. This was a stunner; the quartet was dispersing for vacation the next morning, and we needed the cash so that it could be divided among us. Moreover, the next day was 1 May, a holiday; the only way into a bank would have been with dynamite. Fortunately, a Lovere citizen solved the matter: I endorsed the check to him and he got the cash for us from his shop safe.

Early next morning, I was driving back toward Milan airport to turn in my car and take flight to Spain to meet Jill. *Toward* Milan was a lucky direction; the highway leading away from Milan was absolutely bumper-to-bumper with citizens bound for the countryside for their holiday weekend. After some pleasant days with Jill in Majorca, Barcelona, Madrid, Oxford, and London, it was back home to finish up on concerts in America. It had been great to be free for a while from the quartet's many-headed schedule.

In May 1966 our quartet flew to London for a concentrated week of music-making. We spent a few days taping the six Bartók quartets for the BBC and performed Samuel Adler's Quartet No. 4 for a symposium at the American Embassy Theater. The day before our return home, we gave a concert at Royal Festival Hall, part of a series sponsored by the BBC. The four of us were taken to lunch the afternoon of the concert day, and I must have consulted the wine decanter with some gusto. When I got back to our hotel, I fell into a sound nap from which I was roused only by a phone call from the other three, who were waiting for me in the hotel lobby to be driven to the concert hall. I flung my concert togs on, joined the others, parked my fiddle-case and music in the auditorium dressing room, and hastened to the theater's café for a bracing dose of caffeine.

Our program was an interesting one: Haydn's Op. 50, No. 2, Webern's *Five Pieces for String Quartet*, Stravinsky's Concertino, and Beethoven's Op. 130 with the *Great Fugue* as its finale. The stage at Royal Festival Hall is in itself larger than many a small auditorium, and the audience space in the hall is sized to match. I wondered, then, whether the listeners in the balcony would be able to hear the very delicate sounds of the Webern. Both the acoustics and the lively attention of the public allowed us to get the music across. The robust sounds of the Haydn and Stravinsky had no trouble, and the outcries of the *Great Fugue* spoke for themselves. As for myself, I am happy to report that I performed with all due sobriety.

In the spring of 1967, we flew to Japan to begin a tour of the Far East, Australia, and New Zealand under the sponsorship of the U.S. State Department. Clarinetist David Glazer, our colleague from the New York Woodwind Quintet, came along as guest artist. The wives of the musicians (except for Carol Sopkin) and Ruth Roberg, longtime friend and supporter of the quartet, were also with us.

We landed in Tokyo, where we spent a couple of days recovering from jet lag. Then we flew on to Hokkaido, the north island of Japan, to start the tour with a concert in Sapporo, which in 1972 would be host city for the winter Olympics. From there we went by train and ferry down the west coast of Japan for concerts in Akita, Niigata, Okayama, and Taka-matsu; then it was two days off in Kyoto and back to Tokyo for a pair of concerts, and finally on to Sendai and Morioka for our last performances in Japan.

At each stop, we were met by a welcoming party of Japanese men and women, graciously offering us flower bouquets. The audiences were un-failingly warm and appreciative, and—as was true in the other countries we visited—clearly knowledgeable and enthusiastic about the classic chamber music repertoire. We enjoyed everything about our stay: the people, the scenery, food, train service, and the care with which the State Department representatives and our Japanese hosts assured the smooth-ness of our visit. I even became accustomed to the Japanese pronuncia-tion of my name: Aburamu Rofutu (as near as I could catch the phonet-ics involved).

Our next stop was Taiwan, with an itinerary starting in the principal city, Taipei, and including Taichung, Tainan, Kaohsiung, and Hualien. A standout of our visit to Kaohsiung came at a reception after our concert there: a young violin student was roused from his bed to dress and come to the gathering to perform for us (very well indeed) several movements from the Bach solo violin sonatas. This was another sign of the now very familiar prowess in Western music of performers from the Far East.

For our concert in the small, east-coast city of Hualien, we were driven by bus through the spectacular Taroko Gorge; actually, by two buses, for a rockslide from a cliff of the gorge had blocked the highway. The second bus awaited us on the other side of the obstruction to take us the rest of the way. When we got to Hualien, we were met by the mayor, a physician known by the cheery title "Dr. Lucky," who conducted us to our hotel. From the reception desk in the small lobby, a rather steep stair-case ascended to the upper floors. I was impressed by the fact that the owner's daughters were quick to wrestle our luggage up the stairs to our rooms.

When I stepped into the hallway to pick up my briefcase and shoul-der bag, there was a middle-aged Chinese gentleman looking at me from outside a doorway a short distance down the corridor. He was arrayed in his cap, underwear, shoes, and stockings. We regarded each other for a moment with aplomb, then turned back into our respective rooms. Strange, I thought, but there is no arguing with local custom. It was not until we left Hualien the next day that it dawned on me: the "daughters" who had helped install us in the "hotel" were in fact on the staff of the local bordello.

The Hualien concert was held in a kind of large, open-walled shed, obviously used for various communal festivities. The peeping of what I took to be some type of frogs could be heard from nearby shrubbery as we played. Our audience was appreciative and mixed, composed of Chinese and native Formosans. Some had arrived in helmet and other road gear, having motorcycled in from the surrounding highlands. After the concert, our party was entertained by a large dance troupe, arrayed in native costume. We were not allowed to remain mere spectators but were all eventually pulled into the dance lineup to add the exotic touch.

The evening of our arrival in Seoul, Korea, we all had dinner in the hotel dining room. Wanting to get into the spirit of things, I ordered a meal of native cuisine. It came in a partitioned tray. Unknown to me, one section contained a portion of kimchi, Korean pickled vegetables. W-w-wow! Koreans are accustomed to kimchi from their childhood years. For my uneducated palate and digestive system, the impact was formidable. In our remaining days in Korea, we were several times hosted by the families of the Korean students who were in our instrumental classes back at the Milwaukee campus. Kimchi was always part of the elaborate repasts served us. I thought I dealt bravely with this new taste sensation, though my eyes watered and a certain amount of steam must have been issuing from my ears. Toward the end of our stay, over lunch in the city of Pusan, I realized that I might be overcompensating. After serving myself from the dish of kimchi, I offered it to a Korean member of the Pusan symphony, seated across the table from me. "Oh, no thank you," he replied, "it's too strong for me!"

Younger readers may wonder why kimchi came as such a surprise to me. The wider availability of Korean foods, as well as other ethnic staples, in America today was less the case in the 1960s, and I had not encountered kimchi before my visit to Korea. Had I tasted it earlier, I would certainly not have forgotten.

We got to Hong Kong as the city was in the grip of the Red Book riots. From our hotel room windows we could see the lines of marchers wind their way down the street, each brandishing the red book containing the

inspirational sayings of Chairman Mao. In minor consequence of the tur-
moil, our concert was canceled. Instead, we gave a performance for a
small audience at the American consul's apartment. We also conducted
a workshop session and did two tapings at the city's television station.

On our arrival at the Thailand airport, the immigration officers
refused to let our violist Jerry Stanick and his wife enter the country, because there were then no diplomatic relations between Canada (the couple's home country) and Thailand. Staffers from the American consulate
finally arranged with the Thai officials that the two could stay for a couple of days until we had given our concert and workshop, after which
they were to depart. Thus, Jerry arrived in Australia (our next stop) two
days before we did, and Mary Stanick flew back to the United States
sooner than she expected. The other women in our party also returned
home when Len, George, David, and I went on to finish the tour in Australia and New Zealand.

Because of concern about the incidence of cholera in Asia at that
time, the immigration people at Sydney airport had insisted that Jerry be
inoculated against the disease upon entry, even though he assured them
he had received shots before leaving the United States. When the rest of
us entered Australia, the same demand was made. It was finally agreed
that we need not repeat the shots, provided we checked in daily at the
local health departments along our route. This procedure went on without incident until almost the last city on the itinerary, Melbourne; here
the medical officers wanted to give us the shot! Following some intense
discussion, we were allowed to finish our stay in Australia and leave the
country, unpunctured.

The tour ended with five days of concerts in New Zealand. In the
South Island city of Christchurch, on a cold and sunny afternoon before
our evening performance, we went to see the new film *Ulysses*. We were
part of an all-male audience in the theater. Coming out into the chilly
late afternoon, we learned the reason for the segregation: a New Zealand
legislator had insisted, most improbably, that viewing by mixed audiences would lead to "fornication in the streets."

Our last concert of the tour was an afternoon program in a theater in
Auckland. We were due to start our return journey to America that
evening, but only if we could get a connecting flight to Wellington airport, and we understood that the local airfield could get so fogged in that

flights would be canceled. All of us were anxious to be on our way, but none more so than George, who had been away from his family all those weeks. From my seat onstage, I could see out a window in the wings of the theater. Where George was seated, however, his only view was through a window out in the auditorium. The glass in that window was either misted or dirty, so George played the concert while tormented with the thought that the weather was turning foggy. Not so—our plane flew on schedule, and we started the long trip home.

A mixed memory is summoned up by a segment of our itinerary later that season. In mid-November we flew from Milwaukee to Fairbanks, Alaska, for concerts and related events on the campus of the University of Alaska. After a pleasant though very cold weekend there, we flew back to Milwaukee. What with the early-morning starts and the long layover between planes in Seattle, the jaunts to and fro were almost as tiring as a journey to Europe. We spent the ensuing week carrying out our teaching duties in Milwaukee and then flew to San Francisco for three concerts in California. I will say it again: in quartet travel, even when self-imposed, a straight line is definitely not the shortest distance between two points.

As a break from the steady round of teaching and of quartet rehearsals and concerts, I indulged for several years in duo repertoire programs with a faculty colleague, pianist Armand Basile. In early 1968 we performed all seventeen of Mozart's mature sonatas and the two sets of variations for piano and violin in a series of programs on the Milwaukee campus. We decided to present the same package at New York's Town Hall in autumn of that same year. Since we could not be away from our chores in Milwaukee too long and because any extended stay in New York would have been prohibitively expensive, we programmed the entire set of works into three concerts, to be presented on consecutive evenings. Armand and I were back in Milwaukee teaching on the morning after the third concert. Continuing in our enthusiasm, we performed the ten Beethoven sonatas for piano and violin the following year on campus.

In the aftermath of the Town Hall series and a favorable review in *The New York Times*, Armand and I had visions of a minicareer as a violin-piano duo. We enjoyed playing together and continued our collaboration for a couple of added seasons on the UW-M campus. Though we had management for a time, nothing came of our hopes. I was further discouraged by Armand's seeming unwillingness to recognize that promotion of a concert career, whether for a soloist or ensemble, takes significant investment in printing and publicity.

The deciding factor in my own thinking about the duo project, though, came when I attended a sonata recital by Pinchas Zukerman and Daniel Barenboim at the Edinburgh Festival in 1971. The sizeable auditorium was filled to absolute capacity; had there been bosun-chairs slung from the chandelier, I believe they would have been occupied as well. I realized that there was no point in trying to sell into a market that would inevitably be dominated by star soloists—and very good ones, at that.

In March 1968 our quartet joined with the New York Woodwind Quintet in presenting the entire *Art of Fugue* in the Grace Rainey Rogers Auditorium at the Metropolitan Museum of Art in New York. As is well known, Bach's failing energy and blindness in his last months prevented him from completing the last fugue (Contrapunctus 19) of the composition. In accord with our custom when performing the entire work, we followed the truncated end of the fugue with an ensemble setting of Bach's organ chorale "Before Thy Throne I Stand." This had served as a postlude in the first (posthumous) publication of the work. And, as always, the effect of the chorale at the end of the monumental composition left our audience spellbound and pensive, scarcely able to offer anything so mundane as applause. After our bow, we were all filing offstage behind the movie-screen that served as an acoustic reflector at the back of the platform. We were not quite into the wings when Sam turned to me and said, with straight face and proper solemnity, "Abe, perhaps now the public will at last be able to accept the fact of Bach's death." I looked at him, absorbed the statement, and responded with a loud "Hah!" that rang through the hushed auditorium. My brother was among the listeners, recognized my voice, and later took me to task for having so broken the mood of the moment. I assured him it was all Sam's fault.

In late 1968 I found myself working on a book, to be called *Violin and Keyboard: The Duo Repertoire*, for Grossman Publishers. Sam Baron, who was working on a book about wind ensemble music (a book he never had time to finish) for a projected series for Grossman, had suggested me to the general editor of the series, Oscar Shoenfeld. By 1973, when my book was published, Grossman had become part of Viking Press. During the intervening years, I would haunt music stores in the more likely cities of our tours: Hamburg, Amsterdam, Berlin, Cologne, Paris, London among them, not to mention the important music stores in America. This was in addition to checking the resources of music libraries, to make sure that I covered as much of the in-print sonata literature as possible. Also, I started taking sonata scores with me on some of our tours in America, so that I could keep up with my writing homework on the road. (There is more on this in chapter 13, where I describe some experiences from our tours in the 1970s.)

I can close the present chapter, though, by repeating what I said at its opening: the 1960s added up to one busy decade.

12 ✧ ILLNESS, INJURY, AND OTHER PROBLEMS

N ewspapers from time to time carry the information that a prominent opera singer or instrumental virtuoso has had to cancel an
appearance owing to ill health. In the case of the singer, a replacement
can sometimes be found swiftly enough to keep the given opera performance from having to be canceled. So also, if the instrumentalist is scheduled to be soloist with a symphony orchestra or to be heard in solo recital,
a comparable virtuoso can often be recruited to take over the assignment.

In the case of a chamber ensemble, replacing one member of the
group on short notice is difficult. The stand-in must be very familiar with
the compositions that have been programmed for a particular concert
(or with those that have been switched to suit the emergency). He must
also be so seasoned a chamber musician that he can respond to the style
and reflexes of the ensemble's players on the strength of a bare minimum
of rehearsal.

Most likely, the ensemble that has suffered illness within its ranks
will choose to cancel its appearance rather than go on with even the most
able pinch-hitter. In that case, the sponsors of the engagement(s) in question may choose to call in a substitute ensemble rather than disappoint its
audience. That happened twice to our quartet: once when we substituted
for the Budapest Quartet in a concert in the Chicago area and again (as I
relate in chapter 13) when we replaced the La Salle Quartet in the Edinburgh Festival of 1971.

Usually the indisposed member of an ensemble will make every effort
to carry on, despite active discomfort, so as not to put his colleagues to the

strain of a temporary replacement or to the actual loss of an engagement. This will be especially true when the group is on tour. The expense of travel has already been incurred by all, and it is ordinarily not realistic to fly in a substitute for just one or two engagements on the itinerary. There is every impulse for the indisposed player to tough it out and remain in action.

Then, too, if the sponsors are willing or even insistent, there is another solution. The ensemble members who have not been stricken will manage to put together a program, even at short notice and with music that has been locally supplied, of works that do not require the participation of the missing player. The possibilities are obvious. For the wind quintet, the repertoire yields compositions for smaller assemblages from among the available instruments of the ensemble. In the case of the piano trio, there can be sonatas for violin and piano, cello and piano, or duos for violin and cello, depending on the circumstances of the moment. With regard to the string quartet, the range includes violin duets, violin-viola duos, violin- or viola-cello works; string trios for two violins and viola or for the more usual combination of violin, viola, and cello. As a last resort, the program can be filled out with a selection from the sonata-alone repertoire for this or that instrument. Ingenuity, determination, and a dash of can-do (desperation) will dictate the answer.

By way of illustration, here are some of the (fortunately few) instances when illness or injury affected our quartet's activity during my years with the ensemble.

It was the morning of the day in the 1950s that the quartet was to fly to New York for a recording session at the Everest studio (Debussy, Ravel, Britten, Vaughan Williams). Jill was vacuuming our living room carpet in preparation for a visit by her cousin, a Chicago pathologist, and his wife. The vacuum seemed to be drawing poorly. Completely forgetting commonsense safety procedure, I explored the bottom plate of the machine with my left hand and immediately received a blow to my index finger from the rotating brush.

Our visitors arrived shortly before I had to leave for the airport. Displaying the already stiffened and slightly swollen digit for a medical opinion, I asked how long it would take for recovery. The sage response by our visiting pathologist was that ordinarily it would take some time for limberness to be restored, but since I had to record the next day, the finger would of course be better by then. And so it was: I recorded for some hours over the next two days and was able to use the ailing finger without apparent impairment. Medical science is truly wonderful.

We were lucky to be able to start our first tour of Europe, in 1958, for cellist George Sopkin began his stay in France by falling ill. He managed to play our first concert, but felt worse and worse over the weekend that followed. A doctor had to be called to his hotel room. The shot of penicillin that was prescribed was administered with a hypodermic so large that George thought he was being treated by a veterinarian. The injection seemed to turn the trick, however, for George was able to play our next concert, an all-Bartók program. I personally suspect that the applause contributed to George's speedy recovery.

Our winter tour of 1959 began with a concert at the Abbaye de Royaumont, fifteen miles north of Paris, in a program that ended with Schumann's Piano Quintet, with Mieczyslaw Horszowski as guest artist. I was already feeling poorly and, by the time I finished the drive to Rotterdam a couple of days later, had a vigorous cough and running nose. An elderly doctor came to examine me at the hotel. He prescribed two medicines, one to make me cough and clear the plumbing, the other (to be taken before the concert) to suppress coughing while in the throes of performance. The apothecary gave me a tall, square brown bottle, complete with large cork, containing the expectorant. One swig convinced me that the elixir was basically a combination of varnish and rust remover, and I emptied the bottle down the bathroom drain. I made it through the two concerts at the Boymans Museum, and the cold began to taper off.

I had been having bouts of uneasiness during our stay in Israel in early January of 1960, and now at home I was feeling increasingly tired and off my feed. This bothered me especially because we had a concert impending at the 92nd Street Y in New York. As we approached that date, I had a chance encounter with our family pediatrician. She noticed my eyes and complexion and immediately arranged an appointment with an internist. He sent me straight to hospital, for the diagnosis was hepatitis. Thinking back to my first attack of faintness in Athens (en route to Israel), I realized that I must have been incubating the illness since at least our stay in Greece, if not in Italy before that. In any event, the quartet had to cancel the New York concert, the only such instance brought about by illness during the twenty-five years of my membership in the group.

Remarkably a stay of ten days at the hospital pulled me out of danger, and I was able to get back into harness, though still pretty weak. Very soon after I was in action, we gave a concert in Green Bay, Wisconsin. Leonard and I shared a dressing room there. When it came time to suit up for the concert, I mistakenly reached for Leonard's full-dress trousers on the clothes rack. Leonard's waist size was bigger than mine, so when I got the pants on, I had a worrisome moment during which I thought I had lost an alarming amount of weight during my illness.

Toward mid-January of 1966, Milwaukee streets were slick with ice. Leonard Sorkin slipped, breaking his fall with outstretched arm. Unfortunately, he suffered a slight wrist fracture in the process. While the break healed, the rest of us had to scramble to provide a program for four concerts on four consecutive days, in Milwaukee, Chicago, Wilmette (our North Shore series), and Indianapolis. We were fortunately able to have violinist Oscar Chausow—soon to become concertmaster of the Utah Symphony—flutist Robert Cole, and guitarist Rey de la Torre join Jerry Stanick, George Sopkin, and me. The program roster:

Flute Quartet in D, K. 285	Mozart
Quartet in G, D. 96	Matiegka-Schubert
String Trio in C minor, Op. 9, No. 3	Beethoven
Quintet in D	Boccherini

As I look at this lineup now, it does not seem very adventuresome. However, it was constructed under some time pressure and around the forces we could muster at short notice. Leonard mended quickly enough that our regular foursome was able to resume concertizing together by the start of February. We were especially lucky that the emergency had arisen when we were at home, and not in far-off places.

When we resumed our European tours in January 1970, we (quartet members and wives) started with two days of tape recording at the BBC studios in London. The next morning, when we were due to fly to the Continent for concerts in Holland and radio sessions in Cologne, we learned that Carol Sopkin had decided to remain in London to undergo medical tests that suddenly seemed necessary. It was courageous of her not only to undertake this in a city so far from home but also to urge George to go on with the quartet and leave her behind. Needless to say, George had to fight his own reluctance to be away from his wife in this situation. It took fully a week for Carol to learn that all tests had turned out favorably and that she could fly to Stockholm to rejoin George and our entourage at the start of the Scandinavian segment of our trip. We were, all of us, delighted and fortunate at the happy resolution of this emergency.

In May 1970 we flew to New York for two concerts at Lincoln Center's Tully Hall. Both programs were made up of commissioned works. The first comprised Beethoven's Opp. 127, 132, and 130, as bespoke by Prince Galitzin. The second evening offered quartets of Seymour Shifrin, Karel Husa, and Milton Babbitt that had been commissioned for our quartet and—as a kind of programmed encore—Ruth Crawford's lone string quartet of 1931. When I boarded the plane, I had a head cold. By the time I landed in New York, the cold had settled in the inner canal of my left ear. At our rehearsal for the first concert, I found myself hearing the violin primarily through my right ear, an unsettling aural perspective. I had a stopgap consultation with a New York physician but was still not well when we flew back to Milwaukee.

By now my ear was really acting up. This led to an extended course of examinations and treatments with an ear specialist. With medication, there was a slow recovery. While it lasted, I was forbidden to fly, in order to avoid the air-pressure changes that flight would have imposed. Luckily our European tour for the year was over with, or I would have had to make a slower ocean crossing by ship. As it was, Jill and I had to travel to and from Albuquerque for the June Music Festival session by train. By summer's end, however, my ear had settled down, I was spared the necessity of any surgical procedure, and I could once again hear the violin with both ears.

What with the last-minute details of teaching, concerts and home arrangements before leaving for a tour abroad, I usually arrived in Europe with a cold, particularly in the winter season. Sometime in the early 1970s I landed at Amsterdam in just such condition. A bottle of Irish Mist, purchased at the airport shop, went into my shoulder bag. In the course of the first week of the tour, my shoulder bag grew lighter and my cold steadily diminished and disappeared. My readers, as well as the medical profession, may draw their own conclusions.

Our European tour in the winter of 1972 spanned twenty-five days in November, taking in Germany, Switzerland, France, Holland, and England, with a total of nineteen engagements. As always, there was some doubling back and forth between countries to accommodate the schedule. We arrived in Rotterdam from a week in England. The weather was raw, and we had a strenuous day: first the flight, then a newspaper interview at our hotel in the late afternoon, disrupting our dinnertime. There followed a rather strained (and unnecessary, I thought) warmup rehearsal at the hotel, so that energy and temper levels were already tested by the time we reached the concert hall.

Our rushed hotel conclave had already included some "free lessons." At the concert itself, we had just come offstage after the first work (an early Haydn quartet) and were about to go on for Britten's Quartet No. 2. Leonard now received some advice from within the group about the way the Haydn should have been handled, and I felt constrained to say, "Please! Not *now!*" I was still annoyed after the concert. By the time we left the auditorium building, there was only one cab on the street. I had Jill take the last remaining seat with the others. (It was not gallantry alone. Be damned if I was going to share a cab with the errant colleague who had been so free with instructive comment.) No other taxi materialized, the box office and its telephone were closed, and I had no choice but to walk back to our hotel in the cold rain. That night, I really began to feel bad and sat up in our room, swigging tea to fight the chills.

The next day was a doubleheader, with a taping at the radio studios in Hilversum and a concert in the evening at Utrecht. Jill and I had ordered dinner in the hotel dining room at Utrecht, but when my dish came, I could not confront it. I ducked out the front door of the hotel to get air, and came to myself by hanging over the railing, I suppose to get the blood to move to my head. I got through the concert and was able to travel back to England the next day and on to the city of Leeds. At that night's concert at the University of Leeds, I had to hug the radiator in the dressing room during intermission. By next morning, I was so ill with the flu that Jill again had to summon a doctor.

This was the last day of the tour, and again it was to be a doubleheader. The quartet was scheduled to give a broadcast concert at Manchester in the early afternoon, then go on to Nottingham for an evening performance. None of that was possible for me, according to the doctor.

He ordered me to the hospital (via ambulance, no less) for X rays to determine whether it was flu or something worse, and whether it would even be possible for me to travel back to America the following day as scheduled.

The other three of the quartet had a nerve-wracking ride to Manchester by chauffeured minivan (the erratic ways of the driver, combined with a wet roadway, kept my colleagues on the edge of their seat most of the way). At Manchester, music was obtained from various sources, to make up a program of string duos and trios. Len, Bernie, and George performed without time for any rehearsal whatever. From Manchester to Nottingham was an even longer drive (with, I believe, less frantic-making conveyance), and they had the pleasure of delivering their impromptu program for a second time that evening.

As for myself, the X rays at the Leeds hospital were taken soon enough, but then I spent some hours lying on a cot until the busy hospital staff found time to read the films. The diagnosis was that I was well enough to undertake the journey home next day. I was conveyed back to town in a small hospital bus, surrounded by cheerful Britishers old enough to be my parents. Back at the hotel, Jill met me to report that our room had been preempted. We had not been expected to stay for a second night, and all space was needed for a visiting Bulgarian chamber orchestra that had booked rooms well in advance. Jill and I had been transferred to a room at another (rather grungy) hotel nearby.

Next morning, the weather had closed down Leeds airport. So Jill and I now had, in our own turn, to take a cab to Manchester airport. The weather there was none too good either, but our plane for Heathrow was able to make a delayed takeoff. It was going to be a very tight connection to our transatlantic flight at London. Our plane landed late at Heathrow, but the airline had very kindly arranged for an official car to take us directly to the trans-ocean plane. Our attendant ushered us up the gangway and into the plane, bypassing waiting room, passport check, and all. (He implored us, when next we came to England, not to tell how we had made our unusual departure.) As we entered the plane, my colleagues and their wives were coming down the aisle of the plane from the other cabin door.

We got home on a Friday evening. That weekend, we were to give the UW-M concert of a Milwaukee-Chicago set. Early Sunday morning,

George phoned to tell me that Leonard himself was now down with the flu, and that it was my turn to join George and Bernie in a duo-trio program. We had time for a rehearsal that afternoon, but it was a fairly grim day nonetheless, since I was not yet entirely out of my own bout of illness. Len felt well enough by Monday to undertake the scheduled quartet programs at Chicago and Wilmette, and we were back on track, though with some feeling of being the walking wounded. In fact, I dozed on the floor of George's station wagon during the drive down to Chicago.

A pain in his right arm that had been bothering George for some months persisted into early 1977. As a result, the excellent cellist Michael Rudiakov was invited in from New York to substitute in our late-January set of Milwaukee-Chicago concerts. Michael, fine player and congenial guest that he proved to be, was a hit with all of us, including George (who had a chance to hear the group as a member of the audience). This was auspicious, for we would be calling upon Rudiakov again a year later.

George's problem with his arm subsided enough so that he was able to carry on with the quartet's various assignments, both on campus and on tour in America and Europe for the rest of the year and on into the beginning of 1978. By then, however, he was also having some eye trouble. He decided that he could not make our European tour, scheduled for four weeks in February and March, through Holland, Germany, Switzerland, Austria, and France. Rudiakov (who has since then been lamentably and untimely taken from us) was fortunately able to join us for the trip, fitting into the ensemble, the tour repertoire, and the air and train itinerary with unflappable energy and skill.

All in all, I think our ensemble was lucky there were not more medical mishaps and discomforts during the twenty-five years I was member. From the preceding account, though, it should be clear that it takes a combination of a strong constitution, determination, and good luck to get through season after season of rehearsal, travel, and performance without serious downtime.

By the way, I once explored the possibility of a quartet insurance policy to guard against loss of income because of accident or illness. It transpired that rather complex calculations would be needed to set the premiums for each season's coverage. And in any case the projected cost of insurance would have been prohibitive. The moral: stay well, and play.

On a European railroad platform with our four loaded luggage carts. Left to right: Michael Rudiakov (filling in for the ailing George Sopkin on this 1978 tour), Abe Loft, Bernard Zaslav, Leonard Sorkin.

And if you are not well—try to play anyway. In fact, I recently heard a thoroughly outstanding performance by a young quartet whose cellist had been confined to his hotel bed the previous day by severe bronchitis. Even though he was still under the weather by concert time, you would never have guessed it from his sound and artistry. And he was proceeding to the airport with his colleagues after the program for their flight back to their home city. It is all part of the job.

What is definitely *not* part of the job, though, is for the ensemble members to leave themselves unprotected against the expense of illness or injury that can befall. In our quartet, each member was carrying individual health insurance for himself and his family. This was true during the years when we maintained our recording company, for the business was too small to qualify for a group health policy. After we became faculty members at UW-M, of course, we were able to enroll in the university's health plan.

Whether through individual coverage or as part of a group plan, it behooves every member of an ensemble to carry medical coverage. The player owes such protection not only to him- or herself, but to spouse and children and, beyond that, to the other members of the ensemble. Sickness of any member is enough of a strain on the work of the group. Colleagues should not have the added stress of a moral obligation to fund medical treatment for a member who has neglected the necessary coverage.

Further, the coverage chosen must provide reimbursement for medical treatment that might be needed while the ensemble is away on tour, whether in the home country or abroad. It is also simple common sense to take flu shots and other preventative measures to maintain health generally. These steps should be followed in good time before departure, so possible adverse reactions are dealt with before leaving home. The players also need recommended or required protection against infection or disease conditions that may exist in the areas to be visited while on the road.

The performer should have learned how to play without excessive strain on muscles or joints. Strain will show in the sounds made, impede facility, and be harmful physically. A competent instrumental coach and, if need be, a sports physician or physical therapist should be consulted to remedy any pains or problems. When one member of the group suffers, the entire ensemble suffers.

And if, as was the case with our ensemble, spouse and kids accompany the group on tours, count on similar foresightedness—and a strong dose of luck—to carry all the party safely through the time away from home.

13 ✦ THE 1970s

My Last Years on the Road with the Fine Arts Quartet

Following our trip to London for the BBC in 1966, we made no European visits for the rest of the decade. The Winderstein agency in Munich had been general managers of our previous two tours on the Continent. After the 1964 circuit, I wrote to Herr Winderstein asking that fees be raised for our next visit. He responded that we had to "introduce" ourselves in Europe before such an increase could be obtained. We in the quartet, however, felt that our six European tours already completed must certainly have introduced us sufficiently. As a result of this difference in viewpoint, we did not tour Europe again until 1970 and also placed general management of our concerts there in other hands.

Even with higher fees, however, our travel to Europe remained more a source of personal satisfaction and publicity ammunition than a profit-making venture. As always in the concert world, commissions on the gross fees were split between the general manager and the local management, if any. We also paid commission on our European fees to our American management of those years, Melvin Kaplan, Inc. Truth to tell, it was Kaplan who placed us with the Fritz Dietrich agency, in Frankfurt, the general manager of our European tours in the 1970s. As the decade advanced, however, I grew increasingly strenuous in my objections to the Kaplan agency's cut on our European touring, for I was in direct and continuous correspondence with Dietrich concerning tour details. After the several commissions, our travel and living expenses, publicity costs within Europe, and taxes on our net concert income, our European tours were by no means a get-rich-quick affair. By the mid-1970s, I felt the time had come to ask Mel to give up his commission for our European engagements. We reached a compromise: for each of our next three tours, he would get only a nominal commission, and from then on, nothing. The rub was that, as matters turned out, I left the quartet after that third tour, so my complaining did not get me very far. Some day, I will have to read up on Pyrrhic victories.

Along with our European jaunts, of course, we were still keeping on with our travels in America and Canada. I must say, though, that temperaments within the ensemble made the experience progressively less alluring. By the time I left the quartet in 1979, I was not through with travel, professional or otherwise, but I was quite ready for voyaging without a musical entourage. Twenty-five years earlier, I would not have imagined this change of heart. However, it was a bit like the inimitable Jimmy Durante's quip about a romance from his past: "I met an old flame—but the pilot light was out!"

From 1968 through 1978, the FAQ was the featured quartet at the June Music Festival in Albuquerque, New Mexico. We were able to fit this event each year between the end of the spring semester at UW-M and the start of our summer session duties there. In our Albuquerque concerts we had the pleasure of performing with guest artists including, among others, distinguished pianist Ralph Berkowitz, director of the festival, and Josef Gingold, legendary violinist-teacher and long a participant in the festival concerts.

Our return to European touring in 1970 took us back to audiences of former years and to new ones as well. We visited again the studios of the BBC in London for two sessions of recording for their tape library. Once again we played at the Boymans Museum in Rotterdam, at the Concertgebouw in Amsterdam, at the Dutch radio studios in Hilversum, and twice at the studios of Cologne Radio. For the first time, we visited Sweden, traveling to several cities along the eastern edge of the country and north to Kiruna, beyond the Arctic Circle, then south again for a concert at Stockholm. From there, after a brief return to Denmark, we went on to Germany. There, by way of a kind of reintroduction after our years away, we played in Hamburg, Hannover, and Berlin under Amerika Haus aus-

In 1970, during its years as the featured quartet in Albuquerque's June Music Festival, the Fine Arts Quartet with the festival's director and pianist, Ralph Berkowitz, and eminent teacher and festival artist, the violinist Josef Gingold. Left to right: Abe Loft, Ralph Berkowitz, George Sopkin, Josef Gingold, Bernard Zaslav, Leonard Sorkin.

pices, recorded for Radio Freies in Berlin and the studio in Baden-Baden, and ended the three-week circuit with a renewed appearance at Zurich's Tonhalle and at Basel radio.

Back home in early spring, we returned to our academic and concert schedule in Milwaukee and Chicago, gave a couple of concerts elsewhere in Wisconsin, and took a week-long jaunt to Washington, California, and North Dakota.

The month of May brought with it a blockbuster assignment: the two concerts (mentioned in chapter 12) of commissioned quartets at Alice Tully Hall in New York. The first of these programs contained the three

Galitzin quartets of Beethoven, Opp. 127, 132, and 130 (with the *Great Fugue*, of course)—a very long evening. I imagine that many in the audience had come for the unique experience of hearing the three works in sequence in one concert and, perhaps, also to see whether we could stay the course in this musical marathon. There were two intermissions to separate these three imposing works. It was a challenging session, and though we brought it off, one we never repeated. Incidentally, one reason the idea of the program had occurred to us in the first place was that George Sopkin was proud owner of a silver samovar that had once belonged to Prince Galitzin himself.

The second evening, the concert was scarcely less demanding. Here the program consisted of four quartets. The first three of these had all been commissioned for us on behalf of the Fine Arts Foundation of Chicago: Seymour Shifrin's Quartet No. 4, Karel Husa's Quartet No. 3 (Pulitzer Prize for Music, 1969), and Milton Babbitt's Quartet No. 3. The concluding work on the program was that landmark composition, the String Quartet of 1931 by Ruth Crawford. We included it because it is short (just eleven minutes), of interesting sound throughout, and innovative in ways that influenced chamber music in the years that followed. The works in this concert contrasted vividly with one another, and I am surprised to note, here again, that this was a grouping we never repeated.

We began our 1971 tour of Europe with a concert at Wigmore Hall in London, certainly one of the best performances of our career. It was the first of two programs devoted to the Bartók cycle. The second concert, equally fine, took place at Wigmore ten days later. In between, we played in Oslo and Bergen, Norway, a radio taping and concert in Berlin, and a concert at Ettlingen Castle in Germany. This tour had earmarks of sanity: it lasted just three and one-half weeks, comprising only thirteen engagements in five countries. I almost felt as though I was on vacation.

Our 1970–71 concert season ended with a pair of performances of the Brahms Viola Quintet in G, Op. 111 (with Francis Tursi as guest artist), in accompaniment to a choreographed setting danced by American Ballet Theater in New York. After the last performance, we dispersed, the other three quartet members going off to their various vacation spots while I took the plane to rejoin the family back in Milwaukee. As luck would have it, there was a prolonged stop en route, so that I did not get home until three in the morning. I took comfort in the fact that I now had a few weeks of relaxation ahead of me. I was mistaken.

That first day of vacation a telegram arrived, asking whether we could play at the Edinburgh Festival. The invitation had been a long time coming, so I was happy to think we would at last be performing there the following summer. Then I took a second, more careful look at the message: it was in fact asking us to play the festival that very month! I did not know until later the reason for the sudden call: the La Salle Quartet had been scheduled to play, but its first violinist, Walter Lewin, had to undergo knee surgery in Switzerland and would be out of action during the span of the Edinburgh season. We were being asked to pinch-hit.

Fortunately I knew where each of the other three in the Fine Arts was vacationing and I quickly phoned around to tell them about the offer. With their yes-votes in hand, I told our New York management to proceed with arrangements. As finally scheduled, we were to give three concerts: one at the Three Choirs Festival in Gloucester, England, and two at the Edinburgh Festival. All three concerts went well. So favorably was the Edinburgh pair received, in fact, that a reviewer wrote in the Glasgow *Herald* (27 August 1971) that it would be only proper to invite the Fine Arts to return to the festival in its own right. In the wisdom of the festival's manager, Peter Diamant, such an invitation was never forthcoming.

At some point in the early 1970s we came to Seattle for another of our concerts at the University of Washington. As on earlier occasions, we stayed at the Edmond Meany Hotel, whose brochure proclaimed, "Every Room a Corner Room." True enough: the structure was a tall cylinder, with the rooms on every floor arranged, spokewise, radiating off a central core. On this visit, I found the setup most helpful. The airline had sent my suitcase to parts unknown, and though they retrieved and delivered it to the hotel in late afternoon, I had no clean shirt for the concert. I had counted on doing some fast wash-and-dry in good time for the evening event.

I raced a shirt through soapy water and rinse in the bathroom sink, wrung it out in a towel, and hung it up to dry in an open window. There was a decent breeze—my room was not only on an upper floor but was indeed a "corner room," and the shirt dried remarkably quickly except for the cuffs. They were still slightly damp when I arrived at the concert hall. Giving a concert with slightly damp cuffs is interesting. It feels as though some ghostly mentor from the past is guiding your arms through the motions of violin playing.

In early February 1973 we had a concert at the Metropolitan Museum in New York (with John Browning as guest artist). I stayed on a few days at my brother George's apartment in New York, going over galley proofs of the text of *Violin and Keyboard,* the book I had been working on since late in 1968. The end of the production schedule was in sight when an unexpected hurdle appeared. With the kind permission of the respective music publishers, I was illustrating my text with many musical excerpts from modern editions of the various works discussed. Early on, I had consulted my publisher about a problem I faced with the musical excerpts. The examples were to be cut from the printed music page, mounted on illustration board, then photographed. I had noticed that, almost without exception, when an example fell at the end of one brace of staves and then continued on the next, there was a difference in the staves' spacing between the two portions of the excerpt. A Grossman officer had told me that the book designer could adjust the discrepancy photo-graphically so that both portions of the excerpt would align in one hori-zontal printout.

When, at this late date, I mentioned the procedure to the designer, she said she could not contemplate any such undertaking for the several hundred illustrations involved. I would have to find a replacement for each of the many excerpts in question. This meant searching through recapitulations, end-sections in ABA movements, and so on. It also re-quired that the illustration captions be changed to supply new measure numbers and other relevant information.

A few weeks later, our quartet was in Portland, Oregon, for a con-cert. I had left home not only with my suitcase and violin case, but also with a small valise crammed full of music pages containing the new exam-ples. After our concert that evening, I retreated to my hotel room and spent the night, well into the small hours, catching up with the coding of the new excerpts. Groggy but unbowed after a few hours of sleep, I fin-ished up early in the morning, wrapped the marked pages, and sent them off by express to the book designer in New York. I treated myself to a restorative lunch, then joined my colleagues for the drive down to Eugene for that evening's concert. Once again, playing a program of three quartets seemed an easy way to make a living.

And now, an account specifically for second violins. Early in our November 1973 European tour we played a broadcast-concert in Helsinki. This program ended with Beethoven's Op. 59, No. 1. The last part of the slow movement in that quartet has the second violin emerge from several measures of oscillating sextuplets to alight briefly on the low F of the D-string, then take off for the B-flat, an interval of an eleventh higher (Example 1). For coloristic reasons, it is desirable to play the B-flat high on the A-string, rather than jump over to the too-bright equivalent, low on the E-string. Consequently, the voyage to the B-flat involves a longish upward shift, with a short and delicate glide at the very end to bring the finger into the target note, all this carried out in solitary splendor by the second violin. I always felt as though the whole world was watching and listening, with critical senses honed to a razor edge. In fact, so exposed did I find this little solo that for me, once I had negotiated the shift, the concert evening always seemed over and done with. In reality, I had never had any trouble with the spot in performance, but it was something I would see getting closer and closer, no matter how many times I performed the work.

Example 1. Beethoven, Quartet in F, Op. 59, No. 1, Adagio molto e mesto, mm. 89–91, first and second violins.

During the intermission this particular evening, I was backstage warming up this slide-for-life. The thought occurred to me (and not for the first time) that there was really no good reason why I should agonize over the matter. I turned to George and asked him whether the B-flat on the E-string would not, after all, be a perfectly acceptable sound. He replied that it could not match the effect of the note as played on the A-string. Out we went to perform the second half of the concert. The fateful spot arrived, I launched into my grand, upward trajectory, and—as luck would have it on this particular evening—when I turned up my bow-pressure to reveal to the world the final glide to the B-flat, I was still a bit shy of the mark. There was nothing for it but to effect that last small fraction of the journey in a rather juicy *glissando*. I had attained my goal, but in rather sentimental a fashion. After the concert, I asked George whether he liked the effect. "I liked it," he said, but I found his tone of voice a bit on the dry side.

I don't believe, incidentally, that my impromptu display of violinistic emotion had much to do with the Helsinki critic's review of the concert. "Very very rarely have we heard better chamber music than that presented by the Fine Arts Quartet in the Riddarhuset on Sunday" (*Hufvud Stadsbladet*, 20 November 1973).

We went on to several engagements in Holland, including yet another return to the Concertgebouw. Following a morning rehearsal in the elegant, small auditorium where chamber concerts took place, I stopped in for lunch at the De Keyser café, just across the street from the concert building. I was already having my dessert when I realized that, in that most benevolent of seasons in the Dutch fisheries calendar, I had neglected to have herring. I asked the waitress whether I could order herring after my dessert. She must have trained at the Stage Delicatessen in New York, for she answered, "You can eat the way you want," and brought me the fish.

The last stop in our European tour of March 1975 was Marseille, France. The weather was fine, and we had an interesting day in the city, complete with some great seafood. Soon enough, though, it was time for work. The four of us (wives were to follow) came out of the hotel and started to install ourselves in one cab. It was not a very large one, and when we put the cello across the knees of three quartet members in the back seat, our leader had an attack of claustrophobia and said that we would have to take two cabs.

Accordingly, we arranged ourselves in two autos, cello and second violin in one, first violin and viola in the other. Our hotel clerk was able to make clear to the Algerian drivers that we were to perform in a clinic. The cabbies declared themselves ready, and we drove into what must have been a suburb of Marseille. In the dark of evening, we pulled up to a broad span of steps fronting a large building. Things looked encouraging, for a man in surgical green was coming down the steps. I asked where the concert-hall was. After some bafflement, he realized that our drivers had come to the wrong medical establishment. While he was giving directions to one of the drivers, an elderly woman came down the steps, got into the other cab, refused to be dislodged, and insisted on being driven home. We yielded, but Len still would not have the four of us crowd into the remaining car. It was now getting dangerously close to the concert hour, so cello and second violin sped alone to the proper clinic to reassure the chamber music sponsor that the quartet would indeed be on hand for the performance. Not much later, the other half of the group caught up with us.

It was now very close to concert time, so there was fortunately no time for one of our nettlesome stage warmups. However, since this was a clinic and not your average concert hall, there was no greenroom either. We unpacked our instruments and did our individual noodling in one end of the long room that served as the box office. It was just as well that we were already wearing our full-dress outfits, for this also would have been our dressing room.

The evening held yet further excitement. We ended with a performance of the Witold Lutoslawski quartet. Forward-looking though it is, that work can no longer be regarded as the very peak of difficult listening for tender ears. Still, it is nothing like a rendition of "Tea for Two." Thus, as we finished, we were greeted with a mixed chorus of bravos and boos (or the Gallic equivalent thereof). Happily, nobody rushed the stage or threw things. But it was a stimulating, even chastening experience.

I should note here that all of us in the quartet were keeping ourselves on our musical toes by doing extracurricular performances during these years. Leonard conducted concerts at holiday season by the school's student orchestra. With Len and the orchestra, Bernie played the Telemann concerto, he and I performed Mozart's *Sinfonia concertante*, and Len and I joined in Bach's Double Concerto. George played sonata recitals and also duo and trio programs, respectively, with Bernie and with me. In solitary splendor I presented a program for violin alone, and off-campus as well as with the UW-M orchestra, I came to grips with the Beethoven concerto and Bartók's Concerto No. 1. And Len played the Bruch concerto. No one sat idle.

It is October of 1975. We are in a taxi, bound into the city of Baton Rouge for a concert on the campus of Louisiana State University. A motel with restaurant attached comes into view. Our violist, a man of impulse and quick decision, says, "Let's stay here!" That none of the rest of us, including myself, said much in opposition baffles me. Had we not made reservations at the hotel suggested by the concert sponsor? If we had, were we able to cancel at short notice? What I do remember is that we stayed at the lodging singled out by our colleague.

That evening we went to the student union of the university and gave our concert. At program's end, the union manager came back to the greenroom, thanked us, and went off to check on a basketball game in progress in another wing of the building. A moment later, the woman in charge of the chamber music series stopped by to thank us in her turn, then left, saying that she would be seeing us at the postconcert party being held for us.

After her departure we realized none of us knew where the reception was taking place. We soon decided, though, that we ought to go in search of some food before the evening got any later. Not knowing our way around town or where eateries might still be open, we ended up in a bar near our motel, ingesting thawed, microwaved pizza. I phoned the motel a couple of times to ask if any calls had come for us, hoping, of course, that someone might have phoned to give us directions to the party. In vain— no one knew where we were staying. Nor, it seems, had any member of the chamber music society been designated to shepherd us to the reception.

I once heard tell that the Quartetto Italiano were given supper in the dining room of a large home in which a postconcert party for them was taking place. They finished eating and left, without ever seeing or mingling with the assembled guests. The Fine Arts Quartet went the Italiano one better; we never got to the shindig in the first place.

We arrived in Israel for our second tour there on New Year's day of 1976. The sponsor of the visit had arranged for a television interview of the quartet at Tel Aviv airport: all well and good, especially since tea and cookies had been laid on. Still, this was not too easy a chore, coming on the heels of a very long plane trip.

During our stay in Israel, we performed at the Mann Auditorium in Jerusalem. When the theater attendant opened the stage door to let us in,

I saw he was wearing army khaki and a pistol and holster—definitely a sight calculated to give a player concert nerves.

From Israel we flew to Denmark for the beginning of the itinerary on the Continent, including a return engagement in Svendborg, south of Odense. The program opened with a late Beethoven quartet. As we were about to begin, I noticed in the front row of the small auditorium a line of elderly gentlemen, apparently dyed-in-the-wool chamber music aficionados, each with an opened score spread across his knees. After this trial by jury at the concert, there was conviviality at the home of a physician member of the chamber concert committee. Glasses of ice-cold aquavit warmed the very cockles, both of the four quartet members and of their respective wives. Carol Sopkin remarked how much she liked the flavor of the particular liqueur being served. Next morning, on checking out of our hotel en route to the train station, we found waiting for us four bottles of that very same aquavit to speed us on our way. Never did we find warmer sign of hospitality in our travels.

Concerts in Stockholm completed our Scandinavian portion of the 1976 tour. From Sweden we took a train southward to Plön in the Schleswig-Holstein region of Germany. Our program there ended with Beethoven's Quartet Op. 131. This is the one that runs nonstop from beginning to end, spanning more than a half-hour's duration. I was suffering from a cold that evening, with my nose dripping actively. If you get to play the work under such condition, be advised that there is no chance for the second violin to grab for a handkerchief until a very brief rest just a few minutes before the final double bar. I got through the concert without disgracing myself or drenching my fiddle.

There were two days off before our next concert in Graz, Austria. Rather than sightseeing for the break, Jill and I elected to go directly to Graz to rest up at the hotel that had been designated for us. I used some of my time off there to write a letter about quartet travel to my students in Milwaukee. The piece would eventually become an article in *The New York Times* (see the end of this chapter). The day after our Graz concert, we took the railroad for Heidelberg, with a change at Bischofshofen to a train that would be "directly across the platform," according to the conductor. About half an hour before arriving at Bischofshofen I showed George and Carol Sopkin what I had written. They pronounced it apt and amusing.

The Bischofshofen platform was snow- and ice-covered, and directly across from us I saw an empty track. "You said the train would be on the opposite track," I remonstrated to the conductor. "It *is*," he replied, and pointed to a short train waiting on the opposite track, sure enough, but about a good 200 feet up-platform from our railroad car. There ensued a mad rush of four men, four wives, instrument cases, shoulder bags, and assorted suitcases from one train to the other. There were no baggage carts or porters to be seen, and no time to bother with them anyway. Once aboard our new railroad coach, George turned to me and snapped, "Your story isn't serious enough!"

It was late January, and we gave a concert in Pforzheim, a city that proudly declares itself the *Schmuckwaren* (ornamental jewelry) center of Germany. The next night we had to perform at the Queen Elisabeth Hall in Antwerp, Belgium. To get from one place to the other involved taking five trains, and that morning when we got to the Pforzheim station, the weather was fierce: snow, sleet, and ice.

Our train was late. Consequently, we missed our connection with train number two. So, of course, we had to miss trains three, four, and five as well. The day turned out to be one of improvisation on a theme of musical trains, generally with a scramble from one to the next. We reached Antwerp just a couple of hours before concert time.

Our general manager for the Holland and Belgium part of our tour, ever concerned for our expenses, had booked us into an Antwerp facility grandly titled Hotel des Sports, near the railroad station. The hotel turned out to be a rather small one, peopled by a clientele who looked a mixed lot to my innocent eye. In due time, we proceeded to the concert hall, making our approach through a corner of the city zoo. The acoustics at the hall proved to be exceedingly dull—a bit like giving a concert in a mattress factory. All in all, a somber end to an exhausting day.

We finished the tour almost a month later with a concert in the Canary Islands. Our plane change in Madrid airport took just long enough for our cellist to exchange some currency into *pesetas* and be immediately divested of the proceeds by a pickpocket. (Something else they do not teach at the conservatory: keep your hand on your wallet.)

A local concert manager was to have been on hand when we arrived at the airport in Las Palmas but did not show up. Fortunately we had the name of the hotel that was expecting us. Lacking the information about concert time and locale that the manager was to have provided, I looked for announcements in the hotel and its environs for the next day's event. No posters, nothing; nor could the hotel staff offer any details.

It was not until next morning that we heard from the manager. He had expected us to be arriving a day earlier than our actual schedule; when we *did* come in, he was off on the sister island for some chore. Now, though, we learned that the concert was to take place at the opera house of the city. Because the stage was intended for opera, its floor tilted slightly toward the audience for better sight lines from the orchestra seats. So we had to be a bit cautious about making our way on- and off-stage with our instruments. That went OK, but during the first half of the concert our cellist's right arm started to ache. There was a shower in the dressing room, and during intermission the sufferer stood with his shirtsleeve rolled up, holding his arm under a stream of hot water. The treatment soothed the limb enough so that we could play the second half of the program.

It was during intermission, too, that the chamber music society officers gave me the fee, in the form of a stack of bills only slightly smaller than a grapefruit. The rub was that it was then forbidden to leave Spain with a significant amount of the currency. The next day was Saturday, and our plane for New York was to leave that afternoon.

Even if we had wanted to spend the fee on local goods, there would have been little time for intelligent buying. I understood I could exchange the cash for a check at a bank, open on Saturday morning. The large bank to which I resorted told me they could indeed provide a check, but only with the authorization of the bank manager. He, however, was not in that morning. Stymied! I had to divide the loot among the four members of the quartet, and in the end nobody at the airport questioned us about currency. We flew off safely, along with our cash.

By the time we set off on our European tour in late February of 1977, George had recovered from the previous season's aches and pains in his right arm. All went without remarkable incident until mid-March. We had finished our evening concert in Limburg, Germany, and were picked up—quartet members, wives, instrument cases, luggage, and all—in two cars chauffeured by our general manager Fritz Dietrich and his assistant. They had come from Frankfurt to shepherd us to the train station at Mainz, where we were to embark for our transit to Venice for a broadcast

A misty morning in Germany, 1977: Leonard Sorkin, surveying our luggage and peering down the road for the bus to the railroad station.

concert the following evening. At Mainz we settled accounts with Dietrich for the commissions and expenses owed him for the tour.

This done, we boarded our sleeping car, changed trains at Milan next morning, arrived at the Venice train station on the mainland, and took a motor-taxi along the canals to our hotel. As we checked in, I asked the desk clerk to phone the radio station to report our safe arrival. The radio spokeswoman told the clerk there had been a technical snag at the office, so they would not be able to pay us our fee directly after the concert that evening. Knowing that bunches of lire were needed for the most ordinary purchases in Italy, I blurted out, "No money, no concert!" The clerk repeated this into the phone, hung up, and told us that the officer had replied, "OK, no concert!"

My colleagues assured me I had been undiplomatic and insisted I phone the management in Rome to enlist their advice. As the Rome office was assuring me that Venice radio was being ridiculous, the guys at the desk were signaling to tell me that the radio office had just phoned. The staff had figured out how to give us cash on the barrelhead after all.

The concert was held in a beautiful old building in Venice (are there any other kinds of structures in the city?). As we approached, it became clear why the radio people had been so speedily resourceful in the matter of payment. The concert was part of a popular subscription series, and there was a long line of people waiting to get in. Announcement of a cancelation would probably have resulted in the radio staff getting tossed into the nearest canal.

We were to play at the University of Padua the next night and had been scheduled to stay at a hotel in that city. Our violist had the good idea that we stay on instead at the Venice hotel. This would spare us a move and give us the chance to enjoy the daylight hours in Venice, in exchange for making a round trip to and from Padua for the concert. The weather was sunny, conducive to walking and sightseeing in Venice, so we had a good time of it.

We returned from our excursion to Padua about midnight and found a motor-taxi to take us directly to the side dock of our hotel. So swift was the taxi that we asked the driver to pick us up the next morning to take us to the airport for our flight to Rome. We got our room keys at the desk, each key with a very large escutcheon plate attached to discourage guests from leaving with the key in their pocket.

Jill and I took the elevator up to our fourth-floor room. I had a shoulder bag for my music and folding stand, in addition to my violin case. The better to grapple with the key and unlock the door, I set my case down on the corridor floor. The next morning I had shaved and dressed, and wanted to check the hour to see how much time remained for breakfast before the appointed arrival of the taxi. I could not find my wristwatch, then remembered that (as I habitually did) I had parked it in my fiddle case before going out onstage for the Padua concert the preceding night. A quick scan of the room showed no case. Nor did Jill know where it was. With growing concern, I picked up the phone and asked the desk clerk whether he had a violin case down there. At his "Yes," I ran out of the room, sprinting toward the stairs and paying no heed to what Jill was calling after me.

This was no time for a slow elevator. I tumbled down four flights of stairs, pelted up to the desk, and asked for the violin case. The clerk handed me an attaché case. "No!" I cried, "not that kind of case, but one *this* size," indicating the dimensions of the instrument case with my hands. "Well, I don't have it."

This was getting serious. What with the violin and two bows, I had over $115,000 worth of equipment at stake. Just before going to Italy, I had read in a newspaper article that Italy was suffering a wave of thefts of wallets, purses, and other valuables. I could now imagine the violin and bows making their way through criminal hands into the possession of unsuspecting buyers.

With panic setting in, I drummed up possibilities. Had I left the violin on the motor-taxi? Well, the driver was coming back to pick us up. But what if he didn't show? I had no record of the taxi number. I went out onto the hotel's side dock; not only was the dock bare, but a garbage scow was moving away, far up the canal. Could the crew possibly have picked up an apparently abandoned item? I went back into the lobby and looked behind sofas and planters. Nothing! The porter noticed my searching and asked what I was looking for. "Your violin case? It's on the floor outside your door!" *What?* I ran up the four flights of stairs, flew to my door, and—nothing. I tried the door and knocked—silence.

What had happened was that, in my anxiety to reach the hotel desk, I had run out my door and straight past my violin case, which had been sitting there on the floor all night. Jill saw the case, could not stop me in my flight, so took the case into the room and phoned down to the desk. Unable to get through, she locked the door and took the elevator down just as I was running back up the stairs. Now she hurried back up, opened the room door, restored me to my violin case and sanity, and gave me a chance to catch my breath before we at last went down to breakfast.

The taxi came right on time, we all boarded and proceeded to the airport. I said nothing to the others about the morning's agitation, and they seemed totally unaware. It was only later that I learned that Jill had already revealed all to the rest of our party. What a snitcher!

Shortly before leaving home for the flight to Europe for our 1977 tour, I had finished typing the text of my quartet-travel article. I mailed it off from the airport to *The New York Times* travel section editors, who had asked to see a draft of the item. A few months after our return to the States, we were in Albuquerque for that season's edition of the June Music Festival. The *Times* reached me by phone there to ask why I had not yet sent them the article. When I told them I had mailed it six months earlier, they deduced that it might still be on the desk of an editorial staff member who had suffered a heart attack at about that time. This proved to be the case.

After reviewing the text, the *Times* editors asked me to make some introductory additions to the article to acquaint readers with the general layout of the typical European railroad passenger car. The revised script appeared in the travel section on Sunday, 11 November 1977. At least one touring quartet musician told me that—in the light of his own exertions on the road—he found my piece "amusing, but not funny." I think it still makes enlightening reading for the novice wandering player. With the kind permission of the *Times*, I reprint it here. It distills the thrills of many seasons.

How musicians keep fit to keep traveling

In 1958 the Fine Arts Quartet, of which I am the second violin, set forth from its home base, Chicago, to make the first of its European tours. Fifteen times since then we have made the rounds of European auditoriums, large and small, from Kiruna to Rome, from Edinburgh to Berlin.

In the early years, we did much of our touring by car. In recent seasons, our European managers have insisted that we minimize the obstacles of weather, which can ice a road, fog a territory, and close an airport, by using European trains.

The ensemble, constantly on the move, has to learn how to live with the realities of train travel. Luggage is always in hand. Hotel-to-hotel baggage service is available from the railroads at nominal cost between many points, but concerts do not always take place in such cities, and the necessities of concert life make it difficult for the performer to entrust his suitcase to the chances of misshipment. Not every European audience would understand the appearance of a string quartet in blue jeans and flannel shirts instead of not-yet-arrived tails and white tie.

So, picture the musical four, fiddle case in one hand, suitcase in the other, music-and-sundry bag slung over the shoulder, piling out of a cab and entering a railroad station. Whether large or small, these structures have long platforms, pedestrian bridges or underpasses with stairs connecting, and during the concert season more than a little cold, damp, snow, and fog. The typical long-distance train is made up of a long string of cars. The typical European railroad car has a short, steep set of steps leading to a vestibule at either end, a narrow corridor running the length of the car and from this corridor a series of sliding doors opening onto compartments, each with two three-person seats facing each other. Consider also that, above each of these seats there are a couple of shelves for hats, parcels, and suitcases.

Some railroad platforms are built on a level with the threshold of the car's entry doors. Usually, however, the platform is at track level, and the passenger must use the car steps upon entering or leaving. This is no great shakes for the unburdened passenger. When luggage and instrument cases are involved, however, and when there are other passengers equally eager to enter or escape, will power and organization are required. Long ensemble togetherness has made us skilled in forming a suitcase bucket brigade to get the bags on or off the car before the train moves. Travel has hardened us, also, to the rigors of getting the bags not only down the corridor to the appropriate compartment but into the compartment and onto the baggage shelves.

You may have pictured this for one station and one train. But concert itineraries do not involve just one train. We have taken as many as five trains to get from one city to the next night's engagement. And progress through as many as five trains in any kind of weather, or even under cover, is something that builds character. Of course, there is always the porter to ease the burden from one platform to another. Always? Often not at the moment you need him for a fast connection. But then, there are always the luggage carts on the station platform—when there are enough to go around. We once deferred to a woman as she made her way from the car, only to see her latch onto the only cart in sight and then stand there in smug possessiveness while we ran all over creation looking for a conveyance.

Our rail festivities are given added zest by the fact that two successive trains can be at opposite sides of the station as often as on adjoining tracks. Even neighboring tracks can sometimes be deceiving. We once entered a terminal on one train, saw our next train standing on the adjacent track, and then realized that the platform giving access was on the far side of that train. With not too many minutes to make the connection, there was a grand dash down the length of the arrival platform and an equally tumultuous progress up the departure platform.

All is not athletics in train travel. There are long stretches of sitting, dozing, reading, looking out the window, taking photographs that one hopes are not obscured by fleeting power and telephone poles.

And there are trips to the dining car or beverage counter (depending on the particular train). Though there is a certain standardization to the menus, the fare offers palatability and reasonable range in price, with beer and wine available.

The routine of the dining car can be enlivened by an occasional discussion with the help. Last year, for example, on a German dining car I ordered lentil soup with sausage bits and roll, and it came without roll. Why no roll? The allotment of rolls had not been delivered at the depot, explained the waiter. Could he reduce the price to compensate? No, he could not. The prices were set by the administration. Could he, then, let me have a small refill of soup instead? No, he could not, the size of the portion was again strictly set by the administration. Checkmate.

For overnight travel, there are the train sleeping accommodations. One way is via the couchette arrangement: people-shelves that fold down to hold the six sitters in a compartment (in first class, four) in a horizontal mode for the night. I have never experienced this kind of togetherness myself. Besides, if I have to sleep in my clothes, I would just as soon do it sitting up. I have, however, shared an upper and lower sleeping compartment with a fellow ensemble member or with my wife and can testify both to the relatively good design of these facilities and also to the fact that dressing and undressing and performing the toilette in these compact quarters is good training for the prospective submariner.

Perhaps I have painted the picture enough to set the stage for the bulletin that I wrote from Europe to the students in my violin class at the University of Wisconsin–Milwaukee. It depicts the regimen of the railroading musician.

Dear Class:

I am writing to suggest some important exercises to add to your daily round of arpeggios, scales, etc. In fact, you might skip the fiddling for a while and concentrate on these essential preparations for concert life.

1) Run up and down at least two flights of stairs and along a 100-foot hallway, carrying a 30-pound weight in one hand, a 10-pound weight in the other, and about 15 pounds in a shoulder bag. Be sure to do this while wearing full winter dress, including heavy overcoat and galoshes. Repeat three or four times daily. To achieve virtuoso rating, work up to a five-a-day regime.

2) Try for speed in the above exercise. Repeated time trials should enable you to run the course in 30 seconds.

3) Get a telephone booth, mount it on top of a short stepladder, and practice heaving yourself up the ladder, weights in hand. Squeeze rapidly, coat, weights, shoulder bag and all, into the telephone booth. Also practice doing this out of the booth and down the ladder. Repeat four to six times daily. See if you can increase your speed by having a colleague urge you on with cries of, "Hurry, the train is about to leave!"

4) In a long narrow hallway, not more than 26 inches wide, squeeze past each other, carrying or pushing the weights. Repeat four to six times daily.

5) Stand in front of a deep shelf that is six feet off the ground. Heave your 30-pound weight onto it. Pull it back off, carry it 30 feet away, return, and heave it onto the shelf again. Repeat six times daily. Have a colleague sit in a chair under the shelf and eye you apprehensively as you fling the weight onto the shelf over his head. Take two demerits if you hit him.

6) Cut one leg of a chair short by one inch. Put the chair next to a window. Have a colleague shake the chair while you sit in it. Look out the window and try to focus on the scenery. Keep this up for two hours (you can change chair shakers in shifts, if need be). Try to catch catnaps, read a book, or write a letter while the chair is in motion. Repeat in two-hour shifts, three times daily with no more than half an hour between shifts.

7) Sit at a small table that has been set up on an eccentrically vibrating platform. Fill a plate with boiled peas, cooked small onions or anything that will roll and bounce, ladle some clear soup into a bowl and pour very hot tea into a glass. Practice until you can do this without spilling on yourself or your neighbors.

8) Arrange a number of shopping carts haphazardly along a course 200 feet long. From a starting line 50 feet from the nearest

cart, have all members of the class run, in full regalia, down the line of carts. The object is to grab an unclaimed cart (even a semi-claimed one), push it back to the starting line, load it with your weights and then push the loaded cart to a finish line 100 feet from the starting point. The first one to complete the course wins. If he wins with a cart whose brake sticks or whose wheels are out of round, then he gets two additional points.

9) For variety, extend the race to include unloading the cart at the finish line, carrying the weights down two flights of stairs, along a 100-foot hallway, up two flights of stairs, then continuing another 100 feet to a step ladder–phone booth combination and into the booth. The first one to survive wins.

10) Hire a smallish taxi. Practice filling the cab until you can get four people, luggage, shoulder bags, and a cello into the cab (plus the driver). If you find you have to take two cabs, take two demerits. Practice arguing with the cab driver (who will urge you to leave his cab and find two others) in either German, Swedish, Flemish, or Dutch.

11) In a small trip around town at rush hour use various conveyances, porters, etc., with each member of the class paying for different items. At trip's end, figure out who owes what to whom to make everything come out even. Use a calculator.

12) Call a mythical concert client, introduce yourself in German, announce when you want to try the stage, ask whether dress is formal or informal, and whether there is to be any reception after the concert. (This last is ostensibly, and actually, to guide you in your eating routine before the concert, but it is also—if tactfully possible—to find out whether the after-concert festivities are hosted or Dutch treat. This is designed to avoid the embarrassment of reaching—or not reaching—for the check. But the wiles of a Metternich will still not protect you from surprise at the eventual outcome.)

13) Report to a mythical theater at the appointed concert time and tell yourself that the hall is too cold, too hot, too dry, too resonant, too big, too small, too dark, and too glaringly lit. Discuss the lighting and temperature with the stagehand in one or another language. The student taking the role of stagehand must be sure to be cooperative but not able to do very much about the situation. The

performers must assure each other that, no matter what the drawbacks of the hall, all will be better with the audience in place. This is almost never true.

14) You've done all the above? Then sit down and give the concert. Careful. Today is Wednesday, you're in Groningen, and it's Mozart K. 387, not K. 428.

15) With your colleagues taking the role of applauding audience, try to have them coax an encore out of you with the fewest possible number of bows. If they persist, slip another encore to them before they have a chance to suspect your eagerness.

16) If you've gone this far, then repeat daily for six weeks. And, just to keep your hand in, travel that day, taking at least two trains. If you catch cold, learn to wipe your nose without dropping a note in Beethoven's Op. 131. (Yes, it is nonstop for forty minutes, but you do have a two-measure rest in section 6.)

17) Anyone for tennis?

14 ✧ HOW I LEFT THE FINE ARTS QUARTET— AND LIVED ON

In 1979 I left the quartet that had been my musical home for twenty-five years. I hope the passage of time now gives me some perspective on that event. Let me describe what happened and see if I can offer any enlightening comment thereon.

By autumn of 1978 George Sopkin was in his thirty-third year in the Fine Arts Quartet. He was feeling the strain not only of arm and eye troubles he had suffered during preceding months, but of decades of quartet life. In rehearsal at the start of the winter semester, George said that he intended to retire at the end of the academic year. Hearing this, I knew immediately that I could not continue in the ensemble without him and said that I would be leaving, too. This could not have been a complete surprise to my colleagues. In a June 1977 rehearsal, Leonard had given me—not for the first time—the kind of gratuitous paternalistic comment that was the more irksome because he was only six years my senior. Nettled, I responded that I had for some time been looking for a suitable avenue to take me out of the quartet. I had not yet found one when George's impending retirement triggered my spontaneous decision to leave. But it was clear to me that quartet routine without George's at least partially calming presence would have been very bleak.

I certainly had not had time to consult with my wife about my decision. When I reported events to her later that day, she again concealed whatever doubts she felt, just as when, twenty-five years earlier, I had switched careers by entering a concert ensemble. At this point, however, the situation was slightly less problematic because our children were already grown, had left home, and were either finished with their academic training or already involved in their work. Even so, both Jill and I knew we were again embarking on a new phase in our lives.

At the moment, however, I did not have much time for reflection. Via Leonard and Bernie (and somewhat against academic protocol, even if not against ensemble priorities), word of George's intended retirement and my resignation flew to the dean of the school. I was summoned to his office that very afternoon. He asked me to stay on in the quartet for another year during which a new cellist could be integrated into the ensemble. This was not too appetizing a prospect, for to help in this arduous process and *then* leave was on the face of it unrewarding. Moreover, though the dean said I would remain on the faculty after the year, it would be on the basis of the academic (nine-month) rather than the administrative (eleven-month) year, for I would no longer be participating in the summer concerts and lectures. This change would involve a reduction in salary, a rather curious treatment for someone who had already served sixteen years on the faculty and been given distinguished professor status. That I agreed to these terms was a reflection on my sanity, consistency, or both. Certainly George seemed surprised by my assent. At the very least, I should have requested time to consider the matter, but the day had moved so rapidly that I was not thinking clearly enough.

Had I considered the matter thoroughly, I might have recognized that by staying on at UW-M after finally withdrawing from the quartet, I would have been in much the same fifth-wheel role that would have confronted Jerry Stanick as ex-member of the ensemble a decade earlier. Tenure notwithstanding, my continued presence in the music department would probably not have been a happy one.

As it happened, events were to save me from myself. During the December semester recess, Jill and I went to Paris for a family wedding. While there, I received a phone call from Robert Freeman, the director of the Eastman School of Music, inviting me to be a candidate for a position in the string department there, with my interview visit scheduled for early February of 1979. I had been nominated by Francis Tursi, long a professor of viola at Eastman (and now untimely gone from us), with support also from Robert Sylvester of the cello faculty of the school. We had come to know each other through their various appearances as guest artists with the Fine Arts and, in Tursi's case, his collaboration in our recording of the Mozart viola quintet cycle. In one of the quartet's concert visits to Eastman, in fact, we had given a program of Mozart quintets with Francis. On that same occasion, there had been an informal play-and-talk session about the quintets, with commentary by me. Accordingly, I already had some introduction to the school.

The night of my trip to Rochester, New York (home of the Eastman School and its parent, the University of Rochester), there was a blizzard in Milwaukee. Flights into and out of the Milwaukee airport were canceled. I tried repeatedly to let Eastman know about the tie-up, but because of the late hour could not get through to the school. I was pretty haggard when I managed at last to fly out of Milwaukee on a 4 A.M. flight that Friday morning. What with a plane change in Chicago and the difference between time zones, it was midmorning when I got to Eastman. With the help of coffee and nervous energy, I pulled myself together, went through an abridged set of administration interviews, had lunch with several string faculty members, and was then escorted to the small recital hall where I was to present a master class before an audience of faculty and students.

I had envisioned that I was applying for a position focused on the coaching of small ensembles. It was a surprise, therefore, to find that the student roster awaiting me consisted of four violinists, each with different accompanist, and only at the end, a string quartet performing the first movement of the Dvořák "American." My own performance experience with the duo repertoire, along with the study I had done in writing *Violin and Keyboard*, helped me deal with the situation at hand. I offered what I thought was relevant advice on various points to each duo, then gave my attention to the string quartet.

At that point, and without my knowing it, I ran into a hidden boulder in the roadway. There is a somewhat militant G-string fanfare, played by the second violin, not long before the recapitulation section of the quartet's opening movement. The student playing that part was not giving the solo enough beef, and I took over his chair to demonstrate how I thought his phrase should be played and how the others should react to it. I did not learn until much later that this evoked criticism from the student onlookers. They thought I was making fun of the weakness they themselves recognized in the approach of the student in question. Such was not the case at all; I was simply trying to demonstrate the passage in sound rather than words, and did so via the part familiar to me through my quartet experience. (Fortunately, director Freeman recognized the true state of affairs and tempered the role of the students' verdict in making his eventual decision.)

I met briefly after the class with Dr. Freeman and his associate director, Jon Engberg, and told them that, if brought to Eastman, I would want to teach chamber music, not violin. They already had a panel of excellent teachers of the instrument, whereas the professor of chamber music, violinist John Celentano, was retiring. In point of fact, the current string faculty search was aimed at filling not just one, but two positions. If both were to be for violin, there would be a dilution of studio teaching loads. Also, this would leave no single faculty member in charge of coordinating the chamber music program of the school. That was how I saw the situation, and fortunately it seemed to match the school's perspective as well.

As we said goodbye, the director told me that, if chosen by the school, I might also be designated chair of the string department (succeeding John Celentano in that assignment as well). "I don't insist on it," I replied. This was sincerely meant, for I had never held that kind of responsibility before. Some weeks later, I was informed I had been selected to serve as chamber music professor at Eastman, and indeed would also act as chair of the string faculty. Greatness was thrust on me, and I carried out both functions until my retirement. (Incidentally, in 1984—with, I was told, solid support from Eastman's students—I was given the university award for undergraduate teaching. Bob Freeman's judgment of my candidacy had been vindicated.)

That hectic Friday visit to the Eastman School, incidentally, was not the end of an athletic weekend for me. From Rochester I flew to Chicago to meet the Fine Arts at the studios of station WFMT for a Saturday of fundraising talk-and-play for our Chicago-Wilmette concert series. Then by bus back to Milwaukee to check in with Jill. Early Sunday morning I flew to New York for a planning meeting on a projected new magazine for instrumental players (I was to be its string chamber music editor). As matters later turned out, a principal investor took ill and had to withdraw his support, and plans for the publication were aborted. Meanwhile, however, I flew back to Milwaukee Sunday night and was back at UW-M for my Monday-morning violin class.

For the sake of the quartet, I meant to keep my departure quiet until the last possible moment. However, word of my impending move reached the ear of a Milwaukee music critic, and the cat was out of the bag. Leonard was pretty annoyed, but things moved smoothly enough for the rest of the transition process. In fact, the reconstituted quartet was performing already in that summer's series of concerts on the university campus. (How smoothly the changeover went, I cannot say. As I shall relate, I was already in the throes of moving to Rochester so never heard a note of the new lineup.)

The leave-taking of George and Carol Sopkin and Jill and me, not only from Milwaukee but also from Chicago, was an event of some sentiment. George, a native Chicagoan and pupil of famed virtuoso Emanuel Feuermann, had joined the Chicago Symphony Orchestra at the age of twenty, after two years as cellist in the Kansas City Symphony. He came to realize that, as member of a large orchestra, he did not have control over his musical decisions. After six years in the CSO, he left to join the Pro Arte Quartet at the University of Wisconsin, Madison, with professorial rank. He entered military service two years later. Upon being mustered out, he formed the Fine Arts Quartet with his colleagues Sorkin, Stepansky, and Lehnhoff, so his ties with Chicago were then newly reinforced.

Though Jill and I are native New Yorkers, we raised our children in Chicago and Milwaukee and have dear friends in both cities. We made our home there for a significant portion of our lives. I worked, taught, and performed so many years there that the move to new surroundings was sobering. If anything made the transition easier, it was the experience of having traveled to so many places during the quartet years. The sense of uprooting was somewhat lessened.

Our dean at UW-M arranged that George and I were each named Distinguished Professor Emeritus and hosted a warm send-off party for us at the university, with town and gown well represented in the gathering. In Chicago the many friends and staunch supporters of the Fine Arts Quartet Concert Series bade us farewell at what had become a traditional, annual party at Chicago's Arts Club. For both George and me, it was a signal evening, bringing back many happy memories.

And the journalists, too, sent us off with fond words. In the *Chicago Sun-Times* of 8 May 1979, reviewing the last concert in which George and

I performed in the city, Robert C. Marsh wrote that hearing George's cello he "was overcome with nostalgia" and that "Watching Loft at work, boldly asserting the replies the second violin must make in great chamber literature, it was clear, as always before, that a great second violinist plays second fiddle to no one." In the *Milwaukee Journal* of 7 May 1979, we read, "Things just won't be the same anymore without George and Abe."

Our eleven years at Albuquerque's June Music Festival had ended with the previous summer season, with the Guarneri Quartet succeeding us for the 1979 session. The Fine Arts had already been slated to conduct a chamber music workshop and concert series at the Instituto Nacional de Bellas Artes, in San Miguel, Mexico. That was the last expedition with the quartet for both George and me. Then it was back to Milwaukee to prepare for moving: for George and Carol, to their new home in Maine; for Jill and me, to Rochester.

Our Milwaukee home had been sold the day before we left for Mexico. We returned to Milwaukee on a Friday, flew to Rochester that Sunday to search for a new residence, and were fortunate enough to find a very pleasant home in the city in short order. Then it was back to Milwaukee for a concentrated and exhausting three weeks of sorting, packing, holding a garage sale (Jill masterminded that), transferring ownership of our house, and driving to Rochester. Once there, we went through the details of taking title to our new home, receiving the moving van, installing our furniture in some sense of order, and unpacking some of the many cartons of possessions that surrounded us.

The Rochester phase was crammed into ten days' time. At that point we locked the door, went to the airport, and flew to Salzburg, Austria. I had signed on to serve as chamber music coach at that summer's session of the International String Workshops. Very soon after that two-week event, we flew back to Rochester, continued to settle in, and prepared for the start of my first semester at the Eastman School.

George Sopkin's "retirement" really needs to have quotation marks around it, for he has continued on for years of performing, teaching, coaching, and judging, both in America and abroad. In recent years he has enjoyed service on the faculty of the Kneisel Hall sessions at Blue Hill, Maine, and is director of that same school's adult chamber music workshop. His most recent distinction is a special award in his honor, instigated by János Starker and bestowed by the University of Indiana.

In a festive ceremony at Bloomington, George was anointed Chevalier of the Cello.

As for myself, when I left UW-M to go to the Eastman School of Music, my life changed radically. I would again be acting within a department. That division, however, was devoted entirely to string instrument instruction, with its own faculty totaling almost as many members as the entire roster of the music department at UW-M. Moreover, the string department was part of a school wholly dedicated to the training of musicians rather than of one encompassing the various performing arts. Eastman was part of the University of Rochester, a privately supported rather than state-funded institution. The school had its own endowment, established by its founder George Eastman in the early 1920s. And its students came from a much wider area than had been the case in Milwaukee. In fact, some of that city's most talented young had left town precisely in order to enroll at schools of music such as Eastman. The faculty was large, of virtuoso caliber not only in the performance departments but over the broad spectrum of musical disciplines.

I was at last, at the age of fifty-seven, going to be responding to my work context on my own, after all those years of having to reach consensus with three ensemble colleagues. That I was now, as chair, to be responsible for facilitating the work of fifteen strong-minded artistic souls and their 150-odd students, graduate and undergraduate, had its own challenges. But that is a different story, to be told at another time.

In the ensemble world, I was one of the lucky ones. My feeling of unrest and discontent had been building for some time. Not only did I want to leave the quartet when I did—I felt I had to. And an exciting new career avenue opened for me at just the right moment. Moreover, though I was no longer in the full flush of youth, I still had enough time and energy to take hold of fresh opportunity.

What happened to George and me shows that, with a combination of lucky timing, determination, and the ability to apply past experience to new challenges, there is in fact a life to be lived after leaving an ensemble. Moreover, the transition need not be the narrow one of stepping from one musical family into another that is exactly the same except for new personnel. Acquired experience is both malleable and adaptable.

15 ✧ FORMING OR JOINING AN ENSEMBLE
Some Words to the Wise

In the course of telling more or less all about my life in chamber music, I have folded in various pointers for young chamber music aspirants. It is time for me to offer, in somewhat more formal guise, further sage counsel to those now looking to an ensemble career, or even to those who enjoy participation in an amateur ensemble. (And who does not have to survive in an ensemble of some sort?) As I confessed in my preface, I did not in my own career follow some important aspects of the suggestions I now urge upon you. Wonder at my impetuousness if you will, but profit from my experience.

Throughout, be aware that it is not a matter of "Simple Simon says, 'Do this!'" Whether dealing with colleagues, management, clients, or service agents, keep your wits about you. Whatever I suggest is subject, in the last analysis, to your alertness and judgment in applying it to the situation at hand. This is especially true because everything—technology, communication, business organizations, and relationships—moves and changes with increased speed today. This is certainly a new era, when an ensemble can have its own Web site, complete with bios, repertoire, review quotes, calendar, management information, and even performance excerpts provided. My advice will almost certainly be in need of amendment by the time you use it.

Above all, do not let details slide and pile up. Correspondence, accounts, travel arrangements—anything can get snarled up if not seen to in timely fashion. When you are focused on questions that really matter (intonation, which ending to take, and other monumental concerns), it is all too easy to lose sight of mundane chores. That is another chance for life in the submarine to grow a bit intense.

Appraising the team

Whether forming a new group or replacing a member of an existing ensemble, be well advised! Ideally, you and your prospective associates should have known each other for some time before contemplating an alliance. Perhaps you have been playing together for a while before the idea of a longer-term association suggests itself. At the very least, all of you should rehearse together over a period of time, even present a few concerts before making any decision about the longer term. First impressions are not always reliable.

Setting up a long-term musical partnership is just as tricky as finding the one-and-only person you want to marry. It might, in fact, be even more difficult. True enough, your judgment will not be affected by the same physical and emotional factors that enter into connubial choices. Still, you are guessing about personality and character traits that will prove to be as important as musical skills during the years of togetherness. There are no easy litmus tests for the items in the list that follows. Some are merely disquieting; others are potentially harmful to the prospects of the ensemble. Keep all of them in mind as you make your explorations and decisions. Here they are, not necessarily in order of importance.

Are all members punctual at rehearsal?

Whether the lateness is random or the consistent fault of one or more players, it wastes the time and patience of those who are prompt. It is also a bad sign if one of the party is clearly ready to leave the rehearsal before the agreed ending time. This reflects either on the seriousness of the player in question or, worse, on the musical interest of the rehearsal itself.

Do your colleagues have any personal quirks or mannerisms?

Of course (just as you do), but are they the kind you will find it hard to live with? Try to imagine how irksome such traits will become after extended time in the ensemble. Unless you are extremely forbearing, something like a nervous tic or stammer may grow very noticeable to you in the course of years of togetherness. The idiosyncrasy may be more subtle. I knew a violinist who, in rehearsal, would stroke his nose with his right hand (while still holding the bow) when he was about to burst out with impatience over a point of discussion. Those who were familiar with this trigger-sign dreaded and disliked it.

Are any danger signals in personality displayed by a member of the group?

One such signal is a tendency to project too loudly in performance, thus distorting the music and aggravating the other members of the group. If a desired sound level has been determined in rehearsal, overplaying at the concert amounts to scene stealing. Every member of the ensemble needs the competence demanded of a soloist but should be sensitive enough not to flaunt the ability when it is out of place. A discerning audience recognizes the display for what it is: grandstanding.

Are all members of the ensemble on an equal level technically?

It goes without saying that just one less proficient player will be sand in the wheels of the group. In an orchestral section, an inept player at best muddies the sound of that voice in the composition. In the one-player-per-part world of the chamber ensemble, the unfit instrumentalist sticks out like a sore thumb. If the group has fallen into this situation, it must tactfully (if possible) and quickly replace the offending member.

Though well matched technically, members may differ otherwise.

Do you all agree about tone quality, intonation, dynamics, vibrato, and so on? The string player who misgauges even slightly the relationship between bow speed and pressure, like the wind player with poor breath control, produces a sound that grates on the ear. If the others in the team work for a freely resonant tone, the mismatch with their colleague is obvious and disturbing. Disagreement in the other areas mentioned here is equally harmful.

Are all players *musically* compatible?

If the entire team chooses to play with an intensity suggesting all have just thrust a finger into an electric socket, that will certainly lend an identifying air to the group. Even if the audience can tolerate the voltage, some in the ensemble may secretly resent this approach to the music. Then again, the member who wants to treat the searing final section of Beethoven's Quartet in C-sharp minor, Op. 131, as though playing an early Haydn quartet, or the slow movement of Brahms's Clarinet Quintet in a manner more appropriate to Bartók's *Contrasts*, clearly has ears that are installed backward. Rehearsal time will go very slowly when major differences in musical outlook or stylistic awareness plague the ensemble. Fuming arguments or bored stalemate will result.

Does "rehearsal" mean pointless repetitions of passages or movements?

Without specific focus on needed change in musical or technical aspects, mere repeats waste time, energy, and endurance. Ironically, it is often the member who calls for such treadmill run-throughs who will wonder that colleagues grow apathetic. In fact, all members of the group are at fault if they let problems be glossed over, reading after reading.

Do some in the group try to settle musical differences by verbal duels?

Their colleagues (unless masters of self-control) will be drawn into the fray or else look on in silent frustration. The combat becomes one of semantics and psyches. Worst of all, the musical point at issue is lost from view under the barrage of words. The orators simply cannot admit that an objective comparison, in sound, of the contrasting ways of treating the passage might settle the issue. Word-games endanger the musical health of the ensemble.

Is there a pecking order among the members of the ensemble?

At one extreme stands the player convinced he or she knows exactly how the music should go. (The unspoken implication is that "Mozart was a close friend of mine.") This is strange, for the composer himself—if alive and available for consultation—will probably not be dogmatic, but open to suggestion from the nuances of interpretation revealed by the ensemble. At the other end of the scale is the player who has no firm idea about the music. He or she will likely contribute little more to the performance than an accurate rendition of the notes.

Between these two extremes stand those members who have a concept of the work that recognizes at least a small range of possible ways to interpret the music. Such players realize that the ensemble's way with the composition must inevitably change with the passage of time, no matter what the carefully considered decisions of the moment may be. As you might expect, my sentiments are with this middle echelon of players. Fortunate, say I, is the ensemble that can avoid (or root out) both the adamant defender of *his* truth and the drudge who lacks either the insight or the will to espouse any viewpoint.

Do the ensemble rehearsals lead to a convincing view of the composition?

The answer will not emerge until the group has been together long enough to present a number of concerts before live audiences. If public reaction is lukewarm, be quick to analyze what goes on at your rehearsals. When the scheme, color, and warmth of the interpretation are blurry in the practice room, they cannot appear as if by magic just because the players step onto the concert stage.

Do all members have concert strength?

The eminent Russian pianist Sviatoslav Richter referred to the "salutary tension" that the soloist should experience in approaching the performance. He was describing that state of controlled excitement that heightens the mental focus and determination of the lone player. This kind of concentration is needed at least as much by ensemble musicians, who control their own musical threads in the work, influence the way their colleagues play theirs, and respond in turn to what they do—all this at every point in the course of the performance. None can be immune to a mishap now and then, but the player who seems particularly accident prone in performance is clearly a threat to the career of the group.

Does any member display a proprietary attitude about the ensemble?

This kind of perspective would attach most probably, but not exclusively, to a founding member. Any such participant deserves credit for having formed the group and helped build its career. If, however, the status of founder translates into a sense that decisions about musical style, technical details of performance, and policy matters generally must defer to the will of a single mind, you may expect trouble. Rehearsal efficiency will be impaired, and resentments will arise and smolder, even if held in check. Music-making is hard enough without any jockeying for control within the ensemble.

Avoid political discussions!

Your ensemble is a musical organism, not a political science conference. The musicians who play together need not vote together. It is comfortable if the members of the ensemble have similar ideas about the way things should be run in our country and in the world at large. That kind of agreement, however, is not essential. If you must discuss politics, do it outside of rehearsal time—and even then, be civil and restrained. Prize difference rather than confrontation.

Last, not least: is there humor in the day-to-day life of the ensemble?

Everyone is an individual; one person's fun is another's buffoonery. A light touch, though, will leaven the essential seriousness of the ensemble's work. And do not forget that the composer—whether Haydn, Françaix, Beethoven, Bartók, Mozart, whoever—can spring a surprise or comic turn on you at a moment's notice. If you cannot recognize a jest when you hear it, you will miss vital opportunities to lend sparkle to the performance.

This is plenty to start with. We will assume you have been with the ensemble long enough to have informed views on the matters I have raised. If the participants (including yourself) come up short on some points, the alternatives are: a) try to improve the weak spots in the ensemble procedure; or, b) if the problems are numerous and serious, find a way to replace the errant member(s). If you do not have the voice or willpower to work your way through a) or b), you had best decide to leave the group yourself and search for a more congenial musical family.

Making an exit will not always be easy. If you join an established group and then leave after only a short period, you might be branded an incompetent or troublemaker. Then, too, the ensemble you enter has the right to expect constancy on your part. Rapid change in membership casts a shadow on the group in the minds of both management and audiences. Even so, do your best not to remain enmeshed for too long in an ensemble environment that has gone sour. We all pass this way but once, and we may as well enjoy it while we can. (See Besen, Dauer, Donnelly, and Robinson in Suggested Readings.)

16 ✧ REHEARSAL IN THE REAL AND IDEAL WORLDS

I find that more than a little of what I have to say in chapter 19 (Teaching Chamber Music) can be applied to the work of the professional ensemble in the rehearsal studio. In effect, each member of the group is also an internal coach. This, however, is a problematic role; if you come on too strongly and self-righteously, you may find yourself evicted from the room to contemplate the error of your ways. Besides, with every member a coach, the air can become too thick with contrary opinion, precluding any resolution of differences of viewpoint.

To resort to an outside coach, no matter how experienced that adviser might be, can only be a temporary, not a long-term, solution. A good coach will offer sound guidance, based on long personal involvement with rehearsing and performing a broad repertoire of fine music. The best coach, though, will also encourage the ensemble members to hone their own musical judgment and their ability to arrive at artistically valid decisions about interpretative questions. As with solo playing, the ensemble is going to be out on stage (even if only playing for its peers, though that is demanding enough!). A concert can be a very lonely and dispiriting experience unless the performers have confidence in their technical command and their ability to react to the musical interplay, moment by moment.

A proper coach will know when it is time to cut the apron strings. The student group will need outside guidance longer than will the young professional team. Adult amateur ensembles will have their own ideas on how much is enough. In whatever category, there comes a point at which the players must sail on their own, calling for advice only when they feel it absolutely necessary.

The ensemble should already have heard and played enough chamber music to understand the niceties involved. The members have to pool their individual musical insights and abilities in the work of the team. Opinions must be voiced but untainted by any suggestion of the proverbial "free lesson." If discussion turns into a verbal brawl, the ensemble will not need a coach, but a referee or marriage counselor.

The real…

No musical rehearsal preserves its real character when exposed to the eyes and ears of an onlooker. The soloist, practicing the lone part, might be the least disturbed by the presence of an observer. But as soon as you have more than one player—whether duo, larger ensemble, or conductor and orchestra—conversation among the musicians becomes part of the scenario. That talk is affected by the awareness that an outsider is on hand. The language becomes self-conscious, salty expressions are minimized, free interchange of opinion is soft-pedaled. The musicians are on best behavior. The rehearsal becomes an act. I remember the time when, early in my membership in the Fine Arts Quartet, we broadcast on the NBC *Monitor* program a performance of the Shostakovich Eighth Quartet, complete with a brief rehearsal segment to precede the play-through. John Chancellor, the radio newsman who was then still in his Chicago years, was the announcer and moderator. I recall the rehearsal portion as being stilted, with the musicians' comments sparse and rather monosyllabic. A broadcast or televised rehearsal would have to be especially carefully scripted and well acted to give any simulation of naturalness, and would still by no means be the real thing.

Paradoxically, and depending on the character of the musicians, the enactment of a rehearsal can become one of bravura display rather than of bashful restraint. Those members who in the privacy of the rehearsal room are ready to impose their viewpoints on the rest of the ensemble can—under the gaze of the lens or the ear of the microphone or the live listener—present their opinions even more strongly than usual. In sum, an ensemble rehearsal reflects the personalities of the participants, and is true to life only when unobserved.

If I attempt description of what goes on in an actual practice session, it must be from personal experience, especially with the one ensemble in which I participated for any length of time: the Fine Arts Quartet. Yet first I will speak as an outsider, for I was not in the quartet at its inception. In 1946, when the quartet formed as a staff unit of the ABC station in Chicago, the four players were already seasoned instrumentalists, with a considerable amount of chamber music experience. But the task of preparing a weekly broadcast meant there was a constant push to learn new repertoire. George Sopkin, who was there when it happened, tells me that the time constraints, rendered even tighter because the quartet members had additional duties as members of the station's staff orchestra, forced efficient rehearsal habits upon the ensemble. Each player knew his part, and the group sessions focused on fitting the voices together to reveal as clearly as possible the interaction that would make the composition come alive.

Conversation was kept to a minimum. Movements were put together —thematic statements, passage-work, sections, developments, all—by skilled trial and error, aural judgment, and musical discernment. This went on for the eight years that the ABC employment lasted (1946–54). The result was appraised not only by the players themselves, but in the light of the fan mail elicited by the broadcasts. There were also the audience responses and printed reviews of the various live concerts that the ensemble gave during this period, not only in Chicago but in the limited number of its appearances elsewhere.

George reports something else about those years: the composer whose work called for more discussion than most was Mozart. This jibes with my own appraisal of his music—that it is the most difficult to perform. To realize the lightning-quick alternations of mood, to reveal the all-but-tangible characters that appear even in his abstract compositions, to find the many colors and densities of sound that his writing demands —Mozart tests the musician every step of the way.

For the last few years of the ABC period, there was a change in the viola slot in the quartet when Irving Ilmer replaced Sheppard Lehnhoff. Irv had been serving as violinist in the Chicago Symphony until he was asked to join the FAQ. He had certainly had exposure to the chamber repertoire before this, but now he had to switch from violin to viola and fit into the repertoire requirements of the quartet's weekly broadcasts.

He was in the same situation I would face when I joined the ensemble a few years later: having to absorb and adapt to the way the three incumbent members of the ensemble prepared and played the repertoire under the pressure of a tight schedule.

During my first years with the group, I was busy learning how Leonard, Irv, and George wanted to interpret the compositions, and also absorbing the shape and detail of the music generally. Within the space of a couple years, however, I came to realize what my several colleagues brought to the work of the ensemble. Irv, excellent player that he was, seemed least inclined to make a determined stand on an interpretative point. George, marvelous cellist and a veteran of the quartet since its founding, was—even within the constraints of our schedule—ready to consider alternative approaches to questions of phrasing, pacing, and shading of the musical fabric. Leonard, having lived through years of building and maintaining a voluminous repertoire, was inclined to rely on ways and concepts formulated during the earlier history of the ensemble. In my role as a new and raw recruit, I could understand that he would resist musical suggestions from me, even after the passing of a few concert seasons. It was apparent, however, that he was also reluctant to yield to the opinions of Irv and even of George, who had been with him from the beginning.

Our repertoire was an overwhelming factor in our rehearsal process. Looking at the list of works at the end of this book, I am dumbfounded at the amount and variety of music we performed—let alone recorded—in my quarter-century of membership. The sheer mass of compositions would have allowed for only the most efficient kind of rehearsing. Technical and interpretative problems would have to be discussed and resolved with calmness and dispatch. Suggestions would have to be made, considered, and responded to with utmost selflessness and the least possible defense of ego. Again, this is achievable by only the most saintly of musicians.

The fact that every member of the quartet, to varying degree, also undertook performance of individual repertoire had two implications. In the first place, it gave the member salutary relief from the constant pressure of dealing with music subject to the four-way appraisal that governed our ensemble work. At the same time, though, it added to the burden of the overall schedule within which each one of us existed.

Looking back, I recognize what could have been a contributing factor to Leonard's mindset. He was giving so much time and effort to the editing of our numerous recordings and to other details involved with our recording activity that he had only limited patience with suggestions for altering his time-tested and ingrained way with the music we performed. There was simply too much to do. Still, it was not always easy for us to be confronted with a musical concept that was resistant to suggestion for change.

Irv left the quartet in my ninth year and was replaced by Gerald Stanick. Jerry was years younger than I had been when I came to the FAQ. Even so, I think he had already had more hands-on chamber music experience in his earlier musical training than I had when I joined. My guess is that, though he did not voice the feeling, he came to resent having to accept as established dogma the ways of the quartet as a whole. In any event, Jerry left the ensemble after just six years and was succeeded in turn by Bernard Zaslav.

Bernie brought to the ensemble a prior chamber music experience greater than what either Jerry or I, and perhaps even Irv, had when we began. Bernie is a man of definite opinion generally, and was almost immediately willing to reveal to all of us his views on various aspects of the music at hand. The points he made were apt more often than not, but the air of certainty with which they were advanced did not always make them palatable to his colleagues. Though he and Leonard got on well personally, Bernie's pointers about phrasing, intonation, and many other details often did not sit well with Len. I did not escape entirely, either; George, as I remember, was usually above the fray, though I know it was no fun for him to contemplate the action.

As the years went on, I was time and again amazed to note that, after the more fiery exchanges of opinion between Leonard and Bernie, all would seem to be sweetness and light on their next encounter. This roller coaster of temperament was not easy to live with, and eventually George retired and I simultaneously resigned, leaving Bernie and Leonard to work out their interaction in the context of a changed ensemble membership.

I firmly believe that it is the rehearsal (whether in the studio or in the preconcert warmup) that most severely tests the character and level-headedness of all the ensemble members. To borrow from that old political saying, the rehearsal is where you find "the heat of the kitchen." But I cannot simply leave things there. I must go on to picture rehearsal practices I think might lower the temperature.

And the ideal

Much of what I will say here seems aimed exclusively at the professionally oriented ensemble. Such is not my intent. My suggestions can also help amateur ensembles proceed more effectively, with greater insight and enjoyment, in working with the music they have chosen to play. The non-playing music-lover, too, will better understand what goes into preparation of a performance (amateur as well as professional) of a fine piece of chamber music.

Something else I should point out here: it might seem that my focus moves for the moment toward aspects of music-making in general, and away from my central concern about the welfare and longevity of the chamber music team. Again, that is not my view. It is precisely on differences of opinion about basic technical and interpretative questions that the ensemble vessel can run aground and capsize. Thus it might be helpful if the crew members could at least recognize what they are arguing about. It is with that in mind that I offer the litany that follows.

Let me dream of the ideal situation. It is one where all members of the group know each other well, have perhaps started the ensemble together; are compatible personally, technically, and musically; and seem able to look forward to a long association. To preserve that best of all possible musical worlds, here are some pointers on salutary rehearsal aims and habits.

Do you really want to work on this composition?

If the piece is from the conventional repertoire, you are no doubt already familiar with it. If new, it may commend itself to you by the reputation of its author. Perhaps it is an opus that has been discovered by a member of the ensemble in a music store or library, or heard in concert or recording. Yet again, it might have been submitted to the ensemble by a composer

or, if your group is already in a position to command this, has been commissioned by or for the ensemble.

All in the ensemble have to agree about spending time on the composition. It is either a work you will be able to program, or even if not, one
that will challenge and sharpen your performance skills. It is not every
ensemble, however, that can afford the luxury of taking on a work on this
last basis alone. Whatever the reasons, you and your colleagues must be
motivated to delve into the music.

Familiarize yourself with the piece

Try to get some idea of the music by reading the score. This can be by eye
alone if you are good at constructing the sound mentally. If you have
competence at the piano, get an aural impression of the score that way. If
the piece has already been recorded, listen to that version, preferably with
score in hand. Try not to let the recording give you too firm a precon-
ception about the way the music should be played. Keep your options
open until your ensemble has been able to come to grips with the work.

Add the work to your rehearsal schedule

Once you all agree to put the piece on the agenda, each member of the
group should have his or her own score of the work. Circulating a score
from hand to hand will slow the learning of the music. Also, each performer should be able to make his or her own marks in a personal score.

Working on your part

Ideally, each member should practice the individual part before the group
assembles for a reading of the work. The player should focus on passages
that are technically or rhythmically difficult. The integration of the several
voices may already be known from prior inspection of the score. In any
event, that will be made clear by group reading. Again, avoid forming any
fixed interpretative ideas before you have all had a chance to play through
the piece a few times.

Putting the parts together

For extended passages involving less than the entire group, it is best that the ensemble split up into the relevant subunits. This will spare the time and patience of those who would otherwise have to sit idly by. When the group assembles, the work of the subunit can be appraised and adjusted as needed.

Thorny passages for the entire ensemble should be practiced below tempo, then at speed to see if the clarity and precision hold up. As in solo practice, the relaxed playing should be as much as possible a slow-motion version of the *a tempo* performance. For example, the string player should use the same amount of bow, at the same placement along the length of the stick, as when playing fast. Otherwise, reversion to proper speed will involve learning a completely different set of physical reflexes.

Questions of balance between voices in the subgroups should have been explored before the meeting of the entire ensemble. Balances within the larger aggregate can now be adjusted as well. Listen objectively to make certain that important musical statements (not necessarily found in your own part at every moment) are given due prominence.

Intonation

This should be a constant concern in practice, whether of the individual part, the subgroups, or the overall ensemble. Start with the judgment of your own ears as you practice your part. Add to this the judgment of your colleagues as the parts are fitted together. All of you should be as dispassionate as possible in the exchange of advice. Do not let comment or temper get in the way of aural appraisal. Practice problematic spots under speed, then see whether the result holds at tempo. Be patient.

Intonation can sometimes be helped by trying an alternate technical approach. For example, the string player might consider changing a fingering or choice of string and position to improve accuracy of pitch in a melodic line or in a chord sequence. Alternatives may be limited by the necessity of adhering to a required tone color in the passage at hand. Decisions are also affected by the speed at which the music must be played.

High-register passages will require special attention, particularly on the violin. The half-step spacing in the upper reaches is so small that the player is tempted to make compromises rather than maneuver the fingertips into the position needed for accurate placement. But the error can crop up in any voice in the ensemble. Deal with it, and do not compromise. If you do not insist on accurate pitch, your audience will hear about it. Reviewers will not only hear, but write. If the ensemble member(s) at fault cannot or will not heed the combined opinion about intonation from those inside and outside the group, you have a serious problem. Give short shrift to any attempts to shift the blame to other, innocent members of the group.

To ignore the problem is to have off-color playing haunt the continuing career of the organization and cast a pall over its day-to-day internal dealings. It is a mistake to think the situation will rectify itself automatically with the passage of time. If matters cannot be settled through painstaking (and sometimes painful) teamwork, and within weeks or months, not years, the moment has come to think of a change in the team roster.

Phrasing

Here the fun begins. I can remember much rehearsal time expended on the first few measures of the second movement of Mozart's Quartet in F, K. 590 (Example 2). In the opening bar as well as at many other points throughout the movement, the composer presents a single chord. He could have filled the 6/8 measure with a sustained sound. Instead, he articulated the chord into a rhythmic pattern of eighth-notes, with a rest on the second pulse, thus: 1-(2)-3 4-5-6. How to get past that eighth-beat rest? To some ears, it seems quite clear that the rest simply offers resonant breathing-space after the sound that has begun on beat 1. From out this silence, beat 3 sweeps us forward into the remaining three pulses of the measure and on toward the resolution that eventually takes place in the second half of measure two. In effect, beat 3 is linked to beat 1, and is split off from it only to lend propulsion to the rhythmic flow.

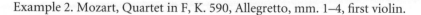

Example 2. Mozart, Quartet in F, K. 590, Allegretto, mm. 1–4, first violin.

I believe we eventually arrived at this effect in our playing of the phrase. However, this came only after some tortuous, quasi-Talmudic debate about the shape of the first half-bar. A tedious waste of effort, especially in view of the composer's heading for the movement: Allegretto. He wanted the music to keep moving.

Decisions about phrasing are important, especially at the start of a movement, where the composer is in effect stating the premise he will explore as the music unfolds. Trial and discussion by the performers is certainly worthwhile, so long as consensus is reached quickly and coolly, and based always on an agreement that the phrase must *sound* as though it moves convincingly. If the performance seems to require footnotes to explain the way you are shaping the music, something is very wrong. And remember again: whatever your current decision, your ideas may change as time goes on.

Breathing points

Singers and wind players are very conscious about breathing. If they do not inhale, they cannot send air through the larynx, the reed, or the mouthpiece. String players, in contrast, pride themselves on being able to draw the bow slowly, sustaining the sound so that even the break between up- and down-stroke is magically concealed. This strategy is not always appropriate to the phrase, which often reflects the breathing pattern of a singer in its structure.

Sometimes, especially in music of more recent provenance, the score will occasionally indicate an important breathing point with a comma above the staff. In music both old and new, the players may want to pencil their own such marks into the parts as a reminder in performance. The actual duration of a break in the line can vary from very slight to quite noticeable. It is a matter of taste and judgment, measured according to the anatomy of the music. The ear must dictate.

For the wind player, the shortest break will simply be an interruption in the sound of the instrument; longer ones will coincide with an actual intake of breath. For the string player, punctuation in the phrase— whether indicated by notated rests or by printed or penciled commas— will affect the way bow-speed and -pressure are graduated at the interruption of the stroke. The pianist will adjust the dynamic level of the succession of notes leading up to the break. In the case of the harpsi-chordist, for whom dynamic gradation of successive notes is not avail-able, the effect must be obtained solely through the timing of the succes-sion. Indeed, whatever the instrument in question, timing is part of the punctuation process. Gradual slowing prepares and embraces the inter-ruption. Maintaining or even accelerating speed makes the punctuation a surprise or shock, depending on the intensity of the maneuver.

With practice, decisions about placement and treatment of breathing points can be made fairly rapidly, certainly more quickly than it takes to write about the matter and usually more smoothly than heated discussion would permit. Your collective opinion will dictate a workable interpre-tation, and you can be sure it may be improved on in the future. Be deci-sive about your choices but flexible in reaching them.

Mechanics behind the phrase

I chose this section heading deliberately. I want to talk about the use of the bow, but I do not want players of other instruments to skip over what follows here. Much of what I have to say can be translated by wind, key-board, and plucked-string players in ways specific to their particular instrument. The breath or the finger stroke may take the place of the bow as the driving force behind the sound, but the ear and mind of the player must still gauge the application of that force in shaping the musical phrase.

As a string player, I know that skill in using the bow is crucial for effective phrasing. In fact, I feel that adroit bowing is at least half the bat-tle in good string playing generally. Choices about phrasing and breath-ing points will affect decisions about bowing. The composer has written slurs into the parts. Consider whether those are simply indications of physically convenient changes from up- to down-bow or are essentially signs that reflect that author's sense of the phrase. If you find that the slurs make for impractical use of the bow, can you alter the bowing while still preserving the phrasing effect that the slurs seem to call for? You may feel the composer's marks do not translate into sound that can properly reflect your concept of the musical intent of the passage at hand. In that case, you assume the responsibility of recasting the bowing pattern to suit your view. Such changes can affect the relationship between your line and others in the ensemble. You will need your colleagues' help in deciding whether your change fits the needs of the overall passage.

Decisions about slurring are just one problem. Your judgment is especially tested with regard to such signs as the dot, wedge, or line. A dot over a note can be understood to mean several things: a) under no circumstance should the note be connected (slurred) to its neighbors in the melodic line; b) the hair of the bow should sound the note with the merest flick against the string; or c) the contact between hair and string can be of somewhat longer duration, so that the effect is one that might be called "legato-spiccato."

To further compound matters, the dot is also used to indicate staccato playing. Here notes are clearly detached from one another by a bowstroke that begins and ends without the hair leaving the string, and with a slight, defining "bite" or grip on the string at both ends of the stroke. And again, the duration of the stroke, the aggressiveness of the bite, the spacing between successive notes, all will be affected by the speed of the passage and the temperament the melody suggests.

A line above the note is also subject to interpretation. Of course, it denotes a sustained sounding of the tone. But sustained how long? That depends on the tempo at which a succession of such notes is to be played. Also, the harmonic importance of some notes in a melodic series will require greater stress or longer duration of sound than for others notes in the line.

The wedge is a troublesome mark. We associate it with a hammered attack on the note, which can lead to a brutal sound if overdone. Use discretion; make musical sounds, except in those rare instances (most often in contemporary music) where the passage demands a particularly rough effect. Some publishers use the wedge in their editions, others do not. The difference can exist even between two publishers' *Urtext* (authentic) editions of one and the same composition. Read the statement of editorial policy that should appear in the publication to see how the editor expects the marking to be interpreted. In the last analysis, you must once again let your ear and musical perceptions be the final arbiter.

Pizzicato: it may seem arbitrary to include this under the heading of bowing. Plucking the string, however, is simply another way of evoking sound from the instrument; distinctive though it is, its uses have some of the variability that the bow affords. Listen to the fourth movement, the

Allegretto pizzicato, of Bartók's Quartet No. 4 to see the variety of effect that the composer can elicit from the plucked technique. He asks for an extremely soft to very loud; an accented and unaccented; a *marcato* and *ben marcato*, strongly "marked" stroke. Then again, there is the snapped stroke, where the string is pulled upward so as to strike against the fingerboard when released. Add to these crescendo and decrescendo, arpeggiated chords, back-and-forth strumming of the strings, chords played near the bridge for the glassy sound thus produced. Everything in the pizzicato arsenal appears here, even the glissando version, where the left-hand finger is slid along the string immediately after the plucked impact, to spread the pitch of the sound over a specific interval.

As in the case of the harpsichord, once the string is plucked the sound subsides from its initial loudness. Both the projection and the apparent duration of the sound of the pizzicato in violin-family instruments can be affected by such factors as vibrating the note or by the choice of the spot where the string is plucked (the more resistant part of the string near the end of the fingerboard as against the more flexible portion somewhat closer to the midpoint of the string's length). There are other choices: the stiffness with which the plucking finger is held, the use of the extreme, bony end of the finger as against the fleshier pad of the more flatly held finger, the use of thumb instead of the index finger, and so on.

Connections

Phrases link together to form larger musical statements. These, in turn, join to form passages, thence on to sections and entire movements. It is important to view the structure of the particular movement on its own terms, set by the composer. The better the work, the more it resists being squeezed into the anatomy of a preordained pattern or formula. In any event, such recipes are drawn up after the fact, by theorists who analyze the writing of composers and extract processes of organization that seem typical of the artists' work.

An interesting composition will often set its own rules. Watch for the surprises, the twists and turns, the detours that mark the flow of musical ideas in the composition and that open into new avenues of musical exploration. Recognize the composer's call for hitting hard on a sudden, jarring shift of harmony—as, for example, the *forte* D-flat chord immediately after a preceding C major resolution at the start of the development section of the finale in Mozart's last string quartet, K. 590 (Example 3). Enjoy the abrupt volleys of pizzicato that break into the scurrying stream of bowed notes in the Presto section of Beethoven's Quartet Op. 131 (Example 4). Welcome the sunlit episodes, in major, that cut through the shadowy cast of Mendelssohn's finale in the D minor Piano Trio and lead to the triumphant coda of the movement.

Example 3. Mozart, Quartet in F, K. 590, Allegro, mm. 132–136.

Example 4. Beethoven, Quartet in C-sharp minor, Op. 131, Presto, mm. 157–168.

A true pleasure of rehearsal lies in working out the subtle pauses, sudden breaks, slight speedups and pullbacks, swells and dips in loudness, that show the players' awareness of the events that mark the progress of the music. Overdo the dramatics, and the listeners will know you are hamming things up. Underplay the effects, and your audience will wonder at the flatness of the performance. There is a happy and necessary middle ground. Arriving at that level calls for the imagination and technical skill of all in the ensemble. The discussion of these essential details should be interesting enough to sustain the patience and mutual respect of all involved.

Timing

The successful speaker, the experienced actor, the stand-up comic, these will all tell you that a keen sense of timing is crucial in their several crafts. Even more is this true in musical performance. The singer's *Lieder* have words to guide the interpretation. For the instrumentalist, there is no text to convey meaning. Everything arises only out of a succession of tones. In effect, the music expects player and listener to learn and memorize a sequence of sounds so that, when it is moved, repeated, or modified, everyone will recognize what is going on.

An obvious demonstration of the role that timing plays in this process is found in the finale of Haydn's "Joke" Quartet in E-flat, Op. 33, No. 2. Haydn has indoctrinated the listener by frequent repetitions of a rather treadmill tune during the course of the movement. In the final measures, he splits the tune into its component units, separating them from each other by two-measure silences. Then he dictates a four-measure break before starting the tune yet again—and comes full stop after just the first unit of the return. Joke!

Haydn could simply have used fermatas to mark the interruptions, leaving the actual length of the stops to the discretion of the performers. Instead, he counts out the breaks to show just what he means. This is a lesson in comic routine. However, once you have been through Haydn's version of the *shtick* (to use the comedian's term) you can just as well pace the interruptions yourself. The audience will probably appreciate the fact that you are not being pedantic about things. And the fact that Haydn, at the end of the movement, calls for a sly *pianissimo* playing of the very opening fragment of the tune seems to be an invitation for a teasing manipulation of the breaks generally.

Do not wait for the composer to give you such bald-faced instruction in timing as in Haydn's example. In all kinds and tempers of music, not just the overtly humorous kind, from Bach to Babbitt and beyond, you will have to be alert to the part that pacing plays in effective performance.

Can timing be rehearsed to the point where it loses all spontaneity? Yes, it can. I would hope, though, that a player's teammates would give warning before any such point is reached. So also, they should be relied on to complain if a phrase is being played without verve or sensitivity. In place of the mournful outcry in the storytellers' enclave—"Look how you told it"—there will probably be the rhetorical question of the rehearsal room, "You want to play it like *that*?" The ensuing discussion and experimentation, if it stays on a civil plane, can lead to an improved musical statement.

Dynamics

Thinking about Haydn's *pianissimo* instruction prompts me to take up the question of dynamics generally. A broadly scaled gradation from soft to loud is a critical factor in the effectiveness of ensemble playing, even in the smallest portion of a musical score. Imagine the first violin's playing of the opening of Beethoven's Quartet in G, Op. 18, No. 2 (Example 5). The composer indicates a piano level for the first eight bars of the piece. Could he, however, possibly forbid that the violin indulge in a slight swell toward the end of the upward swirl of 32d-notes at the end of the first measure? Or what about a corresponding diminuendo toward the resolution on the downbeat of measure four?

Example 5. Beethoven, Quartet in G, Op. 18, No. 2, Allegro, mm. 1–8, first violin.

Improvisatory touches such as these are needed throughout our music-making. They are as natural as breathing, as inevitable as the rise and fall in loudness that marks our way of speaking and conversing. Ensemble members should encourage the habit in each other, again within the bounds of discretion, the composer's indications, and the implications of the music itself. Highlight the flexibility of the melodic line, without carrying matters to grotesque extent.

A small ensemble, at its loudest, can never remotely approach the torrent of sound that an orchestra can produce. To suggest a broad span of dynamics, the chamber group must explore the quiet end of its spectrum, so that its loudest output can stand out in vivid contrast. You will thereby get listeners to adjust their own aural perspective, so that the dynamic range of your small group will seem larger than it actually is.

Repeats

Purists may insist on obeying repeat signs whenever encountered, simply because they are there. I would rather hope there might be some leeway in this regard. If the exposition section of a long movement is itself of some length, a repeat of the section may create a top-heavy effect. To my way of thinking, even some relatively short movements do not absolutely demand a repeat of the exposition.

A case in point: the first movement of Haydn's "Quinten" Quartet in D minor, Op. 76, No. 2. Even when the movement is played with salutary lightness, the melodic emphasis on the interval of the fifth is heard often enough that a section repeat seems expendable. Actually, the last measure of the exposition drives the ear toward the beginning of the development, so much so that doubling back to the opening of the movement comes as a bit of a shock. Still, Haydn displays so many adroit ways of exploiting his rather simple theme that you might feel it necessary to give the listener a second chance to absorb all the composer's musical gamesmanship. (Certainly, though, the indicated repeat of the entire second section of the movement appears to be a formality rather than a necessity.)

Another debatable repeat stands at the end of the exposition in the opening Allegro of Schubert's "Death and the Maiden" Quartet in D minor, D. 810. This first section already numbers an impressive 140 bars out of the movement's total of 341. Moreover, the first fourteen measures of the movement so clearly serve a curtain-raising function that hearing them again in a section repeat seems anticlimactic. Nor is this material brought back by Schubert at the juncture between development and recapitulation. There the return is achieved through music (mm. 186–197) that corresponds to that in mm. 15–40; the composer thereby seems to confirm that the very opening of the quartet is specifically an introduction.

There are times, of course, when the composer insists that a repeat should be made. I do not refer here to such obvious cases as the customary repeats and da capo in a typical minuet movement. Rather, I am thinking of an instance such as the third movement, Allegretto, of Beethoven's Quartet in E minor, Op. 59, No. 2. There, the composer appends the following instruction to the end of the middle section, the Maggiore: "Repeat the Minore [the first part of the movement] but without repeat [of the two sections of the first part] and then again another playing of the trio [the Maggiore]; and after that, once again a return to the Minore without repeat [of the two sections thereof]." Beethoven could hardly be more specific if he were writing a legal contract. Yet after many performances of the piece, I remain less than convinced of the need for all this revisiting. Can it be that Beethoven is trying to balance the ecstatic length of the second movement, Molto adagio, with a full display of the rumba-like rhythm (*pace*, Ludwig!) of the first part of the Allegretto? Or is he, perhaps, making sly obeisance to the Russian nobleman, Count Razumovsky, who commissioned the Op. 59 quartets, by setting the audience up for two hearings of the "Russian theme" in the Maggiore?

I believe, in any event, that it is not sacrilegious to debate the question of repeats in a long or even not-so-long movement on a case-by-case basis. Consider the matter on the merits of the particular movement and in the light of current editorial information about the work at hand. In reaching a decision, try not to let yourself be influenced by such unseemly factors as having to compress the composition to fit the time limits of a record, CD or otherwise.

Recapitulations and returns

Here we are dealing with delayed repetitions. The recapitulation, even with its altered tonality scheme (second theme now in the tonic rather than the dominant, and so on) is a review of the themes and musical processes of the movement's opening. In a minuet movement, the da capo instruction at the end of the trio section takes the performers back to a literal run-through of the opening section of the movement.

"Run-through," however, is not the happiest choice of word. Time was when performers were expected to use repeats of sections as an opportunity to adorn the melodic line with improvised ornamentation.

Conservatively, this could consist of relatively moderate flights of fancy, highlighting particularly expressive details of the tune. At the other extreme, the melody would bloat and sink under an encrustation of virtuoso flourishes. Composers' agitation over this kind of excess may be reflected, for example, in the opening Adagio of Bach's Sonata in G minor for violin alone. Through-composed though it is, it can stand as a model of the kind of enlightened decoration that Bach would have imposed on a melody that had previously been heard in more spare version. Jean-Marie Leclair, more than once in his sonatas for violin and basso continuo, adds the instruction, "[play it] as it stands"—that is, "do not fool around with the way I wrote it."

Whatever the musical sins of the past, we may now have leaned over too far in the other direction. I am not suggesting anything so blatant as adding festoons of notes to the several parts in the recapitulation of a sonata-form movement. I *do* urge the ensemble to take into account what has happened in the composition prior to the return of music that has been heard earlier. Is it possible that a turbulent development section might have an impact on the way in which the recapitulation, or at least its opening portion, is to be played? Occasionally the composer himself will dictate some changes to the performer. This happens in Haydn's Quartet in D, Op. 76, No. 5. The development in the first movement ends with a short passage of fleet-footed 32ds, but nothing especially stormy in tone. Even so, the recapitulation rings some rather fancy ornamentation (Haydn's own) on the basic theme of the movement. This, it turns out, is just a warmup for the coda that follows, now in Allegro rather than the overall Allegretto of the movement. Here there is a race to the double bar, with the several voices by turns singing away at each other or whipping up the frenzy with a veritable hail of sixteenth-notes.

This is, to be sure, an unusual movement in an unusual quartet (the second movement is in F-sharp major, not your everyday tonality). But if the ever-imaginative Haydn can make the players sit up and take notice of possibilities that smack of artistic license, then performers must hold themselves ready to exercise their own imaginations as well. This does not extend to recomposing or rearranging the composer's writing, but simply to nuances of inflection and of tone color that seem justified by the musical context. At the very least, keeping on the alert for such shadings will liven up your rehearsals and your concerts. You will not be bored.

Codas

The legendary Yankee catcher Yogi Berra uttered the famous line, "It ain't over till it's over!" In music as in baseball, keep your eye on the game as you make your way toward the concluding double bar. You might find the composer giving you something fresh and unexpected to deal with before the music ends. Take, for example, the close of Mozart's Quartet in E-flat, K. 428. The Allegro vivace has been sprinting gaily along; you have only to play the saucy theme a last couple of times (starting at the *a tempo* in bar 297) and you will be done. But then, out of the blue, the first violin comes up with a completely new tune, one that could very well be whistled, starting in measure 305 (Example 6). This new idea has consequences: the nonchalant, sustained low and high E-flats in the first violin in bars 320–327 (these again suggest whistling to me), above further recurrences of the original theme. The composer is still reluctant to end, picking his way delicately forward, dwindling at last to the pianissimo leave-taking cadence by the two violins in bars 335–338. But, no! He has not yet finished. There remains a *forte*, full-chorded repetition of the cadence by all four instruments—and that, at last, brings the curtain down.

If you do not play this thoroughly operatic ending for all it is worth, you rob yourself and your listeners of Mozart's musical largesse. Moreover, to miss the fun of working out the dramatic possibilities of this coda in rehearsal means that you deserve to feel like four somber undertakers locked in a room together. (And, if I may be permitted the jest, they at least would certainly know how to take care of an ending!)

Example 6. Mozart, Quartet in E-flat, K. 428, Allegro vivace, mm. 297–312, first and second violins.

Tone

Whatever the instrument (or voice), its tone should resonate freely. Whether the music be loud or soft; jagged or smoothly flowing; mysterious or peremptory, lyric or brazen in mood, the sound must be unforced. This is true not only for the start of the vibration that generates the sound, but even more so for the duration of the note. For the string player, this means that the hair of the bow must glide onto the string rather than descend onto it in a hammering fashion. The string is under considerable tension and must be cajoled into vibration, not forced abruptly out of its static condition. The change in state will sound instantaneous to the ear, but the start of the tone will be free of jarring, gritty noise.

As the note continues to sound, the bow-hair must cross the string with just the right combination of speed and pressure. The player gauges and adjusts this combination to suit the loudness of sound required. Since the strings of the instrument differ in mass, cross-section, and tension, the player has to make rapid and complex adjustments in response to the feedback offered by bow and string. These adjustments happen almost too quickly to be apparent to the player, let alone the listener. If these modifications (or analogous ones in the case of wind or other instruments) do not take place, however, the resulting sound immediately betrays the fact. You may find that a forced, squeezed tone will intensify and make more apparent any flaws in intonation. The ear will truly suffer.

In ensemble terms, players insensitive to the subtle fine-tuning of tone production we have described will mar the overall sound of the group. Slight though the difference in tonal perspective among the players may be, it is bound to be an irritant in the day-to-day working of the ensemble and will in the long run hurt the audience appeal of the group. By all means try to resolve differences in attitude toward tone production. Otherwise, your team of players is headed for trouble.

Vibrato

In contemporary performance practice, and certainly for string players and singers, vibrato is not only an inherent part of tone production, but a way of life. The great activity in recent decades in the performance of early music has led to much doctrinaire discussion as to the appropriate use of vibrato. The most extreme view can scarcely tolerate vibrato at all. Arguments about the matter are almost as intense as those surrounding the question of smoking in public places.

A positive result of the debate is that players generally have tried to evaluate the proper use of vibrato even in music of more recent origin. Clearly, vibrato should not be an automatic component of tone production. Rather, it is an ornament, to be judiciously applied. Using vibrato constantly and unyieldingly is like dousing a dish with Tabasco sauce: you will certainly taste the condiment, but may not be able to discern the flavor of the underlying food.

The speed and amplitude of vibrato should be adjusted to suit the musical environment of the moment. It is simplistic to say that vibrato should be calmer and minimal in slow movements, fast and athletic in excited music. Rather, the player's taste and judgment will modify the vibrato to match the needs of the given phrase. Even within a single note, the vibrato may have to be graded to parallel the rise and fall of dynamics. Further, no matter how loud or soft the musical instant, the vibrato coloration may have to be either intense or restrained, to suit expressive purposes.

In the ensemble, vibrato must match the requirements of the individual voices in the music. Where all parts are of equal importance, the vibratos will be alike in all. Where the voices differ in prominence, the vibrato must reflect the fact. Certain details in any given part will demand special treatment. Decisions about vibrato can be a tortuous aspect of ensemble rehearsal. If the several players are alike in their musical judgments, the matter can be handled expeditiously and effectively. Should the discussion become prolonged and contentious, that might well be the moment to turn on the tape machine, record the passage, and have all listen to it, in hopes of an objective decision.

Style

In another book of mine, I give quite detailed advice about specific compositions (see Loft in Suggested Readings). The operative word is "specific." Each work creates its own expressive dramatic world. Pieces by a particular composer, or even by many composers in a particular time and region, may well have certain traits in common. If a work is any good at all, however, it will have performance demands uniquely its own. Were I invited to sit in on your rehearsals, I would be able to give pertinent advice about the music in question, but might have to offer opposite suggestions about another movement or composition by the same author.

You and your ensemble-mates should be able to arrive at your own musical decisions that will result in a convincing performance of the music you are studying. With continued experience, and with more repertoire at your command, you can hope for reduced discussion and quicker group consensus, based on what you hear yourselves play. Once again, try to remember that, no matter how intensely you feel about a particular musical point at the moment, you will possibly change your ideas as time goes on. But you must first have ideas to change.

Changes have indeed taken place in stylistic attitudes over the years. The quartet that now ventured to play with the very audible slides heard in recordings of the Flonzaley Quartet from the 1920s would cause consternation today. By the same token, the contemporary violin soloist who imitates the well-nigh inimitable—the urbane warmth of the playing of Fritz Kreisler, complete with delicate portamentos—does so as an act of nostalgic reverence for the manner and compositions of a giant figure from our musical past.

It has now been the better part of a hundred years since the fashion for the vigorously emphasized slide has faded from serious performance. The tolerance for that kind of voyage from note to note—or for the superheated and ubiquitous vibrato, the extreme rubato, and so on— might be revived in future. But I would advise players to hold true to their established performance style. If their interpretation of their repertoire has been carefully thought out and seems true to the nature of the particular compositions involved, there is little to be gained by veering to and fro to follow a fashion of the moment.

Some excellent string quartets and small chamber orchestras have elected to use old-style string instruments, bows, and wind instruments. This, coupled with the musicians' interpretations of the evidence from old treatises on performance practice, attempts resurrection of the way composers meant their music to be heard. When this is done by skilled players, guided by well-informed research, the results can make for interesting listening. This by no means, however, negates the validity of performances on modern-styled instruments, again in the hands of accomplished players. The emergence of carefully made editions of the repertoire, such as those forthcoming from publishers like Bärenreiter, Henle, Universal, and AR Editions, puts intelligent performance within reach of expert musicians, whether they use equipment old or new, with attitudes "historic" or of today.

I doubt that any ensemble wants to sound exactly like another. Musicians are not stamped out in a cookie-cutter machine. Carried to the nth degree, slavish imitation would mean we would need just one string quartet, piano trio, chamber orchestra, and so on. The ensemble should approach every work in its repertoire in terms of its own understanding of the given composition. Only that individuality of perspective, attuned always to the special requirements of the music at hand, can justify the existence of an ensemble and keep its performance vital and fresh.

If the group has built a repertoire of some size, most compositions will likely be programmed only at several-season intervals. This gives the players a chance to reevaluate their way with the music and make any changes they find advisable. Musicians should keep their options open, not automatically regard their earlier treatment of the composition as divinely revealed. Tempo, phrasing, dynamic gradations, balancing of voices, all this and more can be reconsidered. Provided the players base their work on editions giving the most accurate picture available of the composer's own written or engraved notation and instructions, they should be offering their listeners their own freshly pondered interpretation.

Homework outside the rehearsal

Valuable rehearsal time is lost if deliberations about interpretation consist only of random, off-the-cuff observations by the members. By assignment, rotation, or volunteer choice, individual movements and entire compositions can be carefully inspected by one of the participants. The results should be held in reserve, to be advanced if trial-by-playing indicates the need for discussion. Two members can collaborate in the preliminary study, investigating the harmonic-structural organization of the music, the dramatic-emotional flow of the piece, and the correlation between these factors. As time permits, recourse can be had to the com-

poser's sketches (if extant) that led to the final musical result, and to com-
mentaries on the music that have been written by various players, theorists, and historians.

This outside time and effort is well spent, for it will stimulate, direct,
and regulate whatever debate takes place among the members of the
group. The study is perhaps most needed when the group returns after a
period of time to a work it already knows. It will assure that a real attempt
to evaluate the music and the ensemble's treatment of it takes place.

Sins against music

I cannot close this chapter without voicing a few heartfelt complaints
about performance attitudes that are all too prevalent today. Many of
you may have been trapped in an orchestra led by a conductor who
refuses to take any expressive risks with the music being played. Each
phrase is spelled out literally, without a hint of rubato to help build the
line or direct it to its goal. The result is a movement that, whether fast or
slow, unwinds relentlessly and metronomically until it expires at the double bar. Minuets become flat-footed exercises, lyric movements are rendered graceless, fast chapters turn into muscle-building machines.

Even with the sonority and tonal contrasts of the orchestra, such
treatment belies the composer's intelligence and imagination. Think how
much more obvious and offensive is this approach when heard in the
more confined palette of the chamber ensemble. You must not do this to
your audience.

A case in point: I have heard a recorded performance by a present-
day string quartet of the finale of Haydn's "Joke" Quartet, Op. 33, No. 2
(see "Timing" earlier in this chapter). The players treat the music very
briskly, as though the ensemble is in training for an Olympic sprint. It
seems the musicians recognize Haydn's joke, are slightly embarrassed by
it, and want to get it out of the way. The technique is brilliant, and the
notes flash cleanly and implacably by. We arrive at the Adagio sighs that
Haydn breathes into the music shortly before the end of the movement.
Because of the tempo in the recording in question, the sighs are griev-
ously diminished. A bit later, the two- and four-measure breaks the composer calls for are similarly contracted, again because of the metronomic
swiftness of the playing. The result is that the last, truncated wisp of the

theme slips away almost without notice. The joke has been obliterated by speed.

Sparkling technique and speed combine again in some renditions of the Beethoven string quartets. The players adhere to the vigorous metronome numbers that Beethoven attached to the quartet movements after his contemporary Johann Nepomuk Maelzel brought out his metronome. Never mind that there is evidence that Beethoven's contemporaries were divided in their opinion as to the appropriateness of these marks. Some ensembles rely literally on these instructions, taking the fast movements at a pace that, immaculate playing and all, rushes the listener through the musical countryside so swiftly that there is little chance to enjoy the scenery en route.

In solo playing, too, there is a tendency these days to play fast simply because the fingers will do so without dropping a stitch. Such virtuosity exacts the loss of expressiveness. The lone player may get away with this as an act of derring-do; and the conductor, too, by hiding behind orchestral color and sonority. The ensemble, however, has no such fig leaves. Dull and uncaring stands revealed as dull and uncaring, no matter how splashy the technical display. Some in your audience may not be aware enough to notice. You should, however, direct your performance to the most discerning ear. If you hew to the highest interpretative standard, all your listeners will in due course learn to expect and appreciate nothing else.

A final thought: We can dream of the ideal, but the real has a way of breaking in again. Imagine this scenario. The ensemble has tried a passage over several times. Adjustments to solve a musical or technical problem have not worked to the satisfaction of all in the ensemble. Concise and cool-headed discussion has given way to a war of words between two or three in the group. Arbitration efforts by the others have only resulted in bringing them into the line of fire. At that point, the noncombatants might consider leaving the rehearsal, by way of showing the miscreants that they are wasting everyone's time.

It pains me to report that, in all my twenty-five years of quartet life, I myself never resorted to this instructive maneuver. Even worse: when— late in that span of time—the ever-patient George Sopkin rose from his chair to read the riot act, I was so alarmed at what I envisioned as the imminent end of our ensemble that I prevailed on *him* to desist. It was craven of me, and a memory that I greatly regret.

In any case, leaving the rehearsal is a drastic gambit. If it has to be invoked more than once or twice, the ensemble had better analyze its habits meticulously—and soon. (See Blum, Norton, Page, and Reynolds in Suggested Readings.)

17 ✧ REPERTOIRE, PROGRAM BUILDING, GUEST ARTISTS

The construction of an ensemble's repertoire hinges on various factors. Does the group perform often in its hometown? Are many of its concerts presented on the road? Does the quartet perform on radio or television (regrettably a nearly moot point today)?

In our case, the answer to all the above questions was yes, though with varying emphasis. The early years of the quartet's existence gave it exposure primarily through weekly broadcasts. This required a large roster of works, even allowing for periodic repeats of some compositions. In my time with the quartet, there was no longer the broadcast calendar, but the yearly series of concerts in Chicago and Milwaukee made the work list grow even fuller.

When you are touring, a relatively limited number of works can satisfy the requirements of the various chamber music societies on your itinerary. You have to offer enough choice so that your ensemble's programs do not overlap too much with those of other touring groups. There is bound to be some duplication, of course, since traveling ensembles are not all under the coordination of one management.

You really head into problems when you perform for your own city's audience more than a couple of times each season. Even a handful of concerts, with three full-length compositions on each program, can eat up a fair percentage of your repertoire. Offering a series of concerts, year after year, in one community will really demand the buildup of a sizeable musical portfolio. In this situation, the ensemble has to plan very carefully because, along with new listeners in your audience, there will be a core of faithful subscribers who will want to hear fresh and interesting musical fare each year. Even when on the road, where you probably perform in a given town at best every three or four years, rarely in two successive seasons, you want to give the impression that you are drawing your programs from a fully stocked larder.

Here are some guidelines we followed in our own program planning:

A given work must not appear on programs too often over the years (though the saturation point for a traditional favorite such as the Schubert "Trout" Quintet has apparently not yet been found).

Try to mix musical styles and periods in any given program. To that end, draw not only from past centuries, but also from the current era. Such combinations of musical fare are good for the ensemble as well as the listeners. Here, though, I must recall the ire of one subscriber to our Chicago series. He complained, "How can you program the contemporary work before the intermission, and the Beethoven quartet in the second half of the concert? You *know* I'll be forced to sit through the modern piece!" Precisely. Let the audience learn along with the ensemble.

Try to mix sounds as well as styles. In your hometown, this is especially feasible if your team is made up of a spectrum of instrumentalists—string, wind, keyboard, percussion, voice—from which varied combinations can be drawn to match the requirements of both homogeneous- and contrasting-sonority music. A sequence of woodwind quintet, piano trio, and string quartet is but one of many lineups that make for a lively concert.

Contrary to the idea of mix-and-match programming, you can also feature the music of just one eminently strong musical personality. Think of, for example, all-Beethoven, all-Bartók, all-Mendelssohn (believe me), all-Mozart, and so on. And while we are talking about strength, some very intense programs can be built by pairing two of our musical great. Consider such "sandwiching" as Beethoven-Bartók, Brahms-Schubert, Dvořák-Hindemith, Britten-Shostakovich, to name just a few. In a program of typical length, there would of course be two works by one of the pair, against only one of the other. But with the proper combination and the astute choice of compositions, the recipe can be effective.

The ultimate contradiction to my emphasis on mixed programming is the series of concerts devoted to a single composer There is the Beethoven quartet cycle, of course. Equally obvious is the shorter cycle of the mature quartets of Mozart ("The Ten Celebrated"). The still shorter sequence of the six Bartók quartets makes a very impressive two-concert cycle. These are popular ideas, judging from the proliferation of "Mostly X" series. All these packages work, though I fear I am slipping into the very type of segregated, "old music vs. new music" diet that I have urged you to avoid. With the passing of the seasons, however, it is possible to demonstrate an ensemble's principled, broadminded view of the musical spectrum.

And of course, there are all manner of thematic approaches to programming, tracing a continuity of some kind through various authors and periods. One example: the piano quintet, not simply with strings, but with winds. Another: works for mixed ensemble built around a single wind instrument—flute quartet, horn quintet, oboe trio, and so on. Plainly, possibilities are as broad as the ingenuity and knowledge of the musician.

I show on pages 214–215 a few sample programs from our concerts over the span of twenty-five years. The programs represent some of the approaches that I have described, and readers may enjoy their own memories aroused by this musical banquet array. At the end of this book is a detailed list of the compositions we learned and performed, some frequently, others only once or occasionally, with the passing seasons. It is as complete as my memory and files permit.

We were fortunate to have the rich literature of the string quartet to explore and rediscover. Yet the world of chamber music offers much beyond the bounds of the quartet. To enter that larger territory, we needed to work with a great variety of sensitive and experienced musicians who knew the repertoire and were able both to add themselves to our ranks with relatively little rehearsal and to blend their own musical insights with ours. The experience of these cooperative efforts was inspiring to us, helping keep our musical horizons open and our performance reflexes keen.

Not least among the benefits of integrating an added personality into the ensemble mix is the freshening impact it can have on the group's rehearsal process. Preparing a concert with a well-chosen guest artist is a bit like injecting a shot of vitamins into the ensemble organism. Differ-

Sample Programs of the Fine Arts Quartet

Bartók cycle, as presented at Wigmore Hall, London, March–April 1971

I. Quartet No. 3   II. Quartet No. 1
    Quartet No. 2   Quartet No. 6
    Quartet No. 5   Quartet No. 4

Two concerts at the University of California, Berkeley, June 1972

I. Quartet in F, Op. 18, No. 1   Beethoven
    Second String Quartet, Op. 26   Ginastera
    Quartet in F   Ravel

II. Quartet in E-flat, Op. 76, No. 6   Haydn
    Quartet No. 1   Wuorinen
    Quartet No. 1 in G Minor, Op. 10   Debussy

All-contemporary program, Kennedy Center, Washington, D.C., September 1972

Quartet No. 3   Babbitt
Quartet No. 3   Husa
Quartet No. 1   Schuller
Quartet No. 3, Op. 73 Shostakovich

Season roster, Chicago concert series of 1972–73

I.   *A Musical Joke:* Sextet in F, K. 522   Mozart
     Lyric Suite   Berg
     Octet in F, D. 803   Schubert

II. Quartet in F minor, Op. 80   Mendelssohn
     Quartet in A minor, Op. 51, No. 2   Brahms
     Bassoon Quartet   Danzi

III. Quartet No. 4   Bartók
     Serenade in C for String Trio   Dohnányi
     Piano Quintet in A, Op. 81   Dvořák

IV. Quartet in A minor   Walton
     Quartet No. 3   Wilfred Josephs
     Piano Quintet, Op. 81   Elgar

V.	Quartet in E-flat, Op. 74	Beethoven
	Quartet, Op. 28	Webern
	Pierrot lunaire, Op. 21	Schoenberg

VI.	Quartet No. 1	Piston
	Quartet No. 4	Johnston
	String Trio in E, Op. 3, No. 1	Antes
	Quartet No. 3	Porter

VII.	Quartet in G minor, Op. 10	Debussy
	Quartet in F	Ravel
	Sonata for flute, viola, and harp	Debussy
	Introduction and Allegro for harp, string quartet, flute, and clarinet	Ravel

Beethoven-Bartók series, Chicago, 1956–57

I.	Quartet in C minor, Op. 18, No. 4	Beethoven
	Quartet No. 1	Bartók
	Quartet in F, Op. 59, No. 1	Beethoven

II.	Quartet in A, Op. 18, No. 5	Beethoven
	Quartet No. 2	Bartók
	Quartet in E-flat, Op. 127	Beethoven

III.	Quartet in F minor, Op. 95	Beethoven
	Quartet No. 3	Bartók
	Quartet in B-flat, Op. 130	Beethoven

IV.	Quartet in G, Op. 18, No. 2	Beethoven
	Quartet No. 4	Bartók
	Quartet in E minor, Op. 59, No. 2	Beethoven

V.	Quartet in B-flat, Op. 18, No. 6	Beethoven
	Quartet No. 5	Bartók
	Quartet in C, Op. 59, No. 3	Beethoven

VI.	Quartet in F, Op. 135	Beethoven
	Quartet No. 6	Bartók
	Quartet in A minor, Op. 132	Beethoven

ences of musical opinion tend to be discussed with more restraint than when the ensemble is unobserved. Also, since hospitality demands that suggestions from the guest be courteously considered, a similar open-mindedness is enforced among the members of the host group. I have attempted to list our many guest artists in the appendix. We could not have done it without them, and if I have inadvertently omitted some, I hope they will forgive me.

Prominent in our roster of guests was the singer Jan DeGaetani, of sainted memory. Over the years, she joined us for music ranging from Bach to Schoenberg and beyond, always with consummate technique and an uncanny ability to meet the particular musical and technical demands of the work at hand, whether old or avant-garde. Similarly gracious and superbly artistic were the violinist Josef Gingold and the violist Francis Tursi. Jan, Joe, and Francis are all untimely departed, remembered as performers, teachers, and human beings.

Also memorable were Victor Babin and Reginald Kell. Rehearsing and performing with Victor Babin was like making music with a congenial and gifted pianist in a court of the Russian nobility. I looked up to him both musically and physically, for he was a good head taller than I am. Reginald Kell was a Yorkshire gentleman, in the best sense of the word, who also happened to play clarinet with wonderful grace and directness. Performing and recording the Mozart and Brahms quintets with him was truly heartwarming.

Another prince among musicians was the flutist Samuel Baron, who combined scholarship and artistry in his playing, whether it was in Bach's *Art of Fugue,* the Mozart flute quartets, or the Jean Françaix woodwind quintet. The recollection of Sam's name brings with it those of the other members of the New York Woodwind Quintet and of the pianist Frank Glazer with all of whom we played many a concert through various seasons. Absolutely unflappable and sterling musicians, every one of them.

A fine guest artist enriches the life not only of the ensemble he or she visits but also that of those who hear the result of the collaboration. Programming, tonal palette, artistic perspective—all take on new color. As is always the hope in chamber music, the changed or enlarged combination of performers often proves to be greater than the sum of its parts.

18 ✧ SURVIVAL

Gigs, Recording, Reaching Your Public

S tarting and sustaining a chamber ensemble is hard work. In the first
quarter of the twentieth century, the Flonzaley Quartet, so named
after the summer estate of its financier patron, was supported during its
formative, rehearsal period until it emerged into its long and successful
career as a concert ensemble. The Juilliard Quartet was established in
1946 as the resident concert and teaching ensemble at the school of that
name. In the same year, the four founding members of the Fine Arts
Quartet were engaged by the ABC network station in Chicago, with duties
to include service in the station orchestra, but—more to the point—to
prepare and broadcast a program of chamber music each Sunday. Within
the past few years, an anonymous patron has provided an annual stipend
for a specific young string quartet to rehearse in preparation for its concert career.

Such examples are few and far between. The usual story finds the
players of the would-be ensemble going through one of the more stress-
ful periods of their lives. They are trying to hold to the schedule of long
hours of rehearsal needed to learn repertoire and crystalize the musical
personality of the group. At the same time, the individual players must
find and work at a variety of jobs to support themselves until the ensemble reaches the stage at which it can provide a reasonably predictable
income to its members.

The strain of balancing the needs of the group and those of the component musicians undoubtedly contributes to the breakup and/or changes
in membership of many startup ensembles. Early on in the work of the

team, some agreement must be reached among the players about the priorities governing the outside job vs. rehearsal schedule. One thing is clear: only a reasonably well-fed musician can function intelligently.

With any luck, the freelance jobs will be musical, not merchandising, garden maintenance, housecleaning, or whatever. You and your colleagues may find yourself playing for weddings, funerals, engagement celebrations, bar mitzvah receptions, dinners, or garden parties. Many larger cities have not only a full symphony orchestra but also smaller, steady or pick-up orchestras with a combination of regular and shifting personnel. You may be called on a fairly regular basis for a few rehearsals and the resulting concert scheduled by such an orchestra.

If some among your team are signed by an orchestra for a domestic or foreign tour, your group's schedule will have to be rearranged around the tour calendar. How feasible this is will depend on whether your ensemble is already established enough to have concert commitments of its own. The matter is complicated by the fact that music contractors tend not to call players who decline job invitations too often. Still, musicians skilled enough for the demands placed on a chamber player can well be so valuable that contractors will keep after the hard-to-get instrumentalists.

Teaching is an activity that is more under your own control. You can give instrument lessons either privately, at a local music school, or (with the necessary credentials) in the city's private or public schools. Chamber music coaching might be of interest not only to schools but also to amateur enthusiasts in the city. As of this writing, in fact, the Amateur Chamber Music Players organization, based in New York, helps fund the occasional coaching of amateur ensembles by qualified local professionals. Also, it is not unusual for an amateur group to pay a professional player to sit in with them as combined participant and coach. (More on this in chapter 19.)

A very meaningful activity is that of speaking to, and playing for, school-age listeners under the auspices of Young Audiences. Make your ensemble known to the administrators of that organization's chapter in your city. The appearances you make will be good for your group as well as for the musical awareness of young listeners who will eventually become your adult audience. In fact, you might not have to wait that long. Kids tell their parents about their school experiences, and some of the grownups may become part of your concert public.

Again in metropolitan centers, there is possible employment in or-chestras for resident or visiting opera, ballet, and "musical" perform-ances. Much of this work is either seasonal or targeted toward specific players who are in the select circles used for such work. However, the marketplace for some of these activities has changed radically over the years, and this leads me to the following plaintive digression.

When I was a freelance violist on radio in New York in the 1940s, there were programs that used one-on-a-part arrangements, with the micro-phones mixing the sound into a somewhat more ample effect. But there were also large bands and orchestras, figuring in programming as well as in yesteryear's radio and TV commercials. This is rarely so today. Instead, there are electronically generated sound tracks and small (read, inexpen-sive) vocal groups mouthing tawdry prose in token of live performance. Musical background of real consequence would be out of place in the hectic jumble of split-second images in today's television commercials.

The supplanting of live music is vividly demonstrated by the release of "sampler" CDs. There the sound of each instrument in the orchestra and of every voice, from bass to soprano, is presented in a succession of solo tracks. The buyer of the CD can copy the sounds into electronic audio machines, there to be manipulated in countless ways, altering the original acoustical spectrum as desired. What originates as "live" emerges as a truly canned end-product.

In exquisite paradox, some years ago the music education depart-ment of a prominent university issued an entire library of such sampler records. Earnest protests by the university's administration and faculty claim that the reengineered sounds derived from the sampler records are for composers' research use and do not help displace live musicians in commercial and theater work. This has been contradicted by evidence from the field.

Technicians (ranging from well-equipped professionals to rank ama-teurs operating with increasingly low-cost electronic machinery) con-coct collages from music in preexisting recordings and from electroni-cally generated tones. The impact of all this on a society that has already been trained to accept reproduced music in place of live performance is obvious. The erosion of live playing is not even noticed by a jaded public taste that has lost the ability to sense the presence of meaning in music.

Among the anomalies of today's music world: imported tape libraries, the source of cheaply produced background music for various purposes; the universal prevalence of radio broadcasts of recordings, usually supplied free by record companies eager to have their releases heard by the listening (and, it is hoped, the buying) public; television programs using background music mostly compiled from the aforementioned tape libraries or from electronically generated scoring.

One might think that alternative radio and television would be avenues of employment for musicians and other artists in this country. To a great degree, this is not the case. National Public Radio and the Public Broadcasting Service, provided with minimal funding by the Congress, have to solicit money feverishly from the listening and viewing public and from corporate sponsors and foundations. NPR broadcasts, like their commercial counterparts, feature recorded music all but exclusively. As for PBS, a great deal of programming comes from abroad, very often from England. No doubt such imports are used because they are generally of high quality and cost less than making new productions domestically. In many cases the production has benefited from government subsidies in the country of origin.

Television has a great deal to answer for in today's culture. It is potentially an instructive tool of great power. But it has instead devoted much of its time, capital, and energy to production of inane sitcoms, lowbrow news programs, mindless game shows, and commercial "messages" designed to represent the public as unthinking and the viewer as capable only of an attention span measured in microsecond duration. Our "educational" stations, along with their more estimable programming, also fund and disseminate such musical treasures as Yanni, André Rieu, and the minimally superior displays of The Three Tenors, to say nothing of endless resurrections of old Lawrence Welk programs.

There is, however, an informed viewer-listener contingent in our citizenry. Pressure from that corps, coupled with imaginative repertoire and presentation ideas from the musicians themselves, may yet carry the day with public station administrators, if not with commercial stations. The professional musician, amateur player, and the all-important music lover have to speak out against what is being done to the public taste by the media, the entertainment industry, the advertising agencies, and the corporate sponsors of meretricious programs and insultingly banal commercials. Our votes must speak for us as well. Politicians rarely think it important to support the arts. Candidates for prominent office even find it advisable not to stress their general smarts, lest they seem too far removed from what they judge to be the intellectual outlook of the voting public at large. And they gauge their public all too well. A populace accustomed from childhood to the stuff that is fed them by the mass media loses discernment not only for things artistic, but for serious thought in general. The potato that rises from the couch to enter the voting booth will not be suddenly smitten with mental acuity.

The young freelancer of today will not find all the same work opportunities we did. Yet surprising avenues can open. I have met, for example, an unusual mixed ensemble: flute, cello, piano, soprano, and tenor. They were moving from one cruise ship to another, spending two weeks on each before giving way to another group, so that passengers could hear fresh entertainment on each segment of the voyage. With the instrumentation I have described, the repertoire of the ensemble leaned heavily on some rather ingenious transcriptions. But these were clearly well trained performers and they took good care of the job they had assumed.

Another ensemble I came across, this time a string quartet, was spending ten months of the year as resident ensemble on a single large cruise ship. They played from thick loose-leaf books that contained not only standard quartet repertoire, but also published or self-made transcriptions of music (operatic, show-tunes, and others) adapted for string quartet. The ship had a full band to take care of ballroom dances and floor and stage shows, as well as a good piano-drums-bass trio to play for more intimate dancing. The string quartet played in the ship's restaurant at tea time, in the main reception area in early evening, and so on. Except for shore leave, there would seem to have been little distraction. With some concentration, it would be possible for an ensemble to rehearse its way through a good bit of repertoire during months at sea.

As these examples show, with versatility, energy, imagination, and tenacity, players today can still find musical ways to support themselves as they follow the yellow-brick road to Carnegie Hall.

Recording

For the relatively few superlative and/or celebrated musicians, royalties from record sales have been a significant source of income. To the greater mass of able performers, the recording has come to mean mechanized competition and the loss of employment opportunities. Moreover, recent declines in the sales of rock and pop records have depleted the coffers of the few record companies who were still willing to put some of their earnings from the pop side of their catalog into fresh recordings of "serious" music. Instead, the limited activity in that sector has focused more on the release of remastered versions of older recordings. The irony is that the recording, while displacing live music, has become an essential part of the performer's façade. The publicity blurb that does not list recording credits on one or more labels is likely to make the potential listener wonder whether the player or singer is worth hearing in the first place. As a result, the performer is under pressure to find a presence in recording in any way possible. Yet record companies are less willing than ever to invest their funds and their staff's energies in players who have not already established some success on the concert stage.

To break out of this vicious circle, more and more new ensembles have resorted to making their own recordings, then either peddling them to commercial firms for distribution or else releasing them on their own label. I hope (and I know that my esteemed colleague, cellist George Sopkin, joins me in this) that the young ensemble starting out on a career will attract enough attention that some established record company will feel inclined to risk an initial release of a CD by the group. This may very well not come the way of your ensemble. In that case, if your concert experience makes you feel very confident about your interpretations, you may take a flier and invest in a recording of your own. In that case, let us hope you can afford the use of a proper recording studio and the hiring of a competent producer-editor. If the first release sells encouragingly well, you might feel inclined to plow added capital into further issues.

You can always use that first recording as a kind of acoustic business card, to help build your concert activity. This last is the area where your work and effort really count. Resist the seductive lure of the microphone. An extremely knowledgeable musician has written that the performer really plays for himself, not for the listener. I disagree. Without the feedback from a live audience, you may never know whether all your work was worth it. Even in a sizeable concert hall, you are dealing with a one-to-one relationship, way up to the back rows in the balcony. You not only have to convince yourself, but also must move your hearers. Without that, everything else is window dressing: decorative but secondary.

With all this said, I confess that we in the music business are heading into uncharted waters in the months and years ahead, insofar as records are concerned. In the brave new Internet world, recorded music, whether serious or pop, is available for downloading to the personal computer— everywhere. The problems of protecting the rights of the performer, let alone those of the record companies, are not likely to be solved overnight. There is, of course, the ultimate irony that radio and commercial recording, which have played a major role in the erosion of widespread, live music-making in this country, are now faced with grave inroads on their own income-producing properties. It will be interesting to see how all this plays out.

The other side of the coin, however, is that recorded music will now have potential distribution of a breadth and rapidity that was never dreamed of heretofore. For the chamber ensemble, the temptation to get its sound out there to concert-presenters in every corner of the world will be irresistible. Keep in mind, though, that what everyone hears should represent the finest work your group can produce. It is still a good idea to focus on your rehearsal and performing, and have a technically equipped and trained studio staff take care of the recording process.

The young (and even not so young) ensemble should also keep abreast of emerging ways to make its recordings known and available. Firms offering marketing services tend to advertise in the trade press, some even offering guidance for attracting tax-exempt contributions. (See, especially, Chamber Music America's publication *The 2002 Taste of Chamber Music*, described in Suggested Readings.)

As readers will know by now, my concerns in this area come from experience, because our ensemble did its own recording for a long time. At first, we had to; then it became part of our way of life. I do not recommend it, for reasons earlier set forth in chapter 6. However, the context of the cultural world has changed significantly, so I may yet come around to new ways of thinking. (Also see Acosta in Suggested Readings.)

Reaching your public through word and print

Clearly, the performing musician's first responsibility is to play beautifully, musically, accurately. This applies to all, whether soloist or chamber ensemble member. An important secondary element in the musician's arsenal, however, is the ability to speak and write well. You do not have to be a latter-day Mark Twain or Charles Dickens, both of whom were masterful in speaking as well as writing. But you have to know how to get your ideas into clear, economical, well-organized English.

Speaking

Leonard Bernstein was extremely good at it: speaking about music in ways that helped his listeners understand what goes on in the art generally as well as in a specific composition. Some may (with a certain envy) consider his approach to have been that of a popularizer. He was, however, a well-trained and versatile musician; he knew what he was talking about and addressed his hearers without condescension. His methods worked.

There are some other prominent musicians with similar abilities. Every young musical aspirant would do well to study what Bernstein and his fellows have done and strive to emulate their approach to the listening audience. The old saw has it that music is a universal language. When you get beyond simple tunes, however, the language has endless complexities. Of course, the music can and must speak for itself. There is nothing wrong, though, with guiding the less initiated listener by means of some verbal "translations." Skillfully given, such guidance will encourage the hearer to return to repeated hearings of a composition, allowing the music truly to speak for itself and reveal its successive layers of meaning.

Be direct, relevant, and plain spoken, and do not rush. If you use a technical term, be sure you understand it and also make sure your listeners understand it before proceeding. A logical sequence of ideas in your talk will maintain clarity and help keep things moving; your audience will be able to follow without any major confusion. Provide time for a question period at the end of your remarks so that listeners can follow up on whatever details they have not yet grasped. The questions will in fact help you to see how you can improve subsequent talks.

By the way, a light touch will help, not stand-up comic style, but certainly not stuffy. Try not to bore your victims into a stupor.

You may choose to organize your thoughts by drawing up an outline or writing out a detailed script. It is important, though, that your actual delivery be either extemporaneous or, at most, carried through with the guidance of an outline. Only the most experienced speaker can read from a prepared text while still maintaining some sense of directness with the audience.

Since you are part of a small chamber ensemble, it stands to reason that the group should be on hand to play passages from the composition under discussion to illustrate the points made. And with all members present, it makes sense to have group participation in the speaking as well. Most likely, the several musicians will vary in their enthusiasm about this. Do not force things. Just try to have enough interaction by all the performers to give the audience a sense of the ensemble's active involvement in the program that is going to be played. At the very least, every player should look interested in what is said about the music. Ideally, there will have been prior agreement among all the players as to the points covered. If one detail or another needs further comment or modification, by all means let there be some back-and-forth between the players. Again, direct and easy is the way.

Having said that all in the ensemble should be involved in the proceedings, let me add that you should rely on them to be straight shooters. Here is a cautionary tale by way of illustration. We were on one of our periodic visits to the Music Center of the North Shore, in Winnetka, Illinois, and were giving the lecture-performance that was a regular part of our visit. On this occasion, the work in question was the Dvořák Piano Quintet.

In rehearsal, I would sometimes utter a cry of "Hurray" at the start of the coda in the first movement, for the music always sounded to me like a triumphant shout from the massed troops of a Czech regiment. Before we walked into the school's lecture hall, cellist Sopkin, my trusted colleague, told me that we should both liven up the occasion by giving the outcry together at the appropriate moment. As the coda approached, George and I exchanged conspiratorial glances. The first measure of the coda arrived, and I shouted a lusty "Hurray"—quite alone. As the audience wondered what was going on and as we continued on toward the double bar, George turned red with barely suppressed laughter. Watch out for your friends.

Not all talk about music need be attached to a concert. For one thing, music lovers making room in their schedule to hear a program of chamber music might prefer to have their music "straight" (without talk) so that they can hear as much music as possible during the allotted program time. In this context, well written program notes, short enough to be absorbed in the time before the performance starts and also during intermission, can carry the commentary end of things. Another possibility is to allow time for a preconcert talk, perhaps with a coffee break preceding the full-length program.

Or consider this approach: a short series of talks, illustrated with musical excerpts or entire movements played by your group, with recorded excerpts where necessary, as well as with projected pages of music, non-music visuals, and so on. An interesting theme could link the several sessions together. The more imaginative the theme, the more likely is it that you can gather audiences for the package. Here are a few suggestions that might jog your thinking, though I am sure you will have better ideas:

Exploiting the acoustic space of the chamber ensemble. The composer leads you to adjust your listening perspective to the ensemble, making you think it larger than it is.

The tonal palette of the small ensemble. Whether writing for homogeneous-toned string group or mixed ensemble, the composer makes you feel as though you are hearing the multicolored sound of an orchestra.

The heavy demands the small ensemble places on the composer. Making clear-cut musical ideas earn their keep, with consistent economy and without "padding." Compare chamber music and orchestral examples, using recorded excerpts as needed.

How changes in the structure of instruments have influenced chamber music. Discuss the evolving technology of wind instruments in the nineteenth and twentieth centuries. Show how older string instruments have been reengineered to suit the demands of public concerts and the larger auditorium. Choose music to show how composers have responded to these new conditions.

When your concert travels take you into foreign lands, it helps if you have some familiarity with the languages spoken in the countries you visit. Even a smattering may be better than nothing. If your command is limited to pidgin, of course, you will meet either with amused stares or with a bit of irritation on the part of your hearer. Try to have enough useful phrases in mind so that you will not have to stand with language guide in hand in order to ask simple questions.

At the very least, you should know how to ask the way to the railroad station, the nearest post office (where you will find telephone, telegraph, and Internet facilities as well as postage), a local restaurant, and such useful places as the American Express office, the police station, and the closest WC ("water closet")!

If you are quite confident about your command of the pronunciation, syntax, and vocabulary of the language of the country in which you are performing, you can venture to give any necessary oral comments at the concert in the local tongue. Since English is understood so widely in Europe, however, you might well decide it is better to be clear and comfortable in your own language than awkward in someone else's.

In the later 1960s and the '70s, our quartet did considerable speaking about the string quartet and mixed ensemble repertoire, whether in courses we gave at the University of Wisconsin–Milwaukee or in lecture-concert series we presented in Chicago. Throughout, we spoke either completely extemporaneously, or else with an outline of the points and examples we wanted to cover.

To carry this kind of assignment off without getting a bad case of foot-in-mouth, you have to know the music and the particular details you want to cover. When fielding questions from your audience, you must be able to move with the conversation. In a classroom situation, be especially careful to make your points clearly. Fuzzy thinking on your part will be reflected in equally obscure writing in the exam papers your students will produce. Even worse, you may notice disbelieving looks or poorly disguised exasperation on the faces of the more alert members of the class. A videotape of one or more of your classroom sessions will help your ensemble improve the organization and delivery of its presentations.

Writing

Unless you can delegate writing chores to paid or volunteer help, here are some of the things that will require attention. There will be business correspondence with your management to cover details of the season's itinerary, repertoire offerings, fees and billing, public relations, advertising copy, and so forth. Some of this may be covered in phone conversation. For the sake of good order, however, you will probably want to summarize the talk in writing, with hard copy or e-mail versions going to all interested parties.

If your management has a public relations officer or your ensemble has engaged a publicity agency on your own, information on your doings must be supplied so that complete and accurate data can be compiled and distributed. Your written memos to these representatives must be clear, and you must also be able to catch fuzzy writing and make sensible corrections in the copy you receive from them. You are better equipped to do this if you have kept up your own writing skills.

You may well have to correspond with managements abroad. Unless you are fluent in the language of the agency, stick to English. The recipient will either be able to read your communiqué as it stands or else will have it translated by someone local. Keep your writing as clear and logical as possible, to reduce the possibility of translation error. Misunderstandings will cost time, patience, and money. English has its own peculiarities, not always clear to non-English speakers. So make your letters as unambiguous as you can.

There will be letters to printers and other service providers. Especially with regard to printing, supply unmistakable instructions and good copy to begin with. Everything that follows will be easier. Editing, proofreading, amending, all will go smoothly and without agony. And keep in mind that a run of some hundreds or thousands of printed material that turns up with a fault that is your doing will be an expensive and immediate loss.

Foreign-language reviews present a two-fold challenge. In the first place, if the reviewer holds forth in flowery, quasi-poetic vein, you will have to be ingenious to keep your translation from sounding silly. A second and more critical pitfall: be sure you understand what the reviewer is saying. I once enjoyed translating a Dutch review because I was reading it as a favorable appraisal. Luckily, I reread it carefully and was saddened to realize that it was a pan, not a boost. I would have felt pretty foolish to have it misquoted in our publicity material. In fact, I chose not to quote it at all.

In your role as teacher, you will probably have to write academic reports. These may concern your own area or, if part of a committee assignment, perhaps other disciplines. Such reports can reach the general faculty and the school administration as well as outside parties. Try to organize and phrase the report for best impact.

Again on the teaching front, you will be grading your students and making written evaluations of their work. These can become part of the students' progress file and will inevitably reflect your own aims and attitudes about teaching. Some of your students may be applying for admission to summer workshop programs. Others will be completing their work with you and transferring to another school for further training. At a more advanced level, your students may be applying for jobs, competitions, or auditions that require references. In each case, your support and endorsement must be concise, to the point, and convincing; otherwise, it could be worse than no support at all.

Today, fax or e-mail will distribute information faster than ever, but speed cannot make up for sloppy or confused language and disjointed presentation of ideas. Your writing represents you, so make sure it does you justice.

19 ✧ TEACHING CHAMBER MUSIC

W hether for love or money, the members of a chamber ensemble will probably be doing some teaching. This can be on the elementary, secondary school, or collegiate level, or in a community music school. There will be teaching also in the context of workshops, especially in the summer months, or of private lessons. My own teaching experience (outside of classroom courses) has included both that of violin and chamber music. My focus here, though, is on effective chamber music coaching.

Let me emphasize, again, that a prime responsibility of the coach is to gauge the readiness of the ensemble to make further progress on its own. The point when that state is reached will vary with the age, musical experience, and specific aims (that is, personal enjoyment, professional preparedness, and so on) of the groups concerned. Even in their academic coursework, some ensembles will make faster headway than others. The coach must know how to recognize achievement, move gradually into an advisory role, and allow the ensemble to assert an independent musical personality. For this evolution to take place, the coach must have ears, eyes, and discernment. No guide can spell everything out.

The successful teacher of an instrument or voice helps the student by observing what *that* particular person (note the emphasis) does while performing. Similarly, the coach of a chamber ensemble needs to focus on the playing of that specific group, admittedly a rather more complex target. You are absorbing information about the group as a whole, and at the same time the playing of each individual member. That takes some doing.

In your own rehearsing, you are inside your group, taking an active role in the realization of the music. As an experienced player, you are aware of how you are playing your own part, and also of the way your colleagues are handling theirs. There will be active criticism of one another's approach to the musical passage.

When you coach, you might join in briefly for a segment of the work to demonstrate the point you are trying to make. Mostly, though, you will watch the ensemble from outside. In effect, you are a member of a hypothetical audience. But you are a very experienced listener, one who knows the sound and part-writing of the given composition intimately. You do not have to bury your nose in the score to follow the action. If you are knowledgeable enough, in fact, you may be able to make worthwhile suggestions to the ensemble after only a couple of hearings even of a work that is new to you.

When I coach, I want to have a score at hand, even if it is music that I have performed frequently. As I listen, I can scribble rapid signs and memos to myself in the score to help me remember the points I want to discuss with the players. Otherwise, if I have had the group play an extended passage, section, or entire movement, I find that one or another detail will escape my memory. Even more important, without an indicative line, arrow, or short verbal entry in the score, I might forget which player(s) to prompt in a given measure or phrase. My jottings help make my coaching more effective.

What are your coaching targets? You will certainly want to zero in on poor intonation, whether of the group as a whole, or of one or more of its players. You may choose to resort to that cruelest of all tests, the slow playing of scales in unison-and-octave, so the players can hone their perceptions of pitch and intervals. Then follow up with slow playing of the problematic passage in the composition itself.

You have to strike a balance between your insistence on a single facet of the music-making and the endurance of the players. Remember that they may start out by hearing Heifetz, Primrose, or Rampal with their mind's ear, rather than the sounds they are actually making. To harp relentlessly on even so obvious a flaw as poor intonation for too long in a given lesson, let alone during an entire semester, will make your victims grow resentful and seek a different coach. Even worse, they may lose all confidence, give up, and fade away, perhaps even losing their love of music.

Besides, there is no need to focus on just one problem; there will be enough to go around. Does the pianist in an ensemble act as though the composition is for p-i-a-n-o with accompaniment? You may find that the player has set the lid of the grand on the long stick. With the lid that high, only the more skilled pianist can keep from outweighing the combined sounds of the other instruments in the group. Try the short stick, or just insert a book under the lid. Even then, make sure the pianist actually listens to the rest of the ensemble. Go back to a higher lid when the player develops enough discernment.

In balancing the parts, check constantly that the "subordinate" voices (something of a misnomer in good chamber music), such as the second violin and viola in the string quartet, project suitably when the music so requires. Pay special attention in this regard to the second violin. The viola has a more individual voice in the quartet family. Also, a competent violist will not be bashful, but will sometimes go overboard in a determination to make that part heard. The second violin, on the other hand, is already in the tonal aura of the first violin and is in any case often playing a part that supports the higher-ranging melody of the lead voice. Support does not always mean deference. For example, when two voices, whether the violins or any other pairing in the ensemble, move in parallel octaves, the lower line actually "supports" by slightly dominating in the balance. The upper voice here provides a sonorous edge to the ribbon of tone. In general, the second violin has to be the friend of every other voice in the group. And it should be possible for friends to converse on an equal footing.

Each voice in a chamber ensemble must recognize when that musical strand should stand out against the rest of the family. In a slow movement, the spotlight ordinarily moves tranquilly from one instrument to the other, so the transition between support and solo roles for each voice is a fairly sedate matter. In rapid movements, however, each player must be ready to catch the "hot potato" and burst forth in the moment of solo splendor before yielding to the next in line.

If you see any players in a string group drawing the bow constantly near the fingerboard, show them how their lines will emerge more strongly when played in the firmer part of the string, closer to the bridge. Also, be sure the musicians do not stay only in the lower half of the bow, but use the upper half as well, right up to the tip. That does not mean that the whole bow has to be used constantly, just because all of it is there. Swishing too much of the bow too quickly across the string will produce glassy, insubstantial tone. A slower stroke, firmly and sensitively applied, with the bow not excessively tilted in the hand and with the ribbon of hair resting comfortably on the string, makes for a more robust, more intense sound than does the slashing stroke. This will apply also to the playing of chords; after a momentarily energetic start of the stroke to get the strings vibrating, the speed of bow can be reduced so that the chord can resonate freely for the remainder of its duration.

Loud and rapid passages of detached sixteenth-notes often sound more convincing if they are played on the string, boldly rubbing with the upper part of the bow. The same music can seem flighty and lacking in substance if the lines are played with a hopping stroke lower in the bow. This is especially true if the bounce is tried at an unsuitable spot along the length of the bow. The frequency of the stroke will be at odds with the physics of the bow, and the player's struggle for control will result in unpredictable rhythm.

Technical pointers such as these have analogies in keyboard and wind instrument playing as well. In a woodwind quintet, each of the five voices has its own, unmistakable timbre, with none of the duplication of tone that exists between the two violins in the string quartet. Focus on the sound of the flute, oboe, clarinet, bassoon, and French horn, and you will agree: every line stands out. The problem here is to achieve the blend of sonorities that is often required.

The question of musical temperament comes to the fore in a woodwind quintet, as in any ensemble. I recall coaching a group in the quintet by Jean Françaix, a piece that has many touches of Gallic wit and humor. The ensemble was taking too serious a view of the music, and certainly so in the case of the oboist, a lovely young woman who was missing all the fun. I had to resort to clowning around and almost to cartwheels in order to evoke the necessary verve from the players. If you dislike what you hear from a group, you must not just sit there and take it. Do everything you can to awaken the players to the opportunities in the music.

Some pieces are more dangerous than others. One case in point is Mozart's *A Musical Joke*, for string quartet and two horns, K. 522: a late work (1787), the kind of caper that only a consummate master could have devised, full of sophisticated gibes and false turns in its writing. The ca-

cophonous chords at the very end of the piece, of course, are overt pande-
monium. For the rest, the fun is most fully appreciated by the listener
who has heard a lot of music that, unlike the *Joke*, has been properly
organized—the way Mozart himself ordinarily writes.

There is a temptation to gear the performance to the kind of raucous
clowning suggested by those closing chords. That would be a mistake, for
it would imply that the players themselves know how foolish a spectacle
they are making of themselves. The performance must be delivered with
proper seriousness and technical polish, letting the music itself score all
the points of its "in" humor.

I once had the dubious pleasure of watching a performance in which
the horn players brought out a deck of cards to while away the moments
during the first violin's lyricizing and mock-bravura cadenza in the third
movement (where the horns are *tacet*). Worse still was having to coach a
student group whose first violin dutifully played every note with solemn
accuracy, but who seemed by nature incapable of recognizing the musical
gaffes imposed upon him by the composer. Nothing I could say was able to
put that glint of true comprehension into the eye (and playing) of this hap-
less fiddler. We all survived, but I think it would have taken nothing short
of neurosurgery to awaken the fellow to all the subtleties of Mozart's jest.

When you coach an ensemble of mixed instrumentation, you may
not know the techniques of one or more of the instruments. Have the
player ask his or her own teacher for help with a troublesome passage.
However, you yourself must provide interpretative guidance, no matter
what the instrumentation. Be sure the players reveal the shifting center of
interest in the web of voices as the piece unfolds. Insist that the leader of
the moment knows how to take over, to give the unobtrusive but clear
signal that indicates the beginning and end of a phrase. Have the players
recognize that beginnings and endings come not only at the start and finish of a movement, but at many points en route.

Already in the course of rehearsing, and certainly after several performances of a work, signaling can be so subtle that it will mostly be
undetectable by the audience. In fact, coordination is effected as much by
hearing as by sight. The connection between voices and the succession
of elements in the music is gauged on the run, by alert listening.

Have the players experiment with choice of tempo, not only in the
overall speed of the movement, but in the slight changes in pace that may

be called for at some points in the music. These changes may be specified by the composer, either for an entire section or—by indications such as accelerando or calando—for smaller areas in the musical flow. Others are left to the taste and judgment of the performer, governed by inference from the musical context. Insist on that blending of inflection, dynamics, and rubato in the performance of melodic fragments and phrases that makes the music come alive. In our spoken language, we use rise and fall in pitch-level, closely spaced shifts in loudness, and equally fine-grained slowing and speedups to make plain the thoughts we are expressing. These fluctuations are all the more important in instrumental music, where there is no text to govern our response to the sounds we hear.

Some contemporary composers try to control the interpretation of their work by loading the page with signs and words of instruction. It is not possible, however, to give each fragment of music its own performance footnote. Partly in recognition of that fact, composers have produced music assembled entirely from electronically generated sounds. Here, the performance and its highly detailed controls are built into the taped rendition of the composition from the very outset. For all I know, it will yet become possible to incorporate as well some of the variability that is characteristic of performances by live, flesh-and-blood players.

I would think, however, that the human brain, at least for the present, is still capable of more subtlety than is available to the sound-generator and the computer. It is up to the performer to make his musical decisions seem logical to the listener. That is where you, the coach, can earn some of your keep. Let the ensemble or its individual members know when they do something unconvincing in the treatment of the musical lines and fabric. I often find myself stopping the group by saying, "You can't do that!" I know, however, that I will have to follow up by showing them *why* they cannot.

The coach may interrupt the players repeatedly during a short span of the movement to discuss details while they are still fresh in the players' attention. They may then experiment a bit with the specific spot in the music, often backtracking to try the passage again in the larger context of the writing. I know that if I were at the receiving end of these interruptions, I might well find them aggravating. Try to be lively and imaginative in the manner and pacing of your discussion. Relieve any stop-and-go episodes in the coaching session by giving the ensemble an early chance to play longer segments of the work.

Whether in the space of the single coaching period or over several sessions, the group must have opportunity to play the entire movement, not just once, but several times. These should not be treadmill repetitions, but opportunities to view and react to the music as a whole. The players should imagine viewing the topography and contours of the movement from a low-flying airplane. They are close enough to recognize musical ideas and details and to trace the avenues and byways in the composer's thinking, but at the same time distant enough to notice the relationships in the overall span of the composition.

It takes time and practice before the player learns to listen, in small detail and in comprehensive view, to what the ensemble is doing with a composition. Even then, it is helpful for the group to be able to hear itself from outside. The tape recorder is a useful tool, both for the coach and the ensemble. Have the group listen with you to a playback of a passage, section, or entire movement. Discuss your collective impressions about balance, conversation between the voices, dynamic gradations, phrasing and inflection, and the handling of the structure and unfolding of ideas in the course of the movement. The players will see where musical repairs are needed.

A tape recorder is equally useful in the rehearsals of a long-standing group. Musical arguments can be resolved, or at least more precisely defined, by hearing on tape what all the fighting is about. A sneaky suggestion: try to tape some of the rehearsal talk that surrounds the passage in question. Listening to verbal fisticuffs is a chastening and enlightening experience for all but the most pig-headed.

Another helpful teaching tool for the ensemble is the video camera. A visual recording will show the players if they are watching each other alertly. They will also see that they can often "look with their ears." You can reinforce this point by having the ensemble memorize a short passage and play it with their eyes closed. Also, have them play from the music, but with their backs to each other. In fact, this unaccustomed seating may make them play with more sensitivity to each other than usual.

A video playback of the group in action will also reveal with cruel clarity whether any of the players are "hamming things up." Histrionics and flamboyant gestures will stick out. The music itself should provide the dramatics in the performance.

The most important teaching tool for the chamber music coach, however, is unremitting alertness and observation. If a player in the ensemble does scant justice to the shape of a phrase, show him how to give it a sense of direction, how to make it a cogent melodic statement. You can use verbal imagery, visual analogy, literary allusion, body English, or any other technique to explain what you are after. The most direct and effective path is to sing or play the line, to demonstrate how it should sound. If any in the ensemble disagree with your view, so much the better. Either your idea will prevail, compromise will be reached, or you may come around to the opposing concept. There is no rule against the coach yielding on an issue, or even learning from his students.

When dealing with amateur players, you will be surprised or nonplused at the range of abilities you encounter. Some ensembles comprise quite competent players who have met regularly over a period of years, even presenting themselves in concert. Other amateur groups make up in enthusiasm for what they lack in technique or familiarity with the literature. They may, however, know too much about the repertoire, flitting from one work to another in the course of their sessions together. Whatever the proficiency level of the groups you work with, old or young, amateur or would-be professional, or ensembles assembled by their school faculty, have them deal with music they can manage. Adult players especially tend to have appetites that are beyond their musical digestions.

For the grown-ups, early Haydn or youthful Mozart will give them something to chew on before moving on to the demands of the mature works. If the players will hold still for it, carefully selected movements from these later compositions will serve as an introduction to the complexities of Haydn's music from the 1770s and later, or of Mozart's writing from the last decade of his life. You may not be able to restrain the adventuresome leanings of your enthusiasts. So your clients will probably be regaling you with their renditions of entire, demanding works, right up to late Beethoven and far beyond. Coach with humor and a light touch, getting the group to focus on the musicality of their playing; you will see progress, no matter how slow.

A sense of humor will also go a long way in your work with younger students. For truly inexperienced players in their early years of study, you might want to explore chamber music method and etude books issued by various publishers. My own leaning would again be toward the earlier, technically less demanding output of the Viennese and Parisian masters of the middle third of the eighteenth century. I would also recommend looking through Luigi Boccherini's work for suitable material. This music will be relatively easy to handle, still challenging enough to encourage the learning of good ensemble habits, and marked with a musical intelligence that stimulates the thought processes of the performers.

In writing this music, the composers were aiming at a broad public, amateur as well as professional. Toward the later eighteenth century and on into the nineteenth, composers of the time (and their publishers) still looked toward an encouraging sale of music among the ranks of amateur players. But the writing was moving inexorably into a technical and musical complexity that could be properly handled only by trained professional players or by well-schooled and dedicated amateurs.

To close, I turn again to the thought that you, the coach, might be able to learn something from your students. By seeking and finding the most effective way of explaining a technical or musical detail to one student, the teacher adds to his own ability to educate all his students. Work hard at retaining your sense of curiosity. Without that interest, teaching is not much fun.

20 ✧ THE BUSINESS SIDE OF ENSEMBLE LIFE

Once during the audition sessions I shared with Sasha Schneider at the Eastman School in the late 1980s and early 1990s, I was indiscreet enough to describe life in a quartet as a "job." Schneider characteristically took umbrage at the word, though I think he must have been well aware of everything that surrounds the core responsibility—consummate musical performance—of a chamber ensemble.

The Budapest Quartet, of which Schneider was so long a member, was no doubt able to delegate much of the nonmusical aspect of its activity to others. That was not the habit in our group, though I think that, especially in our later years, we should have sought relief from much of the peripheral detail. Out of sheer economic necessity, the typical younger ensemble will have to handle much of the joblike side of its career. And to the extent that the players can delegate some concerns, they must still be able to keep a knowing eye on how such matters are being treated. I describe below the various responsibilities the players must either undertake or else oversee in the work of others. There is more to chamber music than practicing your part, rehearsing, and giving concerts.

Keeping accounts

If you are not now comfortable with balancing your checkbook, you will quickly learn to be. Unless your group is busy or affluent enough to have an accountant, the ensemble will have to keep its own financial records in order. A checking account for the partnership (and the ensemble is indeed a partnership) must be maintained. Concert fees will be coming in, either directly from the client or—more usually—via the office of the ensemble's management. The fees, after deduction of commissions and expenses, must be shared among the ensemble members by means of checks paid out from the partnership account.

There will be bills for supplies and services: office needs, travel charges, printing of fliers, duplication of press books, and so on. All this again goes through the checking account. A careful, month-by-month verification of the checkbook arithmetic must be maintained. It is very painful to have to trace through a long backlog of check entries to find an error that should have been caught early on.

Unless the affairs of the ensemble have grown to an impressive size, elaborate bookkeeping may not be necessary. However, careful and consistent record keeping of income and outgo is essential. In these days of the computer and its helpful software, the task of organizing the details of an ensemble's finances is easier than it used to be, though still time-consuming. Yet, to keep track, year in and year out, is all the more important. (See Dauer in Suggested Readings.)

Partnership tax return

Each year, a partnership tax return must be filed. That return is only as good as the records on which it is based. The partnership return for an ensemble will ordinarily not be a complicated document to prepare, so long as the financial information concerning the group's activity during the tax year has been clearly organized. You will probably have a tax adviser helping with the return, but it is up to you to supply the detailed information on which the return is based. Among other things, the return will list the ensemble's expenses and the amount that has been paid out to each member. The latter information figures importantly in the preparation of each individual's tax returns, federal and state, for the year in question. Again, this underscores the crucial need for accuracy, beginning with the ensemble's checkbook and going on from there.

Contact with clients

No matter how you secure your engagements, whether through management or by your own efforts, the concert itself is not the end of the matter. In the course of your visit to the locale of the event, you will have made the acquaintance of one or more members of the concert committee or other supporters of the chamber music series. It is important to extend that acquaintance by follow-up correspondence or even an occasional phone call. These contacts should not be treated as hard-sell overtures. On the contrary, they are best understood as informal updates on your own doings and that of your ensemble. If the letter or call reveals any special interest in some facet of your activity, the sending of a more detailed report on that aspect may be in order. The aim is to keep your ensemble fresh in the memory of the concert sponsors, to foster their responsive attitude toward eventual reengagement proposals from your management.

If the ensemble has been giving a fair number of concerts on the road, the business of maintaining connections with the respective sponsors will require time. Once again, the responsibility for such contacts should devolve on ensemble members who have the necessary way with words, both written and spoken. The particular acquaintance may exist between a specific member of the group and a corresponding member of the chamber music society. In that case, of course, the ensemble player in question should follow up in maintaining the contact.

If this sounds like an overlap with management, it may well be. A chamber group that was on the roster of one of America's larger concert managements found that it was obtaining more engagements through its own efforts than were being booked by the management. Since the agency insisted on taking its full commission on all engagements, as was its contractual right, ensemble and management came to the parting of the ways. I do not know whether the group reached a more satisfactory understanding with the management to which it transferred its business. But this is certainly a worthwhile talking point when negotiating arrangements with a prospective musical representative. The management will very likely resist compromise, saying that it is difficult to apportion accurately the efforts that resulted in a specific engagement. At least, however, you will put the agency on notice that it must demonstrate its effectiveness by landing concerts for the ensemble. (See Scales in Suggested Readings.)

The press book

I mentioned the cost of duplicating press books. Before such a document can be duplicated, it must be written. Here are the kinds of information that enter into the ensemble's image-in-print. You will want to adjust the focus on each area in light of your own ensemble's activities. Try, however, for as inclusive coverage as you can.

First, there must be a brief history of the ensemble itself. This would describe, for example, when and where it began; where it has moved in the course of its existence; and whether it is currently in residence in a community arts program or in a school, college, or university.

Second, each member of the group gets a short but reasonably detailed biographical sketch. This should cover training, including names of major teachers; performance experience (solo appearances, orchestral affiliations, and so on); recordings and prior ensemble memberships, if any; and especially in the case of string players, mention of any highly pedigreed instruments used by the members.

Third, provide excerpts from reviews of the ensemble, both from its native land and abroad. These can be brief but should be as complete as possible in themselves. Too many insertions of ellipses, those dots indicating omissions from quoted material (". . . ."), may make the reader wonder whether some damaging or qualifying comments had to be omitted. Draw your excerpts as much as you can from publications in major cities. The ways of the world being what they are, your readers will tend to give greatest credence to views expressed by big-city critics.

Fourth, make mention of noteworthy events in the ensemble's immediate future. Relevant information would include your local concert series, tour plans, commissioned works in progress, and particularly interesting recording plans.

Fifth, provide a listing of the labels under which your ensemble's recordings have been issued. The labels can be either those of commercial record companies or that of your own, self-produced releases.

Sixth, show representative ensemble program listings from recent seasons and—to indicate the scope of the group's musical interests—some of your repertoire list. Since your press book may also include the musical menu your group is offering for the forthcoming concert season, there is some danger that a concert sponsor will want to doctor your program suggestions by bringing in a work from your larger repertoire list. Consult with your colleagues and your management as to whether you want to risk such complication and, if so, how to handle special requests.

Compiling a press book is a time-consuming matter, and the burden should not fall exclusively on the shoulders of any one member of the ensemble. Translation of foreign-language reviews is naturally assigned to those players with the required linguistic abilities. Composition of the overall text should fall to those members able to write smoothly and succinctly.

Editing the text and designing the layout so that the finished document is attractive and legible can be handled in-house if any of you have the needed skill. In the entire process, you will no doubt be consulting with your management. For that matter, they may want to handle the whole assignment. In such case there might be a charge to the ensemble, but it could well be worth paying if the group can afford it. You would be relieved of this nonmusical task, and the end result might be a more polished product. Whether you or your management assumes the job, there should be consultation between you as the task progresses. And whichever route you choose, the manuscript must of course be completed in time to be of use in the booking calendar.

Obviously, you should not print more copies of the press book than are needed for the next season. You will have to update the information about your ensemble each year. Here again, the computer and word-processing software make it possible to freshen and rearrange the dope sheet more comfortably than in the past. Moreover, the typefaces and other formatting niceties available on computer enable the discerning eye to produce a document that reads easily. Do not run wild with the mixture of fonts, italics, general page layout, and so forth. Simpler is clearer.

Find an attractive, reasonably priced press book binding that will allow for yearly updating. With adroit layout of copy, you should be able to keep on hand a longer-term supply of pages carrying information that does not need yearly change. New data pages can then be printed to supplement or replace pages in the finished assembly, ready for binding into the revised book.

Program notes

If your program notes are any good, they can be habit-forming for your audience, so start them only if you intend to continue them over the long haul. For your concerts on the road, the local sponsors will have their own views about the need for printed notes, and in many cases may have them supplied by a local musician, amateur or pro. Some managements will ask their ensembles to provide notes that can then be offered to the clients who engage the groups. Or again, a given management might prefer to have program notes come from the agency's own larder of such material. In that case, I hope your group will insist on seeing the text of the management's notes before they are associated with your concerts, just so you can check accuracy of detail, writing style, and musical outlook.

There is some merit, incidentally, in having program notes come from within the ensemble proper. That way, the note will more likely reflect the perspectives of the ensemble's own approach to the music at hand. The performance will speak for itself, and the printed commentary will perhaps illuminate the group's playing or at least not contradict it.

Notes about the compositions to be heard can be useful to your home-city audience if clearly written, offering interesting sidelights about the composer, the place of the given work in his output, and the structure and temper of the piece. Brevity is in order. Unless they are to be read at leisure after the concert, the notes must be readily comprehended between the time the listeners take their seats in the hall and the performance begins. Avoid overly poetic style and remember that you are writing a note, not an article.

Concise and helpful though they may be, notes are a definite burden when added to your essential responsibilities in the ensemble: rehearsing intelligently and performing as beautifully as you know how. I wrote program notes for our Chicago series during all the last nineteen years of my stay in the quartet. There were never fewer than seven programs to be thus equipped each year. Even allowing for the recurrence of some works over the seasons, years of such notes make for a lot of writing. In those days before the word processor had become widely available, I had the use of an electric typewriter, but the task of composing new notes, revising or adapting old ones, and typing out a fair copy for the printer was a constant chore. The moral: even with the facilities of a word processor, undertake the project of constructing program notes on a steady basis in the knowledge that you are adding yet another continuous thread to your already busy schedule.

If you decide to provide notes, spread the workload. Each note will reflect the writing style and musical insight of its individual author, and the differences in approach can make for lively reading for your audience. And who knows, there may be even livelier discussions between the perpetrators in the aftermath.

Travel arrangements

We will assume that your ensemble, sooner or later in its career, will be giving concerts on the road, both at home and abroad. "Home," here in America, is almost as big as abroad, so you will still be traveling considerable distances. Consecutive concert engagements rarely arrange themselves along straight lines, free of backing and filling. Moreover, with airline flight patterns tending to move through the hub cities of the given company, you may fly a crooked path even to get from one city to the next. (From my present home city of Rochester, New York, I often fly west to Chicago, an airline hub, in order to change to a transatlantic flight eastward-bound to Europe. Go figure.)

Coordinating airline schedules, railroad timetables, and car rentals, both here and abroad, takes doing. You may be able to delegate this work to travel agents. With airline commissions to those agents constantly declining, however, you will be fortunate if your agent can afford to spend much time puzzling over your travel problems. It is likely, though, that some or all in your ensemble will be traveling together, so the grouped voyage requirements will improve the earnings picture for your agent and, who knows, even make it possible to extract a specially discounted fare if the size of the ensemble and the extent of the itinerary are large enough.

In any event, you will have to be knowledgeable about travel to have any hope of double-checking on the results of your agent's research. With international air and rail schedules and fare information now available on the Internet, you will have an easier time of collecting data now than even a few years ago. You must be Internet savvy, however, and also willing to spend time assessing the best solutions to your travel needs.

If you find a conscientious and willing agency, by all means let them handle your travel chores. Even with a bit of checkup work, you will still save a lot of time to devote to your musical pursuits. If, as a group, you decide to keep much of the travel work in-house, see if any member has a particular flair for the assignment and the time and willingness to take it on.

The local concert sponsor will often suggest a particular hotel, whether for its location near the concert hall, its favorable rate, or both. Here again, with so many hotel chains offering directories as well as on-line information, you can try making your own arrangements or at least verify that the recommended choice is as good a deal as the competition might offer. When contacting a hotel yourself, be sure to ask the management whether a group rate is available.

I have to point out again that doubling up in hotel rooms is not worth it. You will save a few dollars but will not have the relief from ensemble togetherness that a solitary night's slumber provides. It is the kind of safety valve that helps assure the longevity of the group.

Travel by car

Travel by automobile is somewhat more practical in Europe, where countries as well as cities are closer together, than in North America. America and Canada are so spread out that making concert connections by car is practical only for cities clustered in a relatively small area. Even then, the vagaries of weather can make the roads hazardous.

Road conditions can be variable in Europe as well, and there is a further complicating factor: speed. Drive on the *autoroute* in France, the *autobahn* in Germany, or the *autostrada* in Italy and you will see what I mean. You may be driving eighty miles an hour, but you will still see cars passing you and disappearing into the distance (can they really be jet-propelled?). You have to be used to it, as well as to other driving techniques that may be unfamiliar.

I do not recall feeling as unsettled on the roads in Britain, but I have driven less often there than on the Continent. Besides, the experience of driving on the left, whether in a British car or—even more—in an American-style car with the driver in the left front seat is something else that takes getting used to. (What *is* that oncoming driver doing in your lane?) I confess here, for those who read of our auto escapades in Europe in previous chapters, that our general manager in Europe eventually insisted that we make our way from one city to the next by train or plane, rather than rely on the vagaries of car travel. With a network of rail-lines, much fuller daily schedules than here, and increasing numbers of high-speed routes, the alternatives to car travel in Europe for the ensemble certainly deserve serious consideration.

As an additional note, let me point out that on European highways, service-stop restaurants offer wine and beer. I have been stopped at a French checkpoint for a routine breatholator test for sobriety, but this was on the road into a small city where motor speeds are moderate. What procedure is followed by the patrols on high-speed highways, I cannot say. Perhaps there is a logical explanation somewhere.

Self-management

You can try self-management but will probably find that it does not work. If your ensemble has a residency at a state-funded university campus, it could happen that your contractual duties include performing at various branches around the state. In that case, your concert clientele is a known factor. They have probably been primed to expect visits from you. The hard work has already been done for you, and you need only to agree on the date for your visit, settle the choice of program, and provide photos and data for the publicity surrounding the event. It might well be that even these details are taken care of by the public relations office of your home campus.

If you are resident in a private institution, or if your group is free-lance, then you really have your chores cut out for you. Concert clients in the various cities of your own state, let alone those of other states and regions, are probably not known to you, nor are you necessarily a household word with them. Should you already be known among the initiated, you have probably already set up shop with a known chamber music concert management.

You might think it possible to get hold of a useful mailing list and write beguiling letters to the names therein. Consider, however, that any such list would most likely have been built up through years of diligent activity by a management office. That kind of information would certainly be regarded and protected as valuable commercial property. Even if you somehow obtained such a list and sent out letters on your own, the potential response would probably be very small or nonexistent.

An ensemble may have become widely known through its touring under a known management. The contract ends, or there is a split between musicians and management for some reason. In that case, the ensemble might have some success in soliciting reengagements from local concert sponsors for whom they have played in the past, as well as in finding places on the concert schedules of new prospects. Keep in mind, however, that a chamber concert season consists of more than one performance. To fill out its calendar, the local society will probably deal with a management that can offer at least several chamber ensembles for the season's events. By the time those groups have been plugged into the schedule, it will not be easy to make room for the ensemble that is peddling its services on its own.

Then there is the question of the time and energy involved in selling an ensemble to concert clients. There are enough extramusical chores for the members of an ensemble to go around. Thus, if one member of the group seems dedicated and skilled enough to take on a management role without special commission or recompense, well and good. There is still no guarantee of success, but it can be tried for a season to see what the outcome might be. If the spouse of one or another member has had prior experience in an active concert management, that person is another possible candidate for the in-house managerial assignment. In such case, however, there should definitely be some understanding about payment for services. The dedication, time, and energy must not go unrewarded.

Commercial management

Either you have tried self-management without any luck, or you have decided to seek commercial management to begin with. "Seek" is the operative word. Let us imagine you and your colleagues know that a specific management has several well-regarded chamber ensembles on its list and that, season in and out, it lands a satisfying number of engagements for those groups. You approach the management and ask to be added to its stable of ensembles.

The response will be positive only under certain conditions. First, your group must already have some clout. Perhaps an influential musical figure believes in the potential of the ensemble enough to speak up on your behalf. Maybe your bunch has won a prominent competition or received enthusiastic acclaim from one or more critics from major newspapers and magazines. Under these happy circumstances, the management will at least be receptive to your overtures. In fact, it may have a staff member attend a concert of yours, followed by an invitation to visit the management for discussions.

The officers of the agency will then have to consider how your group fits into their overall offering. Perhaps they are known as representing outstanding string quartets. In that event, they could be interested in putting yet another string foursome on their list. More likely, the management will have a varied roster of small ensembles, with space for another piano trio, woodwind quintet, or brass group. There is also the kind of bureau that offers a broader range, including small orchestras, conductors, singers, pianists, and other soloists, and that may be thinking of starting, or adding to, its own chamber music branch.

If the management officers are honest with you and themselves, they have to feel confident they can sell your group to their clients. You will be competing for attention not only with the other musicians offered by that agency but with those who are being marketed by other managements. You will not be pleased if you find you have given the agency the exclusive right to represent you, only to discover that you serve simply as window-dressing in their advertisements. You need concerts, not the glory of the association.

Besides, the relationship is going to cost you. Brochures, press books, your share of the cost of the agency's advertisements and other public relations avenues, these and other costs are up front. In the case of larger agencies, there may even be a call for some retainer fees until your sales results outweigh the need for such infusions. Be on the lookout for such a request and resist it as strenuously as you can. The management must earn its keep by selling concerts, not rest on its retainer.

Each concert sold brings attendant costs in its train. There is a commission to the agency on each concert fee. From my experience, this is typically twenty percent off the top, though some high-fee, in-demand artists may possibly be able to negotiate a lower figure. Then there are shipping costs for distribution of publicity material to each concert sponsor, and so on. And, to figure your net income from each concert, you will have to allocate the relevant share of your travel and living expenses to the event. Remember, incidentally, that a portion of your instrument maintenance costs and wardrobe upkeep must also be assigned to each concert if you are to get a realistic picture of the event's profitability.

It might well be, moreover, that your management will insist on facilitating their sales effort by offering your group at a reduced concert figure in your first couple of seasons with them. You can entertain such an idea at your discretion. If your ensemble is well received, your voice in future negotiations with the agency should and will be stronger. Be sure, however, that your initial agreement with the management provides for setting your asking fee at a proper level by a specific date.

In your first meetings with the management, you may be offered what they call their standard agreement. You will want to be sure that the "standard" is fair to all concerned. As with any contract, review the agreement with your lawyer before you and your colleagues sign up. Be sure your lawyer is competent in the field of contract law, and even more specifically, of entertainment contracts. Expertise can be very specialized these days; your intended management is well aware of this, and so should you be.

If the management in question is one that offers its clients groups not only from the home country but also from abroad, there is another point to consider. Try to find out whether the agency is offering the foreign teams at specially low rates. If so, unless your group has a reliably strong following among concert societies, you will either have to be willing to discount your listed fee or must expect that you will be losing engagements to your stable-mates from abroad.

A last but not inconsiderable point: most concert societies are prompt in paying the management the fee for your engagement. Some managements, however, have the distressing habit of delaying the transmission of the ensemble's share of the fee to the hot little hands of the players themselves. Your group, then, will have paid out the expenses—travel and other—incurred for your tour; meanwhile, your management will be earning interest on the money they are slow to send on to you. It should be possible to include the matter of the timely transmission of fees, with a specified deadline of payment, in your contract with the agency.

Musical America's annual *International Directory of the Performing Arts* lists the various concert managements in America, coast to coast (it no longer seems absolutely necessary for agencies to cluster in New York in order to be effective). Judging from the various offices' advertisements as well as their own reports in the directory, it would seem there are more than thirty agencies that include chamber music ensembles among their offerings. I cannot presume to recommend some of these firms over others. The field is too fluid and must be judged under the conditions that pertain when your particular ensemble goes shopping for representation. You should read the reports and sound out the opinions of your musician colleagues and any concert-buyers of your acquaintance. Narrow the field of possible managements, consult with them (preferably in face-to-face meetings), and try to determine which agency best fits the current status and potential prospects of your group.

In negotiating an agreement with a given agency, ask for a reasonably short tryout period, during which you can judge the effectiveness of the relationship. After a couple of seasons, you should be able to decide whether you are being well served. If not, you must then be free to transfer to another agency. Your management should not only be staffed by knowledgeable professionals, but should also not have so many ensembles of your type that your group gets lost in the shuffle.

Web sites

You probably know that more than one chamber ensemble now has its own Web site on the Internet, or else figures in the Web site of its management. Keep current with this kind of exposure. It is widely accessible and a good way of making up-to-the-minute information about your ensemble available to concert clients. On a Web site you can present your ensemble not only visually but in sound as well. Be sure to use this new promotional tool, and use it effectively.

There are, of course, do-it-yourself software programs for constructing a Web site. It can pay, however, to have an experienced designer do the job for you. The Internet is a very public display window, and you want to be sure your ensemble shows up well.

21 ✧ THE CHAMBER ENSEMBLE IN RESIDENCE

F ortunate is the ensemble that obtains a residency in a collegiate-level institution. To begin with, there is the prospect of working with colleagues well versed in the family of music disciplines. This is especially gratifying if the music faculty does not harbor the mutual suspicion that has too long existed between the "academic" fields (such as composition, theory, musicology, ethnomusicology) and the "applied" areas (instrument, voice, conducting, arts management, and so on). There is the ultimate reward of knowing that you are helping educate young people who will be the professional musicians, critics, arts administrators, or informed listeners of tomorrow. For the ensemble, there is the sense of assurance that comes from a predictable income and schedule base that extends for the length of the contract or, if tenure is involved, for the longer haul.

What are the chances of landing such a position? This is difficult to know. Of the more than seven hundred groups who describe themselves in Chamber Music America's *Chamber Music: The 2002 Taste of Chamber Music*, eighty-some ensembles mention a residency with an academic campus, a conservatory, an orchestra, or a community, although they do not indicate whether these residencies offer the ensemble significant support in the way of stipend, benefits, rank, or length of contract.

The darker side—uncertainty over the renewal of the contract—can be of concern even with a tenure appointment. Does the tenure status apply to each individual member of the ensemble, or does it cover only the group as a whole? A player in the group can prove at some point to be musically unsuited to the ensemble, or incompatible emotionally or in working habits. Or a player might simply refuse to stay in the group but be determined to remain on the faculty in an individual capacity. The ensemble is immediately disabled unless the administration has the funds and the desire to enlarge the faculty by authorizing the hiring of a replacement for the missing player. Further, there must be an appropriate teaching load within the department for the replacement, so that an unequal responsibility does not fall upon the other members of the ensemble. Such questions should be discussed with the administration when the original residency agreement is negotiated.

In fact, the definition of tenure has itself become cloudy. There are ways (such as changing the description or challenging the very existence of the position) of eroding the lifelong job protection that formerly characterized tenure status. To be sure, such nuanced views of tenure cast a shadow on the sanctity of academic freedom generally. They can also render uneasy those faculty members who have not kept up with research in their field, who have grown lazy as teachers, and who are simply coasting along until retirement. More shadowed still is the fact that the new attitudes about tenure reflect a tendency away from faculty rosters filled with older, experienced, expensive, full-benefit professors; and toward part-time, adjunct (that is, transient) faculty: typically young, paid less, and given minimal benefit packages, if any.

Existing faculty may resist the addition of a chamber ensemble to the departmental ranks. If the necessary funds come out of the departmental budget, support for the advancement and research of incumbents in the various musical disciplines may need to be cut, or at least partially frozen, to make way for the new allocation. Is the higher administration able to produce the funds from nondepartmental resources? In that case, members of other disciplines, in addition to those of the music division, will feel their potential support threatened.

Still, the faculty at large may view the campus presence of an accomplished musical ensemble as an aid in recruiting desirable faculty in a variety of fields. This has proved true especially when the college or university is located in a smaller city or town that has not yet achieved significant musical activity. Even in the larger metropolis, a fine resident ensemble may be regarded as a necessary campus attribute, even if of less public allure than a successful football or basketball team.

The path toward residency will be smoothed somewhat if the ensemble, no matter how young in career or in the relative youthfulness of its members, has already won some national and international recognition for its music-making. In today's musical world, of course, winning a prominent competition will figure heavily in the group's favor. The individual members must be competent and sympathetic teachers of their several instruments and able coaches of ensemble repertoire. They should know how to deal with a varied level of student ability and be able to attract students from the available pool of talent, both local and distant.

The teaching load of the ensemble members will have to be reduced to balance the time spent in preparing concerts the group gives on campus. Time away from school will be needed for a reasonable amount of the touring, both domestic and foreign, that the ensemble must continue in order to maintain its standing in the musical scene. Such touring, in turn, must garner the kind of favorable publicity that will lend distinction to the school and attract able students. All this, obviously, affects the negotiation and mutual respect between the ensemble and the school.

As is perhaps often the case, the ensemble may be formed in part or entirely from among existing members of the faculty. It will be fortunate (and remarkable) if such an ensemble is musically balanced and compatible. Even then, the ensemble members will need time to rehearse themselves into a viable performing group. If one or more additional musicians must be hired to fill out the group, balancing the opinions and desires of the ensemble with the needs and makeup of the department overall will be a neat trick.

Any difficulties that may arise after an ensemble is officially in residence should be resolved without recourse to litigation. I cannot stress this point enough. Judges are usually disinclined, and properly so, to deal with questions of artistic or academic merit, and may decide not to consider the case. Should the argument actually land in court, it makes no difference which side "wins"; everyone loses. Whether the disagreement is between the members of the ensemble itself, or between the ensemble and the school administration, the publicity surrounding a court proceeding is damaging to all parties. The press and television coverage will arouse uncomfortable emotions both on campus and within the community at large.

Administrators know this and will sometimes try to sweep difficulties under the rug. This can even go to the extent (as a recent case has shown) of reaching an expensive agreement with an ensemble that has reportedly not done its job satisfactorily on campus but has been able to muster the support of the community at large. The university was possibly influenced by concerns for the long-term fund-raising campaign in which it was engaged. Any threat of litigation would have evoked fears of retribution by potential donors. Also, clouded artistic judgment on the part of the high administration may have played a role.

Another actual case demonstrates the opposite: the administration of a prominent and well-endowed university deciding not to extend the contract of a talented and devoted quartet-in-residence, apparently only to reduce expenses. While by no means overpaid, the quartet had for some years concertized both on campus and away, made well-received records, and given students effective and much appreciated instrumental and chamber music teaching.

In a third instance, a judge agreed to consider a complaint brought by a quartet member who had been ousted by his three colleagues. The court action for a time made it impossible for the remaining three to function, and the university residence of the ensemble was ended. Whatever the outcome of the litigation (now for defamation of character), the ensemble's career was gravely wounded, and the aggrieved member has probably branded himself as too contentious a character for any other musical team or sponsor to handle.

Academic administrators are not always equipped to recognize and appreciate true musical artistry. In that case, they should be at pains to seek disinterested and expert advice in the matter. Administration must be willing both to defend the presence of the dedicated artist on campus and to deal hard-headedly with incompetence, negligence, or both. Such discernment and determination is, after all, part of the administrator's job. I speak, however, of that ideal world where everyone invariably lives up to responsibilities.

Along with my twenty-five years of membership in the Fine Arts Quartet, most of my forty-year active career included service as a member of college faculties. Fortunately, I did not experience the kinds of turbulence I refer to in the preceding paragraphs. I have been involved enough in the academic scene, however, to know what residency can mean for members of a chamber ensemble. For some insight into our team's experience in this area, see chapter 10, "The Fine Arts Quartet in a University Residency."

Despite any caveats I have detailed, be assured that an ensemble should regard a possible residency with lively interest. Discuss the prospect carefully with the institution in question. Its administrators should be made aware of what your presence will mean to the campus. For its part, the ensemble should understand clearly the responsibilities the position will entail. Try to negotiate realistically for conditions that will best serve the interests of both the school and your group. Make suitable arrangements at the outset, rather than wait for trouble to arise down the road. Most important: recognize that, if you do the job right, you are indeed adding to your responsibilities as an ensemble. No matter how favorable the terms of your residency, your candle will henceforth be burning at both ends. Try to be warmed, not singed, by the flames.

22 ✧ RECAPITULATION AND CODA

If I had it to do over again, would I follow the rather circuitous path I traced during my lifetime? My answer is a guarded yes. I am glad I had exposure to what is called the applied side of music-making—in my case, the violin (formally), and viola (self-taught). It is good, too, that I had some variety of performing experience, ranging from freelance radio playing, to participation in concerts of contemporary music, to formal recitals on viola and violin. I was fortunate that this activity between the end of my undergraduate years and my entry into the quartet helped me develop my "chops." Further, I was able to continue that development rapidly during the early seasons of my quartet membership.

I profited from my studies, research, and teaching activity on the academic side of the music discipline. These gave me broadened musical horizons as well as valuable practice in writing, speaking, and—very important —familiarity with the use of library resources. This last was essential not only for research purposes, but also because it showed me the paths to music whose existence I might not otherwise have known: compositions found in careful modern editions that are commercially available; others, in the complete works sets, specialized studies, and rare and early editions in the holdings of major libraries. I learned that, although much music has been resurrected, a great deal more remains to be studied and evaluated by scholars and performers, and, when the quality of the music warrants it (not always so, unfortunately), brought to light and performed.

I have just used a fateful "and" to separate the academic scholar from the performing musician. Let me hope that the word can be seen not as a gulf between two polar opposites, and not even as a figurative bundling-board (the wooden divider that preserved prim separation between the two constituents of a courting couple as they kept warm under the bedcovers in the chill of old-time housing). I am happy to think that the walls of mutual suspicion that divided the various practitioners of music in former years are now being increasingly replaced by the knowledge that scholar, theorist, composer, and performer are all interdependent on each other. Here again, I value my own training for making me receptive to the idea of close alliance between the several members of the community of music.

My readers will, I hope, have had more demanding and consistent instrumental teaching in their early years than I did, and learned more quickly the essential habit of listening critically to their own playing. Practicing intelligently is something teachers can describe, but it is up to the students to make it happen. Also, early and hands-on exposure to the chamber music repertoire is extremely important: you learn what is out there on the musical horizon, and you learn to listen to your ensemble-mates as well as to yourself. Careful chamber music practice makes every player a more intelligent solo performer as well.

What about the instrumentalist's exposure to the other areas of the musical discipline? To go about it the way I and some other performers have done takes years of time and energy. In view of the expense of instrumental instruction, moreover, the cost of pursuing two musical avenues may be forbidding. For those of you approaching college age, one realistic educational option is to seek admission to a school of music that offers a well-rounded humanistic curriculum as well as expert, comprehensive musical training. That kind of school can be either an independent institution or part of a university. So also, some universities have departments of music that (even though smaller than a school of music), both in their own right and by access to their university's courses, provide the student with the breadth of training I recommend.

If you have already finished your undergraduate years, perhaps you were lucky enough to study in that kind of setting. I hope your school curriculum included some solid experience and coaching in chamber music. I hope, too, that you had the stamina and enthusiasm to live up to the opportunities the school provided. If you have gaps in your training (and few of us do not), you will either have to do a lot of reading, listening, and playing on your own, or will have to consider enrolling for graduate work, again at a carefully chosen school. If you can afford the time and expense, the extra study will add to your equipment for a career in professional music. You will need all the knowledge and perceptiveness you can get.

To contemplate a life these days in musical performance rather than in computer science, law, investment banking, and the like, calls not only for proven ability but almost aggressive determination. If you are reading this book, you must be thinking about, or already have entered, the chamber music world.

We are told that these are difficult times for musicians generally, and that chamber music is not high in the attention spectrum even of concertgoers and record buyers. The lament is not new. I remember visiting Russell Potter, director of the concerts and lectures office at Columbia University, the year after I joined the Fine Arts Quartet. When I asked Russell to think about having our ensemble on his series, he replied, "But Abe, everybody knows that chamber music is dying." "OK," I replied, "but I want to play at the funeral!" We were in fact included in Russell's series the following season. All this was back in the middle 1950s, so the obsequies have been going on a long time.

If chamber music is really as moribund as we have been told, why are there concert managements that include (sometimes exclusively) chamber ensembles among their offerings? Why the proliferation of chamber music workshops for amateurs in various parts of the country, numerous enough to be scheduled not only in the summer months but at other times during the year? There is enough interest to sustain the existence of the well-subscribed Amateur Chamber Music Players organization, including its roster of members from many states in America, Canada, and abroad. And there is that important organization for professionals and aspirants, Chamber Music America. Most significant, able young musicians, in a constant stream, demonstrate great aptitude for the art and are eager to study chamber music. They are an interest and human resource that must not be wasted.

Some of these young people may yet go off to study computer science, but until they do, everything possible must be done to help them find fulfillment in their first love, ensemble music. The group that can play well, build a comprehensive repertoire, arrange appealing programs, speak and write in direct and interesting language, and relate well to people has the potential of making a career for itself where it counts most: in the community.

Prominent among younger chamber ensembles, the Ying Quartet, during an extended residency in a smaller city, proved that an ensemble can indeed become an important and much appreciated factor in American municipal life. The spread of such residencies would contribute significantly to music in this country. Equally great would be its impact on the career possibilities for young musicians. Our schools of music would be hard pressed to provide enough trained professionals to fill the ranks of the ensembles that would then be needed. Oh! Happy prospect!

Coda

I referred earlier to Beethoven's Quartet in F minor, Op. 95, and its exhilarating, intoxicated Allegro coda. Streams of eighth-notes, crisply snapped rhythms, jaunty syncopations, all speed "very lightly" past, as the composer instructs. The movement ends with a concerted dash to the double bar, all instruments ascending except for the cello, which darts downward to lend weight to the cadence. This coda is Beethoven's way of resolving the emotional contrasts and displays of indecision that mark the quartet as a whole and the finale in particular. It is a very satisfying ending to a rather enigmatic work.

I am no Beethoven, but I am happy to take a cue from the master in writing this closing to my book. From some of the reminiscences I have set down here, the reader will have noticed that I did not always find sweetness and light flowing unrestrained in our ensemble's life, whether in the rehearsal room or the wings of the auditorium stage. In retrospect, I am aware again that we four were not necessarily saintly characters and that the stresses of togetherness in a challenging occupation could bring out some unpleasing traits in our several natures. Yet, despite all, there were the many, many moments of musical satisfaction in the workroom. And most important, there was the special reward of the concert performances and the frequent sense that we had come close to what the composer had in mind when he fashioned a great work of art. As with Beethoven's coda, these experiences offered a rush of resolution that countered the doubts of the daily round.

Was it worth all the effort? I have to say yes. As our repertoire list reveals, we played a great many compositions, representing a cross-section of the finest output by our greatest composers, both past and present. We had the satisfaction of performing for appreciative audiences in many countries of the world, often winning not only the applause of the audience but also the written plaudits of that problematic tribe, the critics. It was twenty-five years of varied, hard work, oftentimes too hard, in my estimation. But it was full of interesting experiences. One thing I know, however: I will not have to do it again.

Fortunately, as I said at the outset of this guide, there are today many excellent young players bent on taking up the torch of chamber music. I welcome them to a most worthy pursuit and I trust that they may be helped by the advice I have given in this writing. In so saying, I recognize that precepts are one thing, human impulses another. Still, my suggestions about forming or joining an ensemble, keeping it together in as happy a frame of mind as possible, recognizing the many responsibilities that can attach to ensemble life, and confronting changes and departures—these are valid concerns. Knowing the kinds of problems that can arise will help you see them coming and prepare to deal with them intelligently rather than muddling your way through.

Ideally, some serious training in psychology might help the members of an ensemble in their dealings with each other. But I am optimistic enough to think that a measure of common sense and congeniality can go far to smooth the daily life of the group. Above all, try to avoid the sin of egotism and the disease of boredom. Let all participants play so beautifully that they earn each other's continued admiration and respect. And may their musical differences be resolved with reason and humor. Only then can an ensemble hope to endure and prosper.

✧ REPERTOIRE LIST

T *his is a list of works actually performed, some more often than others, by the Fine Arts Quartet or by its several members during the years 1954– 1979. For consistency's sake, the titles are shown in numerical sequence according their usual catalog identification (opus numbers, Mozart's Köchel numbers, and so on), though in some cases—Beethoven, Dvořák, Mozart, for example—the chronological sequence of composition may differ from the numerical order.*

ABBREVIATIONS

b.c.	basso continuo	qt	string quartet (2 vn, va, vc)
bar	baritone	s	soprano
bcl	bass clarinet	str	strings
bn	bassoon	va	viola
cl	clarinet	vc	cello
db	double bass	vn	violin
fl	flute		
hn	French horn	BWV	Bach-Werke-Verzeichnis
hp	harp		(J. S. Bach catalog)
hpd	harpsichord	D.	Deutsch (Schubert catalog)
ob	oboe	G.	Gérard (Boccherini
orch	orchestra		catalog)
pf	piano	H.	Helm (C. P. E. Bach
pic	piccolo		catalog)
qnt	woodwind quintet (fl, ob, cl, hn, bn)	K.	Köchel (Mozart catalog)

Strings

SOLO

Bach, Johann Sebastian
  Partita No. 1 in B minor, BWV
    1002, vn
  Suite in G, BWV 1007, vc
  Suite in C, BWV 1009, vc

Hindemith, Paul
  Sonata, Op. 11, va
  Sonata No. 1, Op. 31, No. 1, vn

Honegger, Arthur
  Sonata, vn

Telemann, G. P.
  Fantasies, vn

DUO

Beethoven, Ludwig van
  Duo in E-flat, WoO 32, va, vc

Crawford, Ruth
  Diaphonic Suite No. 4, va, vc

Kodály, Zoltán
  Duo, Op. 7, vn, vc

Leclair, Jean-Marie
  Sonatas (various), 2 vn

Martinů, Bohuslav
  Three Madrigals, vn, va

Mozart, W. A.
  Duo in G, K. 423, vn, va
  Duo in B-flat, K. 424, vn, va

Ravel, Maurice
  Sonata for Violin and Cello

Seiber, Mátyás
  Sonata da camera, vn, vc

TRIOS

Antes, John
  Trios, Op. 3, 2 vn, vc

Beethoven, Ludwig van
  Trio in C minor, Op. 9, No. 3,
    vn, va, vc

Dohnányi, Ernő
  Serenade in C, Op. 10, vn, va, vc

Mozart, W. A.
  Divertimento in E-flat, K. 563,
    vn, va, vc

Quartets

Adler, Samuel
  Quartet No. 4
  Quartet No. 6 (*A Whitman
    Serenade*)

Arriaga, Juan Crisóstomo
  Quartet No. 3 in E-flat

Aschaffenburg, Walter
  Quartet

Babbitt, Milton
  Quartet No. 3

Bartók, Béla
  Quartet No. 1, Op. 7
  Quartet No. 2, Op. 17
  Quartet No. 3
  Quartet No. 4

Quartet No. 5
Quartet No. 6

Beethoven, Ludwig van
Quartet in F, Op. 18, No. 1
Quartet in G, Op. 18, No. 2
Quartet in D, Op. 18, No. 3
Quartet in C minor, Op. 18,
No. 4
Quartet in A, Op. 18, No. 5
Quartet in B-flat, Op. 18, No. 6
Quartet in F, Op. 59, No. 1
Quartet in E minor, Op. 59,
No. 2
Quartet in C, Op. 59, No. 3
Quartet in E-flat, Op. 74
Quartet in F minor, Op. 95
Quartet in E-flat, Op. 127
Quartet in B-flat, Op. 130
Quartet in C-sharp minor, Op.
131
Quartet in A minor, Op. 132
Great Fugue in B-flat, Op. 133
Quartet in F, Op. 135

Berg, Alban
Quartet, Op. 3
Lyric Suite

Beversdorf, Thomas
Quartet

Blackwood, Easley
Quartet No. 1, Op. 4

Bloch, Ernest
Quartet No. 1
Quartet No. 3
Quartet No. 4
Quartet No. 5

Boccherini, Luigi
Quartet in A, G. 206

Borodin, Alexander
Quartet No. 2 in D

Borowski, Felix
Quartet No. 3 in D

Brahms, Johannes
Quartet in C minor, Op. 51,
No. 1
Quartet in A minor, Op. 51,
No. 2
Quartet in B-flat, Op. 67

Britten, Benjamin
Quartet No. 2 in C, Op. 36
Quartet No. 3, Op. 94

Carlstedt, Jan
Quartet No. 3, Op. 23

Carpenter, John Alden
Quartet

Carter, Elliott
Quartet No. 1
Quartet No. 2

Chadwick, George
Quartet No. 4 in E minor

Crawford, Ruth
String Quartet (1931)

Debussy, Claude
Quartet No. 1 in G minor, Op. 10

Denny, William
Quartet No. 3

Dittersdorf, Carl Ditters von
Quartet in E-flat

Donato, Anthony
Quartet No. 2

Dvořák, Antonin
Quartet No. 9, in D minor, Op. 34
Quartet No. 10, in E-flat, Op. 51
Quartet No. 12, in F, Op. 96
Quartet No. 14, in A-flat, Op. 105
Quartet No. 13, in G, Op. 106

Fine, Irving
Quartet

Franklin, Benjamin
Quartet

Gershwin, George
Lullaby

Ginastera, Alberto
Second String Quartet, Op. 26

Green, George
Quartet No. 1

Grieg, Edvard
Quartet in G minor, Op. 27

Griffes, Charles T.
Two Sketches on Indian Themes

Gutche, Gene
Quartet No. 4, Op. 29, No. 1

Haydn, Joseph
Divertimento in E-flat, Op. 1, No. "0"
Quartet in B-flat, Op. 1, No. 1
Quartet in D, Op. 2, No. 5
Quartet in B-flat, Op. 2, No. 6
Quartet in E-flat, Op. 3, No. 1
Quartet in C, Op. 3, No. 2
Quartet in G, Op. 3, No. 3
Quartet in B, Op. 3, No. 4

Quartet in F, Op. 3, No. 5
Quartet in A, Op. 3, No. 6
Quartet in D, Op. 20, No. 4
Quartet in F minor, Op. 20, No. 5
Quartet in A, Op. 20, No. 6
Quartet in E-flat, Op. 33, No. 2
Quartet in C, Op. 33, No. 3
Quartet in B-flat, Op. 50, No. 1
Quartet in C, Op. 50, No. 2
Quartet in E-flat, Op. 50, No. 3
Quartet in F-sharp minor, Op. 50, No. 4
Quartet in F, Op. 50, No. 5
Quartet in D, Op. 50, No. 6
Quartet in G, Op. 54, No. 1
Quartet in C, Op. 54, No. 2
Quartet in C, Op. 64, No. 1
Quartet in B minor, Op. 64, No. 2
Quartet in B-flat, Op. 64, No. 3
Quartet in G, Op. 64, No. 4
Quartet in D, Op. 64, No. 5
Quartet in E-flat, Op. 64, No. 6
Quartet in C, Op. 74, No. 1
Quartet in F, Op. 74, No. 2
Quartet in G minor, Op. 74, No. 3
Quartet in G, Op. 76, No. 1
Quartet in D minor, Op. 76, No. 2
Quartet in C, Op. 76, No. 3
Quartet in B-flat, Op. 76, No. 4
Quartet in D, Op. 76, No. 5
Quartet in E-flat, Op. 76, No. 6
Quartet in G, Op. 77, No. 1
Quartet in F, Op. 77, No. 2
Quartet in D minor (unfinished), Op. 103

Hindemith, Paul
Quartet No. 3, Op. 22

Ravel, Maurice
  Quartet in F

Read, Gardner
  Quartet No. 1, Op. 100

Revueltas, Silvestre
  Quartet No. 1
  Quartet No. 2

Riegger, Wallingford
  Quartet No. 2, Op. 43

Rossini, Gioacchino
  Sonata for 2 vn, vc, db

Rusch, Milton
  Quartet, *The Garden*

Schoenberg, Arnold
  Quartet No. 3

Schubert, Franz
  Quartet in E-flat, D. 87
  Quartettsatz in C minor, D. 703
  Quartet in A minor, D. 804
  Quartet in D minor, D. 810
  Quartet in G, D. 887

Schuller, Gunther
  Quartet No. 1

Schumann, Robert
  Quartet in A minor, Op. 41, No. 1
  Quartet in F, Op. 41, No. 2
  Quartet in A, Op. 41, No. 3

Sessions, Roger
  Quartet No. 2

Shifrin, Seymour
  Quartet No. 1
  Quartet No. 4

Shostakovich, Dmitri
  Quartet No. 1 in C, Op. 49
  Quartet No 2 in A, Op. 68
  Quartet No. 3 in F, Op. 73
  Quartet No. 4 in D, Op. 83
  Quartet No. 8 in C minor, Op. 110
  Quartet No. 11 in F minor, Op. 122

Smetana, Bedřich
  Quartet No. 1, in E minor

Stein, Leon
  Quartet No. 1

Stravinsky, Igor
  Concertino

Tchaikovsky, Piotr Ilyitch
  Quartet No. 1 in D, Op. 11

Tcherepnin, Alexander
  Quartet No. 2, Op. 40

Telemann, Georg Philipp
  Sonata a quattro in A

Thomson, Virgil
  Quartet No. 1

Turina, Joaquin
  The Prayer of the Toreador, Op. 34

Tuthill, Burnett
  Quartet

Vaughan Williams, Ralph
  Quartet in A minor

Verall, John
  Quartet No. 5

Verdi, Giuseppe
Quartet in E minor

Villa-Lobos, Heitor
Quartet No. 8

Walton, William
Quartet in A minor

Webern, Anton von
Five Movements for String Quartet, Op. 5

Wendelburg, Norma
Quartet No. 2

Wolf, Hugo
Italian Serenade in G

Wuorinen, Charles
Quartet No. 1

Quintets

Beethoven, Ludwig van
Viola Quintet in C, Op. 29

Brahms, Johannes
Viola Quintet No. 1 in F, Op. 88
Viola Quintet No. 2 in G, Op. 111

Debussy, Claude
Danse sacrée et danse profane, hp, str

Dvořák, Antonin
Bass Quintet in G, Op. 77, qt, db

Mendelssohn, Felix
Viola Quintet in B-flat, Op. 87

Milhaud, Darius
Quintet No. 4, Op. 350, qt, vc

Mozart, W. A.
Viola Quintet in B-flat, K. 174
Viola Quintet in C minor, K. 406
Viola Quintet in C, K. 515
Viola Quintet in G minor, K. 516
Viola Quintet in D, K. 593
Viola Quintet in E-flat, K. 614

Peter, Johann Friedrich
Six Viola Quintets

Ravel, Maurice
Introduction and Allegro, hp, [fl, cl], qt

Schubert, Franz
Cello Quintet in C, D. 956

Sextets

Brahms, Johannes
Sextet in B-flat, Op. 18
Sextet in G, Op. 36

Schoenberg, Arnold
Sextet, *Verklärte Nacht*, Op. 4

Octet

Mendelssohn, Felix
Octet in E-flat, Op. 20

Strings and winds

Trios

Beethoven, Ludwig van
Flute Serenade in D, Op. 25, fl,
vn, va

Debussy, Claude
Sonata, fl, va, hp

Quartets

Britten, Benjamin
Phantasy, Op. 2, ob, str

Devienne, François
Quartet in C, Op. 73, No. 1, bn,
str

Heiden, Bernhard
Serenade, bn, str

Mozart, W. A.
Flute Quartet in D, K. 285
Flute Quartet in G, K. 285a
Flute Quartet in C, K. 285b
Flute Quartet in A, K. 298
Oboe Quartet in F, K. 370

Quintets

Brahms, Johannes
Clarinet Quintet in B minor, Op.
115

Heiden, Bernhard
Horn Quintet

Mozart, W. A.
Horn Quintet in E-flat, K. 386c,
hn, vn, 2 va, vc
Clarinet Quintet in A, K. 581

Piston, Walter
Flute Quintet

Sextets

Etler, Alvin
Sextet, vn, va, vc, ob, cl, bn

Mozart, W. A.
A Musical Joke: Sextet in F, K.
522, qt, 2 hn

Septets

Beethoven, Ludwig van
Septet in E-flat, Op. 20, cl, hn,
bn, vn, va, vc, db

Imbrie, Andrew
Dandelion Wine, ob, cl, pf, qt

Octets

Hindemith, Paul
Octet, cl, bn, hn, vn, 2 va, vc, db

Schubert, Franz
Octet in F, D. 803, cl, hn, bn, qt,
db

Nonets

Bach, Johann Sebastian
The Art of Fugue, BWV 1080
(transcribed by Samuel
Baron), qnt, qt

Spohr, Louis
Nonet in F, Op. 31, qnt, vn, va,
vc, db

Strings and keyboard

Duos

Bach, Johann Sebastian
Sonata No. 3 in G minor, BWV
1029, vc, hpd

Beethoven, Ludwig van
Sonata in D, Op. 12, No. 1, pf, vn
Sonata in A, Op. 12, No. 2, pf, vn
Sonata in E-flat, Op. 12, No. 3,
pf, vn
Sonata in A minor, Op. 23, pf, vn
Sonata in F, Op. 24, pf, vn
Sonata in A, Op. 30, No. 1, pf, vn
Sonata in C minor, Op. 30, No. 2,
pf, vn
Sonata in G, Op. 30, No. 3, pf, vn
Sonata in A minor, Op. 47, pf, vn
Sonata in G, Op. 96, pf, vn

Brahms, Johannes
Sonata No. 1 in E minor, Op. 38,
vc, pf
Sonata No. 1, in G, Op. 78, vn.,
pf
Sonata No. 2 in A, Op. 100, vn, pf
Sonata No. 3 in D minor, Op.
108, vn, pf
Sonata in F minor, Op. 120, No.
1, va, pf
Sonata in E-flat, Op. 120, No. 2,
va, pf

Downey, John
Sonata, vc, pf

Franck, César
Sonata in A, vn, pf

Mozart, W. A.
Sonata in C, K. 296. pf, vn

Sonata in G, K. 301, pf, vn
Sonata in E-flat, K. 302, pf, vn
Sonata in C, K. 303, pf, vn
Sonata in E minor, K. 304, pf vn
Sonata in A, K. 305, pf, vn
Sonata in D, K. 306, pf, vn
Variations in G, K. 359, pf, vn
Variations in G minor, K. 360, pf
vn
Sonata in F, K. 376, pf, vn
Sonata in F, K. 377, pf, vn
Sonata in B-flat, K. 378, pf, vn
Sonata in G, K. 379, pf, vn
Sonata in E-flat, K. 380, pf, vn
Sonata in B-flat, K. 454, pf, vn
Sonata in E-flat, K. 481, pf, vn
Sonata in A, K. 526, pf, vn

Prokofiev, Sergei
Sonata No. 2 in D, Op. 94bis, vn,
pf

Ravel, Maurice
Sonata, vn, pf

Schoenberg, Arnold
*Phantasy for Violin with Piano
Accompaniment*, Op. 47, vn, pf

Schubert, Franz
Fantasy in C, D. 934, vn, pf

Stout, Alan
Sonata, vc, pf

Trios

Beethoven, Ludwig van
Trio in D, Op. 70, No. 1, pf, vn,
vc

Mendelssohn, Felix
Trio in D minor, Op. 49, pf, vn, vc

Mozart, W. A.
Trio in B-flat, K. 502, pf, vn, vc

Ravel, Maurice
Trio, pf, vn, vc

Schubert, Franz
Trio in B-flat, D. 898, pf, vn, vc
Trio in E-flat, D. 929, pf, vn, vc

Quartets

Brahms, Johannes
Quartet in G minor, Op. 25, pf, vn, va, vc
Quartet in A, Op. 26, pf, vn, va, vc
Quartet in C minor, Op. 60, pf, vn, va, vc

Dvořák, Antonin
Quartet in E-flat, Op. 87, pf, vn, va, vc

Fauré, Gabriel
Quartet No. 1 in C minor, Op. 15, pf, vn, va, vc

Mozart, W. A.
Quartet in G minor, K. 478, pf, vn, va, vc
Quartet in E-flat, K. 493, pf, vn, va, vc

Quintets

Bloch, Ernest
Quintet No. 1, pf, qt

Brahms, Johannes
Quintet in F minor, Op. 34, pf, qt

Carpenter, John Alden
Quintet, pf, qt

Dohnányi, Ernő
Quintet No. 2 in E-flat minor, Op. 26, pf, qt

Dvořák, Antonin
Quintet in A, Op. 81, pf, qt

Fauré, Gabriel
Quintet No. 2 in C minor, Op. 115, pf, qt

Franck, César
Quintet in F minor, pf, qt

Persichetti, Vincent
Quintet, pf, qt

Porter, Quincy
Quintet, hpd, qt

Schubert, Franz
Quintet in A, D. 667 ("Trout"), pf, vn, va, vc, db

Schumann, Robert
Quintet in E-flat, Op. 44, pf, qt

Shostakovich, Dmitri
Quintet in G minor, Op. 57, pf, qt

Sextets

Chausson, Ernest
Concerto in D, Op. 21, vn, pf, qt

Mendelssohn, Felix
Sextet in D, Op. 110, vn, 2 va, vc, db, pf

Mixed ensembles

Beethoven, Ludwig van
Trio in B-flat, Op. 11, pf, cl, vc

Brahms, Johannes
Trio in A minor, Op. 114, pf, cl,
vc

Faure, Gabriel
La bonne chanson, Op. 61, s, pf,
qt

Hindemith, Paul
Die junge Magd, Op. 23, No. 2, s,
fl, cl, qt
Des Todes Tod, Op. 23a, s, 2 va,
2vc

Loeffler, Charles M.
Second Rhapsody, ob, va, pf

Loeillet, Jean-Baptiste
Trio Sonata in D minor, Op. 5,
No. 3, ob, vn, b.c.

Mozart, W. A.
Adagio and Rondo in C minor
for Glass Harmonica, K. 617,
pf, fl, ob, va, vc

Rameau, Jean Philippe
Pièces de clavecin en concert No. 4
in B-flat, hpd, 2 vn
Cantata, *Aquilon et Orinthie*, s,
str, b.c.

Ravel, Maurice
Chansons madécasses, bar, fl, vc,
pf

Schoenberg, Arnold
Pierrot lunaire, voice, fl-pic, cl-
bcl, vn-va, vc, pf

Orchestral

Bach, C. P. E.
Sinfonia in D, H. 663

Bach, Johann Sebastian
Concerto in D minor, for two
violins, BWV 1043
Brandenburg Concertos, BWV
1046–1051
Harpsichord Concerto No. 5 in F
minor, BWV 1056
Suite No. 2 in B minor, BWV
1067

Bartók, Béla
Violin Concerto No. 1

Beethoven, Ludwig van
Symphony No. 1 in C, Op. 21
Concerto in C ("Triple
Concerto"), Op. 56
Violin Concerto in D, Op. 61
Symphony No. 8 in F, Op. 93

Bizet, Georges
Symphony in C

Brahms, Johannes
Double Concerto in A minor,
Op. 102, vn, vc, orch

Dohnányi, Ernő
Konzertstück in D, Op. 12, vc,
orch

Etler, Alvin
Concerto for string quartet and
orchestra

Haydn, Joseph
Symphony No. 45 in F-sharp
minor
Symphony No. 73 in D
Symphony No. 88 in G

Hindemith, Paul
Cello Concerto, Op. 36, No. 2

Lees, Benjamin
Quartet Concerto

Mozart, W. A.
Divertimento in D, K. 251, ob, 2
hn, str
Serenade No. 6 in D, K. 320
Sinfonia concertante in E-flat, K.
364, vn, va, 2 ob, 2 hn, str
Piano Concerto No. 20 in D
minor, K. 466
Horn Concerto No. 4 in E-flat, K.
495
Eine kleine Nachtmusik in G, K.
525, str

Partos, Oedoen
Yizkor (In memoriam), vn, va, vc,
str

Schubert, Franz
Symphony No. 5 in B-flat, D. 485

Spohr, Louis
Quartet Concerto in A minor,
Op. 131

Strauss, Richard
Prelude to *Capriccio*, Op. 85
Metamorphoses, str
Oboe Concerto

Tchaikovsky, Piotr Ilyitch
Serenade in C, Op. 48

Telemann, Georg Philipp
Viola Concerto

Vaughan Williams, Ralph
Flos Campi Suite, va, chorus,
orch

Vivaldi, Antonio
Concerto in D, Op. 3, No. 1, 4
vn, orch

Wagner, Richard
Siegfried Idyll

Weingartner, Felix
Sinfonietta in D, vn, va, vc, orch

✧ GUEST ARTISTS

T *hese guest artists appeared with the Fine Arts Quartet during the years*
1954–1979.

Piano

Victor Babin
Paul Badura-Skoda
Armand Basile
Ralph Berkowitz
Seymour Bernstein
Easley Blackwood
John Browning
Rudolph Ganz
Frank Glazer
Richard Goode
Jeffrey Hollander
Lorin Hollander
Mieczyslaw Horszowski
Gilbert Kalish
Florence Kirsch
Seymour Lipkin
Lou Luvisi
Leonard Pennario
Menahem Pressler
William Schatzkammer
Clara Siegel
Jeffrey Siegel
Franck Theuveny

Harpsichord

Robert Conant
Kenneth Cooper
Dorothy Lane
Sylvia Marlowe
Gertrude Stillman

Conductors

Thor Johnson
Willem van Otterloo
Kenneth Schermerhorn
Herbert Zipper

Violin

David Chausow
Oscar Chausow
Leonard Felberg
Josef Gingold
Marie-Claude Theuveny

Viola

David Dawson
Fred Klem
Milton Preves
Rami Salomonow
Walter Trampler
Francis Tursi

Cello

Joanna DeKeyser
Dudley Powers
Ronald Leonard
Michael Rudiakov
Robert Sylvester
Shirley Tabachnick
Paul Tortelier
Laszlo Varga

Bass

Joseph Guastafeste
Gary Karr
Roger Ruggeri
Harold Siegel

Flute

Samuel Baron
Israel Borouchoff
Louise Burge
Jean-Pierre Rampal
Paula Robison
Arthur Tipton

Recorder

Morris Newman

Oboe

Ronald Roseman
Ray Still

Clarinet

David Glazer
Hans Hepp
Reginald Kell
Mitchell Lurie
Chester Milosovich
Charles Russo
Jack Snavely
Harold Wright

Bassoon

Leonard Sharrow
Robert Thompson
Arthur Weisberg

Horn

John Barrows
Barry Benjamin
Dale Clevenger
Phil Farkas
Ralph Froelich
Chris Leuba
Barry Tuckwell
Basil Tyler

Harp

Edward Druzinsky
Alberto Salvi

Guitar

Rey de la Torre

Ensembles

The Berkshire Quartet
The Modern Jazz Quartet
The New York Woodwind Quintet
The Pro Arte Quartet

Voice

Betty Allen
Jan DeGaetani
Alice Howland
Martial Singher
Helen Thigpen

✧ DISCOGRAPHY

T his discography includes recordings featuring the Fine Arts Quartet or its members, 1954–1979. All recordings were produced by the Fine Arts Quartet except where otherwise noted.

Samuel Adler

Quartet No. 6 (*A Whitman Serenade*), with Jan DeGaetani, mezzo-soprano. CRI SD-432 (Composers Recordings, Inc.), CRI CD-608. Produced by the Eastman School of Music recording staff

John Antes

String Trios Op. 3 for two violins and cello. Columbia Records MS 6741. Produced by Columbia Records

Milton Babbitt

Quartet No. 3. Turnabout TX-S 34515

J. S. Bach

The Art of Fugue, BWV 1080 (transcribed by Samuel Baron), with the New York Woodwind Quintet. Everest 3335/2

Béla Bartók

Quartet No. 1, Op. 7; Quartet No. 2, Op. 17. Concert-Disc CS-207
Quartet No. 3; Quartet No. 4. Concert-Disc CS-208
Quartet No. 5; Quartet No. 6. Concert-Disc CS-209

Ludwig van Beethoven

The entire cycle of Beethoven quartets is contained in the eight-CD set
Omega/Everest, EVC 9051/52, EVC 9053/55, EVC 9056/58

Quartets Op. 18. Concert-Disc 507/3
    Quartet in F, Op. 18, No. 1
    Quartet in G, Op. 18, No. 2. Concert-Disc CS-210
    Quartet in D, Op. 18, No. 3. Concert-Disc CS-210
    Quartet in C minor, Op. 18, No. 4
    Quartet in A, Op. 18, No. 5
    Quartet in B-flat, Op. 18, No. 6

Quartets Op. 59, 74, and 95. Concert-Disc SP 506/3
    Quartet in F, Op. 59, No. 1. Concert-Disc CS-255
    Quartet in E minor, Op. 59, No. 2
    Quartet in C, Op. 59, No. 3
    Quartet in E-flat, Op. 74
    Quartet in F minor, Op. 95

Quartets Op. 127 through Op. 135, Concert-Disc SP-502
    Quartet in E-flat, Op. 127. Concert-Disc CS-233
    Quartet in B-flat, Op. 130
    Quartet in C-sharp minor, Op. 131. Concert-Disc CS-211
    Quartet in A minor, Op. 132. Concert-Disc CS-241
    Great Fugue in B-flat, 133
    Quartet in F, Op. 135

Septet in E-flat, Op. 20, with members of the New York Woodwind Quintet and Harold Siegel. Concert-Disc M-1214

Ernest Bloch

Quartet No. 5. Concert-Disc CS-225

Piano Quintet No. 1, with Frank Glazer. Concert-Disc CS-252

Johannes Brahms

Quartet in C minor, Op. 51, No. 1; Quartet in A minor, Op. 51, No. 2. Concert-Disc M-1226

Quartet in B-flat, Op. 67. Everest 3266

Clarinet Quintet in B minor, Op. 115, with Reginald Kell. Concert-Disc CS-202, Boston Skyline (CD) BSD-135

Ruth Crawford

String Quartet. Gasparo GS-205

Claude Debussy

String Quartet No. 1 in G minor, Op. 10. Concert-Disc CS-253. Produced by Everest Records

Carl Ditters von Dittersdorf

Quartet in E-flat. Concertapes 22-4

John Downey

String Quartet No. 2. Gasparo GS-205. Produced by the Eastman School of Music recording staff

Antonin Dvořák

Piano Quintet in A, Op. 81, with Frank Glazer. Concert-Disc CS-251

Joseph Haydn

Divertimento in E-flat, Op. 1, No. "0"; Quartet in D, Op. 2, No. 5; Quartet in B-flat, Op. 2, No. 6. Vox SVBX 597

Quartets Op. 3. Vox SVBX 598
    Quartet in E-flat, Op. 3, No. 1
    Quartet in C, Op. 3, No. 2
    Quartet in G, Op. 3, No. 3
    Quartet in B, Op. 3, No. 4
    Quartet in F, Op. 3, No. 5. Concertapes 23-5A
    Quartet in A, Op. 3, No. 6

Quartet in D, Op. 20, No. 4 (Concert-Disc CS-228)

Quartets Op. 50. Vox SVBX 595, Murray Hill S-4366
    Quartet in B-flat, Op. 50, No. 1
    Quartet in C, Op. 50, No. 2
    Quartet in E-flat, Op. 50, No. 3
    Quartet in F-sharp minor, Op. 50, No. 4
    Quartet in F, Op. 50, No. 5
    Quartet in D, Op. 50, No. 6

Quartets Op. 64. Vox SVBX 597, Murray Hill S-4366
    Quartet in C, Op. 64, No. 1
    Quartet in B minor, Op. 64, No. 2
    Quartet in B-flat, Op. 64, No. 3
    Quartet in G, Op. 64, No. 4
    Quartet in D, Op. 64, No. 5
    Quartet in E-flat, Op. 64, No. 6

Quartets Op. 74. Vox SVBX 598, Murray Hill S-4366
    Quartet in C, Op. 74, No. 1
    Quartet in F, Op. 74, No. 2
    Quartet in G minor, Op. 74, No. 3

Quartets Op. 76. Vox SVBX 596, Murray Hill S-4366
    Quartet in G, Op. 76, No. 1
    Quartet in D minor, Op. 76, No. 2. Concert-Disc M-1228
    Quartet in C, Op. 76, No. 3

Quartet in B-flat, Op. 76, No. 4
Quartet in D, Op. 76, No. 5
Quartet in E-flat, Op. 76, No. 6

Quartet in D minor (unfinished), Op. 103. Vox SVBX 595

Paul Hindemith

Quartet No. 3, Op. 22. Concert-Disc CS-225

Octet, with members of the New York Woodwind Quintet and Harold Siegel. Concert-Disc CS-218

Sonata for Viola Alone, Op. 25, No. 1, Irving Ilmer. Concert-Disc CS-218

Karel Husa

Quartet No. 2; Quartet No. 3. Everest 3290

Ben Johnston

Quartet No. 4. Gasparo GS-205

Felix Mendelssohn

Quartet No. 1 in E-flat, Op. 12. Concert-Disc CS-224

Quartet No. 3 in D, Op. 44, No. 1. Concert-Disc CS-260

Quartet No. 4 in E minor, Op. 44, No. 2. Concert-Disc CS-224

Op. 81 on Concert-Disc CS-260
    Andante in E, Op. 81, No. 1
    Scherzo in A minor, Op. 81, No. 2
    Capriccio in E minor, Op. 81, No. 3
    Fugue in E-flat, Op. 81, No. 4

Octet in E-flat, Op. 20, with David and Oscar Chausow, Milton Preves, Dudley Powers. Concert-Disc CS-261

W. A. Mozart

Quartet in D minor, K. 421. Concert-Disc CS-227

Quartet in E-flat, K. 428. Concert-Disc CS-258

Quartet in C, K. 465. Concert-Disc CS-227

Quartet in D, K. 575. Concert-Disc CS-258

Quartet in B-flat, K. 589; Quartet in F, K. 590. Concert-Disc CS-259

Flute Quartet in D, K. 285; Flute Quartet in G, K. 285a; Flute Quartet in C, K. 285b; Flute Quartet in A, K. 298. All with Samuel Baron. Concert-Disc CS-215

Oboe Quartet in F, K. 370, with Ray Still; Horn Quintet in E-flat, K. 386c, with John Barrows. Concert-Disc CS-204

Clarinet Quintet in A, K. 581, with Reginald Kell. Concert-Disc CS-203, Boston Skyline (CD) BSD-135

Viola Quintets K. 174 through K. 614. All with Francis Tursi. Vox SVBX 557
    Viola Quintet in B-flat, K. 174
    Viola Quintet in C minor, K. 406
    Viola Quintet in C, K. 515
    Viola Quintet in G minor, K. 516
    Viola Quintet in D, K. 593
    Viola Quintet in E-flat, K. 614

Sergei Prokofiev

String Quartet No. 2 in F, Op. 92. Gasparo GS-203

Maurice Ravel

String Quartet in F. Concert-Disc CS-253. Produced by Everest Records

Arnold Schoenberg

Pierrot lunaire, conducted by Herbert Zipper, with Alice Howland, Abram Loft, George Sopkin, Gilbert Kalish, Louise Burge, Chester Milosovich. Concert-Disc CS-232

Franz Schubert

Quartet in E-flat, D. 87. Concertapes 23-5A, Boston Skyline (CD) BSD-143

Quartet in A minor, D. 804. Everest 3266

Quartet in D minor, D. 810. Concert-Disc CS-212, Boston Skyline (CD) BSD-145

Quintet in A, D. 667 ("Trout"), with Frank Glazer, Harold Siegel. Concert-Disc CS-206, Boston Skyline (CD) BSD-145

Octet in F, D. 803, with members of the New York Woodwind Quintet, Harold Siegel. Concert-Disc CS-220, Boston Skyline (CD) BSD-143

Dmitri Shostakovich

Quartet No. 3 in F, Op. 73. Gasparo GS-203

Louis Spohr

Nonet in F, Op. 31, with the New York Woodwind Quintet, Harold Siegel. Concertapes 24-9, Concert-Disc CS-201

Piotr Ilyitch Tchaikovsky

Serenade in C, Op. 48. Vanguard VRS 1003

Joaquin Turina

The Prayer of the Toreador. Concertapes 22-4

Hugo Wolf

Italian Serenade. Concertapes 22-4

Charles Wuorinen

Quartet No. 1. Turnabout TV-S 34515

✧ SUGGESTED READINGS

T *he items by Acosta, Besen, Dauer, Robinson, and Scales cited in this list can be read online at the Chamber Music America Web site, www. chamber-music.org. Membership in the CMA brings with it access to the organization's publications and to the pertinent professional information therein.*

Acosta, Paul. "Making a Demo Recording." *CMA Matters*, vol. 11 (April 2000). This article, written by the head of a commercial studio, is a quick and comprehensive introduction to the various facets of making a recording. The information will guide the ensemble when planning a tape or CD to introduce itself to clients, management, and other interested parties. You may well decide to leave the process to experienced hands.

Besen, Robert. "Surviving Personnel Changes, Part 1: The Smooth Transition." *CMA Matters*, vol. 11 (June 2000). Besen, with years of experience in arts administration and artist management, gives clear-cut advice on carrying out a change in ensemble membership. He also discusses the timing and manner of notifying management, concert sponsors, and announcing the change generally.

Besen, Robert. "Surviving Personnel Changes, Part 2: Planning Ahead." *CMA Matters*, vol. 11 (November 2000). The author writes about avoiding and dealing with an ensemble's internal frictions, drawing up agreements to cover potential problems, various legal formats the ensemble can assume, and provision for mediation of ensemble affairs and differences. This is good cautionary reading, helping prepare for the possible rainy days of ensemble life.

Biles, Richard. "Circum-Arts: What's It All About?" *CMA Matters*, vol. 9 (March 1998). Biles describes the unusual agency he heads. Embracing a broad span of performing arts, the organization offers low-cost entry to the professional world and a variety of services, helping prepare the artists "so they can professionally approach managers and artists representatives who then will further their careers." At the time of writing, the agency was already twenty-five years old.

Blum, David. *The Art of Quartet Playing: The Guarneri Quartet in Conversation with David Blum*. New York: Alfred A. Knopf, 1986. This is an interesting and comprehensive book, conveying the quartet members' views on topics ranging from the techniques of string playing, to the nature of the several voices in the quartet, to discussion of the repertoire, with full consideration of Beethoven's Op. 131. It is unprecedented to find an ensemble unburdening its thoughts in such detail. If their everyday musical discussion has indeed been as presented here, it is easier to understand why the membership of the group remained unchanged from its founding in 1964 until the retirement of cellist David Soyer in 2001. Recommended reading for all chamber instrumentalists.

Chamber Music America. *Chamber Music: The 2002 Taste of Chamber Music*, October 2001. A "survey of ensemble music in North America." See especially "Ensembles," pages 253–296. The listing for America numbers more than seven hundred groups of all kinds. For each ensemble, there is a description (varying widely in length and detail) provided by the members themselves. As the masthead has it, the offerings range from "Beethoven to bebop."

Dauer, John L. Jr. "Playing Together vs. Doing Business Together." *CMA Matters*, vol. 12 (November 2000). Dauer is an intellectual property attorney. His brief picture of the legal framework within which an ensemble may choose to conduct its affairs is informative for today's young musicians. However, it is important to consult a trusted legal adviser before deciding on what, if any, agreements are needed or advisable for the ensemble's welfare.

Donnelly, Bob. "Breaking Up is Hard to Do." *Chamber Music*, December 2001. This article, written by an entertainment lawyer, was inspired by widely noted litigation brought by the first violinist of an American string quartet against his three former colleagues for having dismissed him. It conveys fascinating and unsettling information, pertinent for members of any chamber ensemble, whether actual or in process of formation. There are questions of responsibility and liability that would not occur to the layperson. My sense is that, while treating this article as important reading, the ensemble should keep a level head about the matter. With guidance from a lawyer whose primary aim is to keep clients from going to court, try drawing up an agreement covering relationships among the members. Above all, realize that you want to avoid problems, not seek them out. Players must choose one another carefully and then behave with consistent civility and consideration, both artistically and personally. If troubles arise, collaborate, do not litigate.

Loft, Abram. *Ensemble! A Rehearsal Guide to Thirty Great Works of Chamber Music.* Portland, Oregon: Amadeus Press, 1992. I risk seeming self-serving by listing this title here. However, I believe it to be the only work of its kind, offering interpretative and performance advice in considerable detail about a broad range of significant works in the chamber repertoire. Included are string quartets, quintets, and mixed ensemble works, from Haydn to Ruth Crawford, Britten, and Bartók. The reader will undoubtedly not agree with me on every point, but I have been there, played it, and thought about it. My views about a composition can serve as a sidelight on your ensemble's rehearsal.

Norton, M. D. Herter. *The Art of String Quartet Playing*, New York: W. W. Norton, 1966 (1925). This book has long been a standard in the American literature on quartet playing. Essentially aimed at the amateur player, it also makes helpful reading for the young professional. I would take issue with the statement (page 48) that, when it comes to learning the score of a work, "the leader of the quartet is the one who must do most of this studying." This makes me anxious because the author has earlier spoken of the first violin as having some natural rights in the leadership area. All members of the team must do the required homework to contribute effectively to what the writer calls the "cooperative enterprise" of the chamber group. Overall, however, there is good, detailed counsel here on many facets of ensemble playing, with specific reference to excerpts from the repertoire. No one composition is discussed *in toto*. Though addressed to string players, the book includes much of interest for all instrumentalists.

Page, Athol. *Playing String Quartets*. London: Longmans, Green, 1964. Page is described in the Author's Note as being—at the time of publication—a member of the New Manchester String Quartet, England. Though small in format and length, this book provides succinct and well-phrased advice on selecting musical colleagues, technical and interpretative questions, and rehearsal and concert matters. There is discussion of representative quartets from the classic, romantic, nationalist, and modern eras (up through Shostakovich and Bartók). The treatment throughout is brief but helpful, no doubt more so to the serious amateur than the professional ensemble. Even so, musicians will find food for thought in this guide.

Pope, Kenneth S. *On Playing in a String Quartet: A Guide to Performance and Interpretation*. Queensland, Australia: privately printed, 1999. Though Pope addresses his text to the amateur ensemble, his advice—clearly the fruit of long experience—has value for the serious student and young professional as well. The slim volume surveys the development, nature, and mechanics of the quartet, both as a medium and as a performing group; effective rehearsal; signals; tempo; phrasing; and other facets of interpretation, with illustration by musical excerpts. Pope also offers brief descriptions of quartets grouped according to various levels of difficulty. The author can be reached at *kenpope@bigpond.com*.

Reynolds, Verne. *The Horn Handbook*. Portland, Oregon: Amadeus Press, 1997. Though addressed specifically to players of the French horn, this book has much of value to all musicians. The chapter on practice gives sound advice on the effective use of practice time by every instrumentalist. The related chapter on etudes will guide the violinist, pianist, and other members of the musical family to the most effective use of their own study materials. My central focus is on the chamber music chapter and especially its advice about efficient rehearsal, both on the musical and social level. Whether discussing teaching, auditions, intonation, playing with piano, or repertoire, Reynolds writes with an authority and wisdom that reflects his long and extremely varied experience as performer and educator. *The Horn Handbook* is not only suggested, but—in my estimation–required reading.

Robinson, Howard. "When an Ensemble Member is Asked to Leave." *CMA Matters*, vol. 11 (June 2000). There is sage counsel here from a social work expert, but it will probably take more than feel-good discussions to calm the waters if matters have come to the point where a player is being urged to depart the group. Read this article and derive what help you can from it.

Rubin, David M. "By Trial in Virginia." *Chamber Music*, April 2002. This article makes chastening reading, especially in sequel to the Donnelly article cited here. The friction-laden sundering of the Audubon Quartet and the subsequent litigation by the first violin against the other three is a bitter narrative. As the author says, "No matter what happens next, there are no winners in this contest." Several morals can be drawn: ensemble members should choose each other as discerningly as possible (a delicate matter!); participants should be circumspect about legal frameworks and agreements entered into by the group; differences, whether personal or musical, should be resolved early, not allowed to fester; and—most difficult of all—the musicians must be on best behavior for the long haul. Togetherness is a tricky business.

Scales, Barbara. "Artist Management Contracts: The Pros and Cons of Exclusivity." *CMA Matters*, vol. 9 (March 1998). Director of a management agency, the author lets the reader view agreements from the perspective of both artist and management. If you know what the other side is thinking, it will help you with your negotiating.

Temianka, Henri. *Facing the Music: An Irreverent Close-Up of the Real Concert-World.* New York: David McKay, 1973. Truly irreverent, Temianka reveals that he knew many of the great and near-great performers and composers of his time. He also apparently knew all the good yarns about musicians and was personally involved in some of them, recounting the tales to hilarious effect. Temianka has something cogent to say about the various facets of the music business and pulls no punches. In 1946 he founded the Paganini Quartet, serving as its first violin until he disbanded it in 1966. His stated reason for ending the ensemble seems both poignant and forthright: he grew tired of the rehearsing, travel, and repetition of works. He writes (page 141), "I was on automatic pilot, a mere onlooker, objectively observing a meticulously trained machine that had been perfected over the years." There had been two deaths (Robert Maas, cellist, and Charles Foidart, violist) during the twenty-year life of the ensemble, with the consequent work of breaking in their replacements. What happened to the other three members of the quartet after its dissolution, Temianka does not say, but one hopes the ending was by mutual consent. In any event, *Facing the Music* is fun to read.

Villchur, Edgar. "High Fidelity to What?" *Saturday Review,* November 1961. This one-page article by the inventor of the Acoustic Research speaker raises a very important point—that reproduced sound should truly mirror the sound of the original instrument and voice. In the decades since Villchur wrote this insightful piece, electronic sound technology has created a paradox: on the one hand, it has been able to reproduce musical sound with ever-increasing faithfulness. On the other, however, it has also led to amplification and distortion that destroys any resemblance to intelligible sound. Too many ears have been educated to accept sheer noise as the norm. By their concerts and recordings, chamber ensembles can maintain a standard that counters the debilitating uses to which technology has been put. It is high time to fight back.

✧ LIST OF MUSIC EXAMPLES

*A*ll music examples courtesy Sibley Music Library, the Eastman School of Music, the University of Rochester.

Example 1. Beethoven, Quartet in F, Op. 59, No. 1, Adagio molto e mesto, mm. 89–91, first and second violins. *Ludwig van Beethovens Werke. Vollständige kritisch durchgesehene überall berechtigte Ausgabe. Mit Genehmigung aller Originalverleger.* Series 6, volume 1. Leipzig, Breitkopf & Härtel, 1862–1888.   *154*

Example 2. Mozart, Quartet in F, K. 590, Allegretto, mm. 1–4, first violin. *W. A. Mozarts sämtliche Werke. Kritisch durchgesehene Gesamtausgabe.* Series 14. Leipzig, Breitkopf & Härtel, 1877.   *192*

Example 3. Mozart, Quartet in F, K. 590, Allegro, mm. 132–136. *W. A. Mozarts sämtliche Werke. Kritisch durchgesehene Gesamtausgabe.* Series 14. Leipzig, Breitkopf & Härtel, 1877.   *197*

Example 4. Beethoven, Quartet in C-sharp minor, Op. 131, Presto, mm. 157–168. *Ludwig van Beethovens Werke. Vollständige kritisch durchgesehene überall berechtigte Ausgabe. Mit Genehmigung aller Originalverleger.* Series 6, volume 1. Leipzig, Breitkopf & Härtel, 1862–1888.   *197*

Example 5. Beethoven, Quartet in G, Op. 18, No. 2, Allegro, mm. 1–8, first violin. *Ludwig van Beethovens Werke. Vollständige kritisch durchgesehene überall berechtigte Ausgabe. Mit Genehmigung aller Originalverleger.* Series 6, volume 1. Leipzig, Breitkopf & Härtel, 1862–1888.   *199*

✧ INDEX